Praise for *Prisonomics*

'Vicky Pryce is one of the leading figures on public policy in the UK: analytical, thoughtful, experienced and well-respected. It is very welcome that she is writing on prisons, a key issue for public policy, an issue for which analysis and evidence must replace slogans and doctrine. This is a very important contribution.'
Lord Stern, Professor of Economics, LSE, and President of the British Academy

'In my report, published in 2007, I was clear that prison was being used disproportionately for women who all too often were victims rather than offenders. With this powerful critique, Vicky Pryce reinforces these arguments and augments them with her considerable economic skills, to show that there should be far fewer people in our prisons.'
Baroness Corston

'Engagingly human, remorselessly practical. A book that needs to be read by politicians, taxpayers and anyone who wants to know the truth about prison for a woman.'
Erwin James

'This is an important book and one which joins a growing genre of books inspired by personal experience of the criminal justice system. Vicky Pryce's telling account of women and criminal justice should provoke important and timely debate.'
Professor Loraine Gelsthorpe, University of Cambridge and President of the British Society of Criminology

'Vicky Pryce is the best witness to what needs to be done to sort out our ineffective prisons for women. As one of Britain's top economists she explains how education and employability need to be top priorities for prison policy-makers. Timpson has always tried to offer a chance to offenders. With Vicky Pryce they have a new champion.'
James Timpson, founder of Timpson Ltd

'We [at Prisoners Education Trust] sincerely support Vicky Pryce in her quest to shed new light on the prison system by telling her own story, relaying her first-hand account of how education in prison is delivered and by describing the difference it can make for the women she met if learning is properly channelled to meet their specific needs. We know education initiatives work because they are a route for prisoners to avoid reoffending and to contribute positively to society – for example, through employment and through building strong and supportive family ties. This is sound economic thinking.'
Rod Clark and Nina Champion, Prisoners Education Trust

'Vicky Pryce is right when she says that Holloway is full of vulnerable women, many of whom shouldn't be there. What Holloway did in my time is respond to women's special needs in a way that would help rehabilitation.'
Tony Hassall, ex-governor of Holloway Prison

PRISONOMICS

PRISONOMICS

BEHIND BARS IN BRITAIN'S FAILING PRISONS

VICKY PRYCE

Biteback Publishing

First published in Great Britain in 2013 by
Biteback Publishing Ltd
Westminster Tower
3 Albert Embankment
London SE1 7SP
Copyright © Vicky Pryce 2013

ISBN 978-1-84954-622-5

10 9 8 7 6 5 4 3 2 1

A CIP catalogue record for this book is available from the British Library.

Set in Sabon

Printed and bound in Great Britain by
CPI Group (UK) Ltd, Croydon CR0 4YY

MIX
Paper from
responsible sources
FSC
www.fsc.org   FSC® C020471

CONTENTS

INTRODUCTION

In 2012 my ex-husband and I were charged with perverting the course of justice and so began many months of legal proceedings. I admitted accepting penalty points incurred by my ex-husband on my driving licence but I pleaded not guilty on the grounds of marital coercion. During the long and painful pre-trial hearings, and after the collapse of the first trial and the guilty verdict of the second, I began to record my thoughts and experiences in a diary, and continued to do so as I went first to Holloway, then to open prison in East Sutton Park, and after I was released on curfew two months later.

I had no idea what to expect and what issues would come up. But I knew that, irrespective of whether people thought the verdict or sentence was fair or not, I had to abide by the court's ruling and try to survive for both my and my children's sake. I had been found guilty of a crime for which I was to be punished and I felt that I had to give something back to society on release.

I knew that just recounting my experience would be an eye-opener for many, but I hadn't thought on entering Holloway that I would be hit immediately by the senselessness of it all for most of the women I met during my two months. This became even clearer as I talked to people on the outside after my release, including previous offenders, prison governors, current and previous chief inspectors of prisons, and individuals and organisations who comment and campaign for penal reform. I knew I was lucky in many ways and different to many of the women I encountered; I had a home and a family to go back to that would help me after my release. I also knew that even though my prospects for employment in the future were uncertain I wasn't going to be destitute by any stretch of the imagination.

It is said that just a few days in Holloway is all you need to understand the flaws of the current regime towards offenders. I spent two months in prison (followed by two months on home curfew), the standard duration for anyone who is sentenced to eight months, and it was enough to give me a feel of the prison regime. When a separate Ministry of Justice (MoJ) was carved out of what the Home Secretary John Reid described as the 'unfit for purpose' Home Office, it was hoped that a new era would begin. But as the police help to reduce crime, the MoJ and its judges help to increase prison numbers. From a strictly economic and public expenditure point of view, the MoJ bangs too many up but delivers far fewer bangs for the taxpayer's buck than the equivalent ministries in better-run countries.

Combining my prison diary with various data sources and interviews with individuals and organisations engaged with the prison service or campaigns for penal reform, this book has tried to put as much evidence together as possible to show that in fact the system is broken and a major rethink needs to take place. It is absurd that as crime goes down we put more people in jail at a huge cost to society when money is tight and there is a public deficit to deal with. The MoJ needs to deliver a better service with much less money.

On entering prison, I knew that the service was struggling to cope with the repercussions of a government policy towards crime which has until recently focused mostly on punishment rather than rehabilitation. But no matter what the service did and how fair it tried to be in its treatment of prisoners, it was obvious to me that there were too many people in prison – especially women. And I am not alone; Baroness Corston is just one among a remarkable thread of reforming British women who for more than a century have taken up the unfashionable cause of women in prison.

Of course, the first duty of care is to the victims of crime. But the women I met had rarely, if ever, caused serious damage to others. These women pose no threat to society. The custodial sentences mostly male judges enjoy imposing do not act as deterrents for crime; if anything they increase the chance of those released reoffending. In the middle of the ramshackle officialdom that deals with prisons, including specially elected political ministers, there never seems to be an economist to offer some utilitarian calculation on the value for money of our current criminal justice system. There is a clear moral case for not sending as many people, particularly women, to prison. But given the poor return in terms of offending and reoffending there is a clear economic case too. The cost–benefit calculation suggests that the impact of prisons in reducing the cost of crime to society is low

and money could be spent more productively elsewhere. However, the economics of prisons is too big
a subject to leave to the politicians or even to the civil
servants alone. Prisonomics needs to be investigated
seriously. In a more rational, less populist world the
lousy economics of our prison system should generate intense debate in society. For most people 'prison
does not work' – except in removing some offenders
temporarily from our streets who will likely reoffend.

There is also overwhelming evidence that the children of prisoners suffer from being separated from
their parents, and those who lose contact entirely
or end up in care have a much higher chance of
offending themselves than children who stay close to
their families, particularly, but not exclusively, to their
mothers. The direct short-term and indirect long-term
economic costs are large. The despair of many of the
women I met in my brief stay in prison was heartbreaking. What gave them hope was the prospect
of being reunited with their family and being able
to obtain a job that would allow them to return to
society and care for their children. And there are clear
links between education and employment as major
factors in reducing reoffending – but the links need
to be understood more generally among politicians,
press and a public that wants retribution and considers education in prison a 'privilege'.

Throughout this book, I try to give some point-
ers on how money could be saved through different
sentencing guidelines, more community service, more
mental health and other support, by keeping families
together or at least in touch with each other and,
crucially for the economy as a whole, by providing
more and better education in and out of prison to

improve future chances of employment. No doubt there will be counter-arguments. But it seems to me that in the current tight fiscal environment a smaller more efficient prison service is a must. If properly managed, our prison population should reduce substantially without encouraging reoffending. In many ways, the current economic climate and pressures on the public purse give us the ideal opportunity to completely rethink the management of the criminal justice system, something long overdue.

While writing *Prisonomics*, I have been assisted by Nicola Clay from the Cambridge Institute of Criminology, who scoured the academic literature for studies in this area; by International Relations graduate Anthony Elliott, who looked at as much publicly available data as he could find in the time available; by solicitor Kristiina Reed, who has a particular interest in the legal, social and economic consequences of imprisoning mothers and the impact on their children; and by parliamentary radio director Boni Sones, who helped me keep on top of external events occurring during my sentence. The conclusions are all my own but the work done by us all leaves me in agreement with those who argue that Britain is poorly served by an anachronistic, archaic network of male judges who send far too many women to prison. Prison is the wrong sentence for a large number of offences. The special needs of women are neglected and the economic cost of keeping women (and a good percentage of men) in prison is immense.

The various organisations working hard to achieve some progress in prison reform have done a great job and they have been forthcoming, offering me help in the form of research and combined wisdom. The facts are there, though admittedly sometimes not complete, not fully evaluated and contradictory at times, and there will always be differences in the data depending on which years one looks at and the sample size; results and percentages vary from one survey to another. I had to put up with a lot of that as I was researching for this book, which wasn't always easy. This book is meant to encourage people to look at the research, sometimes hard to digest, and try to make sense of it – and ask for more. But for the most part the data available reinforces the view that prison is not a deterrent and that the current system is costly and not fit for purpose and has been allowed to remain so despite the very severe financial pressures upon the public sector at present.

Many close friends who worked with me at senior levels of government and business wrote to me or visited me in prison. It is said you only know who your friends are when the press turns ugly and it is easier to walk by on the other side of the street. I will not embarrass them by listing them here but they and I know who they are. I received hundreds of letters from well-wishers who wrote to say how unfair they thought the sentence was. If I have not replied to them all – stamps were precious currency in short supply in prison – please take this book as a thank you.

But this book really belongs to the amazing women I met in Holloway and East Sutton Park. We are all called 'girls' in prison and although it is a few years since anyone so described me I am proud these girls became my friends. Girls, you deserved better and here's to you, wishing you all the best on the outside and keep your heads up high!

PART ONE

CHAPTER 1

INTO PRISON

11 MARCH

The enormity of what was about to happen hit everyone around me on the morning of the sentencing
as I found myself saying goodbye to the children and
calmly packing a suitcase with clothes to last me for
a few months. Still in disbelief, people came in and
out of the house to hug me, all in full view of the
large number of photographers stationed outside my
front door.

I had assured everyone who worried about me that
in fact I was very institutionalised and could survive
anything. And the good thing is that I believed it. In
the late 1980s, I spent an inordinate amount of time
in the Overseas Development Administration providing an economic recovery plan and then an economic
recovery implementation plan for Zanzibar, which,
because of a collapse in the price of cloves in the
face of increasing competition from Mauritius and
Madagascar, was being forced to move from being a
Marxist region redistributing revenues from cloves to
a more open one based on a functioning market economy with proper price signals and some policies to
encourage badly needed inward investment. The old

Arab stone town was beautiful but in dreadful condition. The main old hotel, which had splendid views of the ocean and the dhows still making the traditional journeys to Oman, the sultanate which they once belonged to, was in complete disrepair and so full of interesting rodents moving between your feet that you couldn't stay there. There was only one serious alternative: the Hotel Bowani. This splendid establishment was within walking distance (thankfully) of the stone city but had two problems: first, it was built next to a swamp so you had to dodge the malaria-carrying mosquitoes on the one side. The second was that after it was built, so the locals told us, representatives of the government had a fit when they realised the one hotel that could attract international visitors was built with no balconies. So they were added on – or rather, sort of glued on from the outside. We were told that unsuspecting visitors would open their French windows and step outside onto their balconies which would then collapse and fall to the ground with or without the guests still on them. Walking back to the hotel in the evening in the pitch dark (there were almost nightly power cuts) and trying to avoid walking too close to the swamp and malaria on the right and falling balconies on the narrow road on the left led to the creation of the 'Bowani test'.

As privatisation and economic reform work spread to other countries in Africa, eastern Europe (which was only just emerging from Communism), the Middle East, India and Bangladesh, and later China, my team and I would always compare the shabby hotels we stayed in to the Bowani, which soon became the bar below which it proved difficult for any establishment, however bad, to fall. So, went my theory, Holloway could not possibly be worse than the Bowani. If I had survived very difficult environments – sometimes threatening ones in so many countries around the world – I could survive a UK prison.

It was clear to me that the sentencing would be a custodial one. I was convinced by the attitude of the judge during my first trial and then the retrial that the judge was intent on passing a custodial sentence and that the judiciary did not like my marital coercion defence at all. The CPS argued that it could apply to a lorry driver's wife but not to someone 'rich and powerful' (if only) like me. I knew that the moment the guilty verdict was announced, to the gasps of the people at court, I would be sent to prison for a while. But I also knew that whatever the sentence, in most cases people only served half except in exceptional circumstances. In addition some of it was spent 'on tag' on Home Detention Curfew (HDC). The chances were that I wouldn't be away from home for long.

Nevertheless, I decided to prepare for the worst-case scenario and on the Monday morning, while the photographers were waiting outside the house (I wondered whether they had camped overnight after following me and taking pictures and I presume bribing the supermarket cashiers to tell them what I had bought, including bin liners, apparently), I was busy making all the arrangements for being away for a while. I left cheques for the pest control man, the milkman and generally for ensuring that the house and my children who lived there would survive my absence, at least financially. So it was with that complete peace of mind that I approached the day: it can't be worse than the Bowani. And if my time away was less than I had provided for then that would also be a great plus and the children, who feared the worst, would be relieved.

I was, of course, lucky insofar as I was able to make these provisions. Some 15 per cent of prisoners report that they are homeless before entering prison.[1] For those women who aren't, many face the possibility of eviction while inside due to rent arrears, as well as losing their personal property. Indeed one in three (32 per cent) of prisoners lose their homes while in prison[2] and there is no help available to pay for the storage of their belongings. Many children end up in local authority care while their mothers are in prison, with the remainder being looked after by an assortment of family, friends and acquaintances. Only one in twenty (5 per cent) children are able to stay in their own home when their mother is in prison.[3] They rarely have to move when their father goes to prison.

The array of judges with high salaries, investment savings from their time as QCs, and handsome pensions plus high social status only have the mother in front of them to send to prison. As many campaigners have observed, those actually punished are the children left behind. What is more, many initial care arrangements are likely to break down as a prison sentence progresses, leading to unstable and uncertain care for the child. Grandparents may be too old, ill or disabled. Sibling carers may be too young and emotionally immature to cope. Other family members may be put under financial pressure with another mouth to feed.

Prisoners in general are statistically more likely to be from backgrounds of social exclusion and poverty and an unexpected additional child may tip the balance and aggravate the hardship to crisis point.

There is not enough information about how many of the initial kinship care arrangements break down, resulting in the child entering the care system further down the line. A small but shocking minority of women in prison have no knowledge or information at all regarding care arrangements for their children while they are in custody. The Revolving Doors Agency based in Holloway prison found in a survey of 1,400 women serving their first sentence that forty-two women (3 per cent) had no idea who was looking after their children. Within this cohort it was reported that nineteen children under the age of sixteen years were looking after themselves.[4] Baroness Corston reflected that 'quite apart from the dreadful possibility that these children might not be in a safe environment, this must cause mothers great distress and have deleterious consequences for their mental health'.[5]

In my case, after many extra hearings and two trials, I received a custodial sentence of eight months for accepting my ex-husband's penalty points onto my driving licence some ten years earlier. This book will not dwell on the case or what went before it but will focus on the things I then learned about prisons, the prison system and the cost to society of sending people, particularly women, to jail who are no real threat to society.

And throughout it all I actually surprised myself. I told everyone that I was flexible and could cope with everything. Though I believed it, my friends and colleagues didn't. One of the first letters I received in prison was from a friend who reminded me that I had just two nights earlier at our local Pizza Express sent my water back because it had lemon in it, sent the wine back because it was too warm and complained that the egg on my pizza wasn't soft enough. This tale apparently caused a lot of hilarity among our friends who were trying to reconcile that incident with my assertion that I was 'flexible'. Point taken! I think he may have made up the bit about the egg but the rest is probably true. But what I had meant by flexibility was being able to change expectations and adapt to new environments, regardless of what was thrown at me. And adapt I had to in many more ways than I might have imagined.

Again, I was lucky; I have generally had few health concerns of any sort in my life. Many other women entering custody bring with them an array of emotional and mental health problems, as well as traumatic experiences. Some 37 per cent of women sentenced to prison say they have attempted suicide at some point in their lives[6] and 40 per cent have received treatment for a mental health problem in the year before coming to prison.[7] Nearly all (97 per cent) have experienced at least one traumatic life event, while just over half (54 per cent) of female remand prisoners were addicted to drugs in the year before entering prison.[8] Just under half of women prisoners have been victims of domestic violence and one in three has experienced sexual abuse.[9] There are countless other statistics I could share to show that the women entering prison often come from chaotic or troubled backgrounds, severely reducing their ability to cope in functional ways with the pressures of imprisonment.

A week before the verdict I had gone to a 'chattering classes' dinner in Islington. No one there – including one distinguished QC and judge – thought I would be found guilty. And if the unlikely event occurred, surely a sixty-year-old grandmother with a spotless record would not be sent to prison. They confessed that they knew no one who had gone to prison and they couldn't imagine what serving time might be like, though it turned out one friend present had been briefly imprisoned in Communist Poland for running money to the underground network of the banned Polish union, Solidarity. He had been caught and the police and judicial authorities explained they were simply doing their duty and upholding Polish law as it was at the time. But vivid as this experience remained in his memory, the story of sleeping twelve to a room on straw mattresses and toilets without loo paper was – I hoped – not relevant to British prisons. All I had to go by was a publication on the net by an ex-offender, giving useful advice on what prison was like, what to take in and how to cope.

My very good friends Nick Butler and Rosaleen Hughes expressed similar feelings as they offered a safe haven from photographers in a house not far from mine the Sunday night before sentencing. With the thought that I might not have a square meal again for a while, they cooked up apple crumble and cream, my favourite pudding. They also gave me books (to pass the time) and a radio so I could listen to the *Today* programme – they did not think it was possible for me to survive without enjoying John Humphrys flaying some shifty interviewee each morning. When I left my friends I could see that they were perplexed about this new category I was going to join: a 'criminal' and possibly about to spend some time in prison.

It is understandable that they should have felt that way. But now that I have experienced it myself I must admit that I am astounded at the misconceptions out there – not only about what makes a criminal but also about how one is treated. What I discovered in very simple terms is that first of all 'criminals' are very much like us and the people we meet in the street. In fact, as a result of a Freedom of Information request by the Press Association in early 2012 it was reported that at the time some 900 police officers and community support officers were serving with criminal records. Though most were for motoring offences, other crimes included burglary, supplying drugs and causing death by dangerous driving. Indeed there are 9.2 million people in the UK who have a criminal record and one in four of the UK's working-age population has a criminal record.[10] One in three males under the age of twenty-five is known to have a criminal conviction other than for a motoring offence. Even the Deputy Prime Minister, Nick Clegg, revealed that when young and drunk, he was given community service in Germany for setting fire to a collection of rare cacti.[11]

The number of people committing offences each year is huge. According to Ministry of Justice statistics more than 1.8 million people were either taken to court or given a reprimand or penalty notice for disorder in 2012. This enormous figure coincides with a reduction in the number of crimes committed.[12]

But the real figures for people who have committed offences will be even higher. In the ongoing, highly respected Cambridge Study in Delinquent Development, it was found that 41 per cent of a sample of males born in a deprived area of south London in 1953, today aged sixty, had at least one criminal conviction by the age of fifty and an average of five convictions each. More astonishingly, when asked,

93 per cent of the men admitted to having committed at least one of the following crimes: burglary, theft of vehicles, theft from vehicles, shoplifting, theft from machines, theft from work, fraud, assault, drug use and vandalism.[13] This suggests that the real number of people who have committed at least one crime may be more than twice the reported figure. All of this is nothing new, of course. Back in the 1940s, a study in New York found that 99 per cent of adults admitted to having committed at least one offence. Even church ministers admitted an average of eight offences each.[14] Other studies have shown that there is no relationship between socio-economic status and self-reported delinquency: middle-class kids break the law as much as poorer kids.[15]

In 2012, the British Crime Survey reported 9.8 million crimes against adults and children in England and Wales.[16] Yet there were only just under 700,000 convictions.[17] That's just 7.1 per cent of crimes leading to a conviction. And that presumes that all crime is captured by the British Crime Survey, which is generally acknowledged not to be so.

If one puts seriously violent cases aside, the division between being able to walk down the street and being put behind 'bars' can be down to a single moment – a wrong decision, a wrong turning, finding oneself in the wrong place at the wrong time, being associated with the wrong people, a momentary misjudgement – something that people do all the time but usually without disastrous consequence to them and their families. In fact, 24 per cent of women in prison have no previous convictions.[18] And for those convicted a lot of it seems to be down to bad luck, often disadvantaged background and little education.

Luck seems to work both ways; it is generally accepted that only 3 out of 100 offences end up in court. That figure has been pretty constant for a while. There are a number of reasons behind this statistic: first, many crimes are not reported at all. Many sexual crimes, in particular, are only surfacing now that norms have changed, but change is slow. In addition many instances of corporate crime are dealt with internally and hushed up to avoid damaging a company's reputation. Very few cases of corporate crime actually end up in court. Second, many crimes are not counted. In order to meet internal targets, police often classify crimes as non-crimes. They have to be convinced that the crime can be solved otherwise the rates of clearing crimes look low. Third, even if there are grounds for prosecuting the police may still just give a caution as it is easier and removes the risk of the CPS throwing the case out. And finally, the CPS might disagree with the police and throw the case out if they feel they don't have enough evidence to secure a conviction. So what we are seeing is just the tip of the iceberg. It would be too much to say: 'We are all criminals now', but there is an astonishingly high level of crimes committed that go undetected or unpunished.

A few days after my release, I walked to a coffee shop with an ex-Home Office senior civil servant who had worked on crime reduction issues. As we covered the 300 yards from Clapham Common tube to Clapham Old Town, my friend remarked that on our way there we had probably passed at least half a dozen people who had committed an offence and had never been caught and a similar number who had been convicted of an offence other than motoring and who may have been to prison. In his view, it was ironic that all the time that people were looking for retribution and punishment in sentencing decisions there seemed to be very little awareness in the media debate that the vast majority of people in prison will be released back into society at some point – and will be walking down the street, as I was doing, without others around them being aware of their past.

There also seems to be a worrying inconsistency in the treatment of individuals by the judicial system in this country. It gets you if it wants to or lets you go at the whim of a judge. There is evidence of a justice and sentencing 'postcode lottery' which defies logic and reason, and hence fairness and confidence in the justice system. In his book *Crime*, Nick Ross reminds us that life sentences more than doubled between 1994 and 2004 as a result of a toughening of sentencing rather than because more people committed particular crimes. So if caught during that period you would be likely to spend much longer in jail than before that date. But even then, data presented by the Howard League for Penal Reform to the All-Party Parliamentary Group on Women in the Penal System at their annual general meeting in July 2013 showed the huge inconsistency in the sentencing of women offenders across magistrates' courts throughout the country; Cumbria imposed almost four times more immediate custodial sentences for women in 2011 than Lincolnshire, Lancashire, Northumbria and Wiltshire.[19] English justice is meant to be blind but it certainly knows the geography of England as these bizarre, inexplicable differences between sentencing in one county compared to another clearly indicate.

What is more, even within a county the town you are attending court in may matter hugely; one girl I met later told me of her frustration at being sentenced to imprisonment in one city in East Anglia for possessing and allegedly intending to sell drugs (which she strongly denies) when caught in possession of a very small amount of cannabis when in any other court in a town more used to this type of crime she felt she would have been given, at worst, a suspended sentence or a caution.

A more lenient sentence would have avoided the negative articles in the press, which seems to be fascinated by any crime, however small, committed by a woman. The problem is, judges, juries and the press often react even more negatively towards women offenders because, in their view, committing a crime, however trivial, goes against a woman's very nature. Ann Lloyd explores this in her 1995 book *Doubly Deviant, Doubly Damned: Society's Treatment of Violent Women*. Women with criminal convictions, she explains, have not only broken the law but also offended people's ideas of womanhood. Yvonne Jewkes, Professor of Criminology at the University of Leicester, argues that 'the media tap into, and magnify, deep-seated public fears about deviant women, while paying much less attention to equally serious male offenders'.[20] Many of the women I later met in prison believed they were given custodial sentences for offences that a man may have been given a suspended sentence or a caution for instead. It is hard to prove this but the feeling resonated and was expressed not just by the women but also by many of the staff.

Inevitably as an economist and former joint head of the Government Economic Service I had spent a lot of time looking at cost–benefit analysis of government interventions and had written peer reviews of many government departments' analysis. But I was acutely aware that I had never looked at Home Office and Ministry of Justice policy appraisals with the care they deserved and though I was vaguely aware of some of the work done on the costs and benefits of keeping men in prison, I was pretty sure that the work on women lagged behind. In fact I recall thinking that a lot of the evidence relied on studies carried out in the US. Well, as the judge handed me an eight-month custodial sentence, I was about to find out a lot more.

Thoughts of economics gave way to thoughts of short-term survival as I was led down to the holding area in preparation for the transfer to Holloway soon after sentencing. Just before, during the break after the mitigation presentations by the two sides and before the judge passed down the sentences, I had rushed to the loo and on the way back noticed my friends Stephanie and Philip Maltman and their neighbour Kate sitting disconsolately on the benches outside the court. I can't recall the exchanges now but they told me afterwards that after they asked how I was, I had answered, 'Never mind that, how do I look?' Yes, that was probably true. Looks are important as you cannot afford to look despondent and beaten in front of the photographers and the court artists, who exaggerate any negatives to make a point. I had taken good care every day to appear smart and coordinated and relaxed. Not easy. But at least now the cameras couldn't follow me downstairs. Thinking that my bracelets would not be allowed with me I handed them to the legal assistant who the press, seeing me hugging her in the morning, immediately described in

the pictures that followed as one of my daughters –
another to add to the three I have already!

The process of enumerating and cataloguing what
I was taking with me so that it would all arrive safely
in Holloway took a bit of time. I was taking a suitcase full of clothes and toiletries, many of which I
suspected would not pass the test of acceptability once
in Holloway, and a black handbag which had to be
searched and bagged in a plastic carrier bag but with
all the valuables in it enumerated. So started a rather
long search through it to establish how much money
I had on me and therefore what I was taking with me
as a 'float', which might keep me going while inside.
People from the outside as I discovered could easily
add to this by sending cash in. But many girls I came
across had no one – or their relatives were too poor
to send money and they were relying entirely on the
wages they received in prison for the work they did to
survive. Most prison services such as cleaning, giving
support to incoming prisoners, library assistance,
cooking, laying and clearing tables, and other routine
work are done by the inmates for usually a paltry sum
of rarely more than £20 a week. The money is used
to make phone calls to their loved ones and to buy
things like tobacco from the 'canteen' – some 'mythi-
cal place' that brought in basic supplies and possibly
a few treats like chocolate once a week, assuming you
had any money to spend. So going in with enough
money was important. I never knew that.

I had no idea what was in my bag. The past few
weeks had been rather unusual. I had gone to the
bank to get cash on a few occasions on the way to
the crown court, mostly intending to leave it with the
children to cover the cost of running the house if I

was sent away for any length of time. I also used it to buy various things – coffee every morning from Starbucks outside London Bridge station, which became my trademark as I was photographed carrying one cup with the name of the coffee franchise prominently displayed each morning (I hope they were grateful for the free product placement), and a vast number of unhealthy croissants and muffins from the crown court trolley. Obviously in those days I was not thinking particularly rationally. And although I thought I was in control that morning before heading to court, I had in fact forgotten that I had been hoarding cash and had written the kids cheques instead. So we started counting what was in the bag: tons and tons of coins which had been weighing me down for some time, nearly £100 worth, lodged at the bottom of the bag or inside various zipped compartments (there were many). To my complete embarrassment but the huge amusement of the security guard, there, in between diaries, packets of tissues, chequebooks, loose credit and store cards, letters, newspaper clippings (it was a big bag) and a red rose that had been given to me earlier as I was entering the court by some lovely gentleman who had come to my trial every day, we started collectively to bring out a tenner here, a £20 note there, even the odd £50 note, a few fivers I had been given as change. As we were transferring the bag's contents slowly into a plastic bag for the journey we found more and more – and more. By the time we finished some half an hour later all the other officers on the ground floor next to the exit where the Serco van was waiting to take me to Holloway had come to watch and could not believe their eyes as we finally established that I was going to prison with a total of £1,490 in cash. Instead of the cheques, this was cash I should have left at home that morning for my children. In the end I was grateful for my mistake. The very expensive phone calls alone during the entire period I was in prison cost around £400, much more than my prison earnings over that period. Perversely, counting out these notes and coins set the scene for what was to come as it actually allowed for a much more relaxed and humorous atmosphere to develop, which had a very calming effect on me and stood me in good stead for what would otherwise have developed into a horrendously tense evening. I had heard of people (particularly women) breaking into tears once they were in the cells downstairs after sentencing and I think that incident and the kindness and humanity of the guards proved to be a life saver for me.

It was this sort of kindness from both officers and fellow prisoners that made a huge difference to me throughout my time in prison. Professor Alison Liebling, a highly respected prison researcher based at the University of Cambridge, has written at length on how values such as trust, respect, fairness, order and well-being contribute to making prison life less distressing, less dangerous and more survivable.[21] Nick Hardwick, the current Chief Inspector of Prisons, later told me that, from what he had seen, the officers' understanding of what is important to you as an individual – even little things like getting a drink or having access to a hairdryer when you need it – goes some way to 'make an unbearable situation a bit more bearable'.

I had a quick chat with my legal team who came down to see me and I was able to keep a book to read, my notebook and a pen to make notes as I was whisked into what is known as a 'black Maria' (actually a white transport van) alongside a girl who was on remand being taken back to Holloway after her court appearance. We were put in separate cubicles in the van and started our journey. It was still daylight and as we exited the basement car park I was not prepared for the photographers who were banging their cameras onto the vehicle's window to try and get a picture of me as I was leaving. As we stopped at some traffic, more of them did the same thing, much to the consternation of the girl I was travelling with and the guards, who thought it all appalling. There was a bit of calm as we drove through the streets of north London, past the Arsenal football stadium, which I knew reasonably well, but it quickly ended as we drove into Holloway, with more photographers waiting, more banging on the side of the car, more flash cameras pointing at my face through the window of my cubicle. Once we went through the prison gates, there was peace at last. And so began my nine weeks of prison life: four days in Holloway and then just over eight weeks in East Sutton Park open prison for women.

CHAPTER 2

HOLLOWAY

When asked whether my experience arriving in Holloway was frightening, my answer was simple: no. Many people think that prison must be a terrifying place with lots of violent women locked behind bars. It isn't. I must confess that my arrival at Holloway was smooth, humane and expertly carried out. Quick fingerprinting and BOSS chair (Body Orifice Security Scanner, essentially a metal detector). No strip search. The little information pamphlet handed out to me on arrival comprised a mere eight pages, with page 7 taken up by a crossword and page 8 by two sudoku puzzles. It was all very different from the environment that had greeted David (now Lord) Ramsbotham in December 1995 when he went to do his first unannounced review of Holloway as the then new independent Chief Inspector of Prisons. He was so shocked he stopped the visit the following day and didn't resume it again for six months. A lot has happened since and after many starts and setbacks under numerous governors, prison director generals and secretaries of state in the Home Office and later the Ministry of Justice (MoJ), the place now seemed to be reasonably welcoming.

But there are rules. It was clear I had brought in far too many clothes. I was allowed to keep just twelve tops (shirts, T-shirts and jumpers) and six bottoms (trousers, tracksuit bottoms and pyjamas). No toiletries were allowed but I was given an emergency bag with prison issue and I bought a 'welcome' bag for £2.99, which would be subtracted from the cash I brought in with me. It contained a bottle of orange squash, biscuits, a bar of milk chocolate, deodorant, toothbrush and toothpaste, a comb and some tea bags and sugar. I had the choice of that or a smoker's bag. But I could take in my books, all eighteen of them and many given to me by my children, as well as my writing pads and a couple of pens. The rest stayed in my suitcase and the handbag which had also accompanied me. I would retrieve everything again when I left for East Sutton Park (ESP) a few days later.

A reception officer took down my details and told me where I was going for the first night and that she was putting me down for a single room; a doctor took my blood pressure, which was dangerously high (no surprise after the last few months); and I was met by a welcoming group of prisoners, an innovation which I am told ex-governor Tony Hassall introduced, whose job it was to answer my questions and ensure I got something to eat (chilli con carne and some pudding). It was certainly not what I had expected.

Then the welcome group and prison guards helped me and some other new inmates move our personal belongings, which had now been transferred into transparent prison plastic bags, to landing A3, the reception landing, which ended up being my home for the next few days. The lovely girl who had secured the food for me told me on the way that she had two more years to do but enjoyed doing the reception work because it kept her out of her cell until quite late in the evening.

Early 2012 was experiencing a very long winter (I had often walked to and from court in the snow) and that bitterly cold night I soon realised that the windows in Holloway cells do little to keep the chill out. At first I was shown a cell with no curtains and my helpers tried to fasten an orange blanket onto the railings, without much success. Fortunately there was another single cell available with curtains, this time near the guards' office, but the TV was not working so there was another quick changeover. Then it was obvious that one thin orange blanket on the bed was not enough. Soon the girls were at my cell door with extra blankets even though that was apparently not normally allowed; within a few minutes I ended up with five and had to turn down the offer of a sixth. And then extra fruit and sandwiches that they must have had in their own cells started arriving and shampoo for the shower and extra toilet roll for the loo in my cell. I couldn't believe the kindness of them all. When formalities were completed and I had spoken to the children and my lawyer using my free phone calls and my door was finally locked, the girls kept coming back and asking me through the hatch whether there was anything else I wanted. Many have commented about the solidarity in women's prisons – yes, there is bitching and some bullying but there is also a lot more demonstrable empathy among the women prisoners than in a men's prison.

They say that when that first lock-up happens and you are left alone in your room, reality finally takes its toll; when they finally lie in bed most new prisoners turn their heads towards the wall and start crying. Within the first seven days of prison, 20 per cent of

all prison suicides occur[22] as well as a disproportionate amount of the overall levels of self-harm.[23] I had
had such an exhausting few weeks that none of this
happened – not on the first nor any subsequent night.
I watched the coverage of my case on TV and fell
promptly asleep.

12 MARCH

I was woken by the guard the next morning around
7 a.m. The cell door was unlocked at 8 a.m. (9 at the
weekend). Breakfast was at 8.15 but let's not get too
carried away: the meal consisted of toast and butter
(no jam) though later, at lunch, we were given an
individual cereal portion, tea bags and a small carton
of milk. I don't normally have breakfast but I had
been advised that whenever food is offered in prison
I should take it; as such I started to eat breakfast and
continued doing so in East Sutton Park, where at
least jam was served with the toast. I also took the
opportunity to smuggle a few slices of toast back to
my room to see me through the morning.

Most women in closed prisons lose an incredible
amount of weight either because they won't eat the
food (it tends to be ghastly) or because the portions
are so small that they go constantly hungry – unless
they are lucky enough to be able to supplement their
meals with unhealthy biscuits bought at the canteen
every week. Indeed, the best thing on the menu while
I was in Holloway was in fact the toast. One of my
roommates in ESP told me later how she had gone
into Holloway a size twenty just ten months earlier
and was now a size fourteen. She looked really good
in her new size but I wondered how I would have
fared having gone in as a size eight.

We all know how important healthy eating is but, interestingly, in his 2003 book *Prisongate* Lord Ramsbotham refers to evidence from clinical studies in many countries that proves that 'correct nutrition is a cheap, humane and highly effective way of reducing anti-social behaviour'.[24] He refers in particular to a study by Bernard Gesch of National Justice (a research charity investigating the causes of crime). Gesch and his colleagues conducted a trial that showed that a group of young offenders given healthy food supplements compared with a group that took a placebo saw a 37 per cent reduction in violent offences while in detention.[25] The results were accepted but the recommendation to provide supplements across all prisons was never implemented even though it would have cost, according to Ramsbotham, just £3.5m a year from a prison budget of some £2.8bn. Indeed, nutritious food could be prepared without great cost. Chef Al Crisci trains prisoners at HMP High Down to work in a gourmet restaurant called 'The Clink', which he started in 2009 and is open to the public.

> Prison food [at High Down] is wholesome, low in salt, fat and preservatives, fits within the five-a-day fruit and vegetable guidelines, and only costs £2.10 per prisoner, per day ... It makes sense. Why serve rubbish for £2.10 when you can, with a little more effort, and within the same budget, cook food which helps improve behaviour?[26]

His call is one that echoes Jamie Oliver's campaign to improve student behaviour by providing high-quality school meals.

After breakfast, I almost missed what is known

as the 'movement'. Described in the induction notes, the 'movement' was essentially a twice-daily great exodus of women from their cells and a supervised walk through the prison to the various places of education, exercise, healthcare and so on. I had gone to the shower and on returning to my cell found a guard waiting to lock me back in. Over breakfast, the girls had told me there was a daily walk in the prison yard, and I managed to persuade the guard to allow me to run behind the trail of women with my wet hair so I wouldn't miss out. Fortunately, the movement was quite slow that morning and I soon caught up. I discovered that as I followed the others I could step into the various offices that lined the twisting corridors (built like a hospital, each part of a prison corridor has a guard office so the guards are able to see and control the few cells in front of them). To my surprise, each office had a hairdryer (among other things) that prisoners could borrow on production of their prison card (I had been given mine at reception when I entered the previous night). Indeed, as Chief Inspector of Prisons Nick Hardwick told me, these are the little things that make life in prison bearable. Being able to borrow a hairdryer from an officer in this way also allows a woman the opportunity to chat about how she is worried about her kids or discuss other matters on her mind. According to Nick, anything that might jeopardise this general interaction is a worry.

By the time I went outside my hair was only slightly drier; thank goodness I had put my hat in my pocket when I left my cell. My daily exercise out in the yard from then on (unless it was raining) consisted of a very brisk walk for half an hour, going round and round with the only other woman bothering to walk.

Everyone else would stand against the walls smoking or chatting or generally being quite rambunctious with each other and with the guards.

It soon transpired that no one seemed to think I should have been in prison at all and throughout the next few days, wherever I went following the 'movement', girls would shake my hand and offer support. During the outdoor walk, as I tried to exercise my legs and breathe in some fresh and very cold air, the girls would tell me how surprised and pleased they were that I was not snubbing them but actually was prepared to mix with them all – and then told me their own stories, which got me thinking about how vulnerable so many of these girls and women were.

In fact, I was shocked at the number of cases where indeed the girls had done something wrong but usually for, with, or forced to by their husbands, boyfriends, brothers or fathers. These girls needed help, I thought, not incarceration. Indeed, according to people I spoke to later, senior officers have been known to say that out of some 460 women prisoners in Holloway no more than around sixty that pose a threat to society should remain in prison, and the rest shouldn't be there at all. According to the Ministry of Justice, and not including courts and policing, each prisoner in 2011/12 cost on average some £37,648 a year in direct prison-related costs. That figure becomes higher still if one adds expenditure met by other government departments in areas such as health and education. One must also consider that women and longer-term prisoners cost a lot more. There could be significant savings from lowering prisoner numbers.[27] No doubt costs would be incurred elsewhere, for many of the women in prison are vulnerable and need some sort of help, but it is argued that Holloway and other prisons like it should not be performing the role of an amateur psychiatric unit, which should really be the job of other organs of the state and society and the community at large.

One particular concern, which people are becoming increasingly aware of, is the significant numbers of foreign females in British prisons who may actually themselves be the victims of human trafficking. Their traffickers may have forced them to commit crime, or they may be in custody because of offences related to their immigration status, such as deception, fraud or use of false documents. A 2012 study looked at the cases of 103 foreign nationals in prison for offences relating to immigration status and identified forty-three of the women as victims of human trafficking. Many will have suffered highly traumatic experiences such as repeated physical abuse, rape or being forced into the sex industry. Past experiences of corrupt officials and repeated abuse leave many too afraid to tell their full story.[28]

The difficulty foreign prisoners face cannot be overestimated. Serena, a highly educated woman I met when I visited the library in Holloway, told me of having been approached by a Brazilian girl who was sharing a cell with another Brazilian woman who had been in Holloway already for four months and who seemed to be at a loss as to why she was being kept in prison. She was in a high state of anxiety as she only spoke Portuguese and was lucky to have eventually found another Brazilian and was therefore able to explain her situation. With the other girl acting as interpreter, it emerged that the Brazilian lady had been arrested on charges of kidnapping at the airport where she was trying to fly to Brazil with her daughter. The lady and the child's father had been living in France but he had moved to the UK. After she let her daughter visit her father he had refused to let her return to her mother. After a time the Brazilian lady obtained a court order against the father for kidnapping, came to the UK, found her daughter and tried to leave the country with her. The child's father contacted the police and the woman was apprehended.

Apparently it turned out that the Brazilian lady had not in fact committed the offence of kidnapping when she was arrested, as she hadn't actually taken the child away for the requisite amount of time for an offence of 'kidnapping' to have been committed. After a long letter on the mother's behalf was written to the CPS by Serena explaining the situation, the lady was released. As far as I understand it the Brazilian mother is reunited with her daughter and all is well. I could not believe the system allows such injustice to take place, but mistakes will always happen and frankly it is not surprising that with such large numbers going through the system and the chaos that seems to prevail there will be cases that slip through the net.

But the importance of prisoners being able to communicate is key, particularly if they are foreign. With this horror story in my mind I later suggested to Helen, who I met in East Sutton Park and who had managed to transfer from what she described as a 'dreadful' and 'dangerous' Brazilian prison, where she was serving time for drugs, to Holloway and then to open prison, that she should brush up on the Portuguese she learned while there and offer her services in prisons or at the court as translator and mentor once she got out given the large number of

Brazilians in the UK at present. I wonder, though, whether current rules would allow an ex-offender like Helen to be employed by the prison system – in my view they should make sure that experiences such as Helen's are put to good use for the benefit of society as a whole, otherwise what is the point of sending people to prison?

After the morning walk, I shared a table for lunch in the 'dining' space of A3. This was a grim unfriendly room with a few basic old but functioning armchairs, and a hatch from which the food was served to you by other inmates, led by a lovely if troubled Welsh girl who was in for grievous bodily harm after one incident when out drinking. You had to form an orderly queue, your name was called and your choice of food served (vegetarian or otherwise – I had not had a chance to make a choice so ate what I was given). Water was available from a drinking tap and you could sit and eat on one of a handful of white plastic tables and chairs, which were rarely used as most inmates took their food into their rooms in time for evening lock-up. Recognising me, however, a number of the girls, mostly quite young, came and sat with me and chatted – and the chats were extraordinary. They told me of some women who were in for low-level drug trafficking, and who clearly were on drugs themselves, and how they were having a very difficult time adjusting to prison. They would wander around mumbling to themselves and girls who slept in cells adjacent to those women could not sleep at night either because of their moans, cries or in one case loud singing every night.

According to recent data 15.6 per cent of women in prison are there for drugs offences[29] with many

more sentenced for property-related offences to fund
their drug habits. Drug dependence in the year before
entering prison is as high as 54 per cent for remand
prisoners and 41 per cent for sentenced prisoners.[30]
I have been told in fact that in some prisons access
to drugs is easier than on the outside. A survey by
the Prison Reform Trust in 2012 backs up previous
academic research in finding that 19 per cent of prisoners who had ever used heroin reported first trying it
in prison.[31]

I discovered that a number of the girls on A3 were
apparently on remand and there was a general sigh
of relief from the other girls for the few quiet hours
everyone was able to have when these troubled girls
were taken to court. And the girls didn't often come
back; those on remand didn't always end up receiving a custodial sentence. In addition to higher rates of
substance misuse, remand prisoners have been shown
to suffer more from a range of emotional and mental
health problems, though whether this is due to the
uncertainty about their future, or the reason for their
being denied bail, is unclear. The Ministry of Justice
found that nearly twice as many remand prisoners
by comparison to convicted prisoners rated highly
for various symptoms of neurosis, including sleep
problems, worry, fatigue, depression and irritability.
Phobias, panic and obsessive behaviour were also
significantly more common among remand prisoners.
When asked, some 23 per cent of female remand prisoners reported having considered suicide within the
previous week, while just over a quarter had attempted
suicide within the past year. In addition, roughly twice
as many remand prisoners are prescribed antipsychot-
ics or anti-anxiety medication.[32]

Others on my landing included Irish 'travellers' who had somehow got into trouble together with their boyfriends, who were also arrested and in prison; a couple of girls in for hurting someone after they got too drunk one night out and who were serving a few months each; and a girl who had an accountancy qualification, had gone out one evening along with her boyfriend and some of his friends and found herself the object of attention by a different gang of boys. Scuffles broke out, she threw a bottle of Ribena at someone but in the scuffle a boy from her group knifed someone from the other group. The girl and one other didn't run away and were sentenced to a number of years in jail on the charge of 'joint enterprise'. This is an old charge but one used increasingly, so it seemed, to deal with gangs that committed crimes in groups. It makes sense as a concept but in the way I saw it exercised – if I were to believe what I was being told – it seemed that this joint enterprise or 'association' was now so widely used and caused so much hardship for many young girls that all proportionality was removed during sentencing.

I resolved to investigate that further while I was in prison and after I came out. It was obvious to me straight away that my position was different to most people there. Some of them were likely to be spending many years in prison or were serial offenders and serving successive short-term sentences. The proportion of women leaving prison who are reconvicted within twelve months is a staggering 54 per cent, rising to 90 per cent for those who have served ten or more previous custodial sentences.[33] Reconviction does not automatically mean a custodial sentence, of course, but there is something wrong with a prison

system that perpetuates itself and is unable to help
the women who pass through it. Imagine the outcry
if half the women treated by the NHS were soon back
in hospital. We would replace doctors, ministers and
executives. I felt I could begin to make sense of it all
by talking to fellow prisoners and looking at all the
evidence that others working in the area had gathered. This was clearly a very weird environment for
anyone to find oneself in and such a waste of time,
public money and misdirected effort as it seemed to
have little impact on reoffending. I knew already that
the past twenty years or so had seen a momentous
increase in the prison population (people can't have
suddenly become that much worse behaved, surely);
indeed, the number of women in prison increased by
85 per cent between 1996 and 2011.[34] Between 2000
and 2010 alone the population of women in prison
had increased by 27 per cent. Despite the election
of so many women as MPs, many of whom became
ministers after 1997, and the commission of Baroness
Corston to complete the first review of women in
prison, we still sadly saw the biggest increase in the
incarceration of women in British prison history. Did
none of their colleagues at the Treasury ever ask if
spending all that taxpayers' money locking up women
(and many men) was efficient public expenditure?

Many of the girls I spoke to had young babies and
children, and more often than not seemed to be in
prison due to or because they were fleeing from an
abusive relationship. Data suggests that the number
of women in prison who have been physically,
emotionally or sexually abused as children is as high
as 53 per cent.[35] And Karen Elgar, governor of HMP
Send, a closed women's prison in Surrey, wrote in a

report on fashion education in prisons that 'often ... women become involved in criminal activity through unhealthy, violent or dependent relationships with men – and consequently have very poor levels of self-esteem and no self-confidence'. Not surprisingly, a highly publicised study by the Prison Reform Trust published during my two months in East Sutton Park drew attention to the fact that although women represent only 5 per cent of the entire prison population they account for a third of all the incidents of self-harm.[36]

Indeed this has been a problem that prisons such as Holloway have been struggling with for some time. Angela Devlin, in her seminal book *Invisible Women: What's Wrong with Women's Prisons?*,[37] points out the difficulty of caring properly for women in a building originally meant to be a hospital, with its twisting corridors built for pushing patient trolleys along. It makes supervision and control rather difficult and obliges the prison to have offices for prison staff in practically each corner to allow a proper view of what is going on. Lord Ramsbotham says that Holloway bears all the marks of a prison designed by a committee. And Nick Hardwick describes Holloway as 'horrible and too big'. In his view, if the prison works it is only because of its location – people prefer to stay there rather than being relocated to, say, Reading prison or Bronzefield women's prison in Kent because it keeps them close to their families. At least in Holloway there are lots of staff around who are visible for the prisoners to approach and discuss various matters. Nick Hardwick explained that in a number of the new private prisons, although you have a nice cell, a lot of gadgetry to order your food, a good canteen and anything else you might need including being able to make appointments for many prison services and education courses, the key element missing is human contact. This reduces the need for staff and also takes away the necessary interaction with other inmates and staff. In consequence nobody really knows you or understands your despairs and no one is able to correctly assess the risk you are in and the real help you need, and therefore care for you. Interpersonal relationships are reduced to a minimum in the quest for greater efficiency and lower running costs.

Liz Padmore is one of the best-known public sector non-executive directors. When still a partner at Andersen Consulting (now Accenture) she took part in a scheme some years ago facilitated by Business in the Community, which encouraged big companies like Andersen Consulting, British Airways, Centrica and also the *Guardian* newspaper to 'adopt' prisons. Liz picked Holloway and she was one of the people who spent a lot of time with the then governor Tony Hassall, sharing knowledge and focusing mainly on how to manage the prison better and reduce the incidence of self-harm and female suicides. She certainly came away with the impression during her mentoring period that women were in jail for having committed much smaller crimes than men and that the impact on families and society of removing those women was, in her words, 'draconian' in relation to their crimes. The vast percentage of the female prison population she encountered and of which she heard of during her mentoring either had a drugs problem, which they were often introduced to by their 'boyfriends' or at times their pimps, or they were made to steal or push drugs for money to feed their and their boyfriends' drug habits, or they had been in an abusive relationship with boyfriends who coerced them into being 'drug mules'. She came across cases of Colombian 'mules' who had been caught importing drugs and who were probably coerced to do so by threats to their families if they did not comply. And many other women were in for pretty short sentences during which they learned nothing to help them survive life on the outside, and instead gained a distrust of authority and bleak prospects for future employment. Indeed a report for the National Offender Management Service in 2012 suggested that only 8.4 per cent of women go straight into employment after short sentences of less than a year compared to 27.3 per cent of men.[38]

During her period of mentoring Liz explained that she supported Tony Hassall's decision to close the rather large officers' gym and have the officers share the inmates' gym. The officers' gym was then converted to a hairdressing salon – and they are now prevalent in all educational annexes of most prisons, allowing inmates to train and take NVQs while in prison and therefore offering some hope of employment after release. I later met girls who had been in Peterborough prison, for example, who also reported that the beauty therapy course there was extremely popular and a good preparation for the outside world. When I later moved to open prison, I found that there was indeed a lot of interest in beauty therapy and girls combined the classes with a business enterprise course, with many of them intending to run their own business in this area after they left prison. I had the chance to look at a number of the business plans the girls were using to raise external funding for their business and to pay for extra qualifications while they were still inside. And many had succeeded in finding potential funders. In the case of East Sutton Park, this was done with the help of the highly rated 'Vision' office, which acts as an interface for the residents and the outside education and employment worlds. Working Chance, a charity run by Jocelyn Hillman, is the main employment agency for women offenders and ex-offenders, and helps run a three-day course on employment skills: the girls apply for a dummy job, then someone comes in from the outside to 'interview' them and they then receive feedback on their performance and tips on how to improve. Working Chance operates inside prisons but also runs courses in its offices in Islington, which are very popular.

The girls on my landing were generally very friendly. Not only did they take care of me but they chatted non-stop whenever we were together. It would often be the case that as I was passing the two phone boxes in our landing girls would shout greetings from their mothers. That is, of course, the way that information sneaks out, unless it comes from the officers themselves. There was huge interest in the press in how I was coping and the story in the papers the following day was that I was fine and spending time socialising with other girls in their cells. It amazed me that anyone should be interested in that. I realised why a few days later once I got access to newspapers following my transfer to ESP. The expectation was that because of the high publicity of the case I would have a hard time in Holloway. In an article for the *Telegraph* a few days after my conviction, the crime writer Lynda La Plante wrote that given that my face was now as 'familiar as a movie star's' what awaited me was likely to be quite sinister, 'a frightening and alien environment', with cat-calls and abuse 'yelled over and over again'.[39] She may indeed have witnessed that sort of behaviour when she was visiting Holloway and spending time talking with and observing inmates and staff, but in truth my own experience could not have been more different. It is true that there wouldn't be many (if any) other women like me in Holloway but I encountered no animosity, sniping, bitching or negative treatment from anyone, either among my fellow inmates or from the officers. Instead there was huge sympathy from all and a general desire, it seemed to me, to make me feel better about being there.

I had always thought that the main impact of being sent to prison was that it took away your liberty for a while. And that should be enough and allow you to pay back society for whatever you may or may not have done, or at least satisfy people that justice was being served. But soon after I went to prison, a number of girls told me that in fact their worst moments were during the trial, where things were said about them that they didn't recognise. During the coverage of their trial they felt they had been singled out by the judge and the press for being a 'bad' female – a rare thing. And once in prison there is the added frustration of having little control over external events. With no mobile phone and no internet, there's no awareness of what may be appearing in the press and little opportunity of putting forward a defence or reassuring beleaguered family and friends. Reputations may be shattered; some girls were so worried about what was being said about them in their local papers they had no idea how they could ever possibly return to their homes. But one just had to put up with it and trust that friends and relatives would rise above it all and learn to cope. Worrying about how their children were coping in their absence was a major preoccupation of all the women with children I met in prison. At least mine were grown up and able, in general, to take care of themselves and make their own decisions. Many others were not in that position.

As I have mentioned earlier, 66 per cent of women prisoners have dependent children (of which 34 per cent have children under five years old[40]), and for 85 per cent of women prisoners, their time in prison is their first prolonged period of separation from their children.[41] Mothers in prison experience a high degree of emotional distress and trauma from the separation and their inability to care for their children. One mother reported, 'If I ever received news from home about my son having problems, it drove me to despair. I would be really distraught at not being able to do anything for him.'[42] The consequences of this trauma can be profound. A female prisoner interviewed by the Women's Justice Taskforce said, 'I went into prison as someone with no mental health issues. I became someone that began to self harm ... the pain inside me from being separated from my daughter was so intense that the only way to stop that would be to bang my head on the wall and to cut to give myself physical pain to stop that in my tummy.'[43]

In 2007, Baroness Corston headed an inquiry into women in prisons after the deaths of six women at HMP Styal within the space of twelve months. Approximately 2,200 children of imprisoned mothers are taken into care each year[44] and the evidence so clearly suggests that the short- and long-term impact on those children can be devastating. Children in care have a very high propensity to

become offenders themselves. Less than 1 per cent
of children overall in England were in care in March
2011.[45] And yet conservative estimates are that up
to half of under-eighteens in young offender institutions have at some point been in care.[46] Children
with imprisoned parents may feel emotions of anger,
distress at separation, low self-esteem, confusion and
fear, all of which may translate into defiant, destruc-
tive and attention-seeking behaviour.[47] A study of
thirty-six children with imprisoned mothers in the US
found that 75 per cent of the children exhibited behav-
ioural symptoms associated with post-traumatic
stress disorder. Imprisoning mothers for non-violent
offences is estimated to cost the state £17m over
ten years, with the biggest expense coming from
increased numbers of young adults whose mothers have gone to prison becoming NEETs – 'Not in
Education, Employment or Training' – drug users or
involved with crime.[48] Even after taking into account
the effects of parental convictions and other childhood risk factors, children who are separated from
a parent due to imprisonment are four times more
likely to display a whole range of antisocial coping
behaviours, including fighting, drinking heavily,
taking illegal drugs, poor relationships with parents
and partners, divorce, separation from their own
children, being frequently unemployed, increased
levels of delinquency, and an increased likelihood
of being convicted themselves for criminal offences.
What's more, this behaviour is likely to persist as the
children enter adulthood.[49]

In short, as Baroness Corston noted in her investigation into the problems of women's imprisonment,
the effects of unstable, uncertain care arrangements

in place for the children are 'often nothing short of catastrophic'.[50]

Yvonne Roberts, writer for *The Observer* and commentator and trustee of the charity Women in Prison, says that many women are too scared to tell the system that they have children when they are arrested as they fear that they would lose them. This was reinforced in discussions with Jacquie Russell of Women's Breakout, a charity representing forty-seven women-focused organisations around the country. I was astonished. I had not encountered such behaviour since the mid-1970s, when I became manager of the economics office at a Scottish bank. One of the women who worked for me, though some years older, confessed that she had successfully hidden from her employers for over a decade the fact that she had a fourteen-year-old daughter, fearing discrimination and quite possibly the sack if she came clean as the equal opportunities law did not exist when she first started working. Because she finally had a woman boss she felt she could tell me.

Though some women facing a custodial sentence make arrangements to have their children looked after by a family member, interestingly research suggests that a large percentage, possibly some 50 per cent of women, don't expect to be sent to prison at all.[51] I spoke to girls myself who had been assured by their solicitors that they would be spared prison and who also trusted that their pre-sentence probation report, which recommended alternatives to custody, would be taken seriously. The result, I am told, is that they often go to court to be sentenced having left their small children in the care of neighbours for the day, fully expecting to be back to pick them up that evening. One woman I met, who had been a HR manager in a software company, told me how when she went to be sentenced for what she thought was a minor fraud charge she had been assured by those who wrote her pre-sentence report and by her solicitor, who she trusted, that there was no way she was going to be sent to prison. She remembers looking at other women who were turning up with bags with clothes and other personal items to take in with them and thinking how sad that must be. When the sentence of eighteen months was passed she was shocked. Not only had she not prepared her husband and children for it, she had nothing of use with her when she went in. All she had in her handbag was a deodorant and a makeup powder container with a mirror inside which the officers removed because it was dangerous and could be used for attack or self-harm. One can imagine the heartbreak, stress and agony these women feel when they are unexpectedly sent down as they have often made no arrangements for their family to survive while they are away and therefore the chances of the children being taken into care increase markedly.

It was clear to me in no time at all that female prisoners were troubled by the very things one expects women to worry about. Their children and their families were their first priority. Prison visitors and ex-governors I have since spoken to confirm that what they encounter in female prisons is completely different to what they observe in men's prisons. Men are focused on getting through it – to quote a senior Home Office ex-civil servant: 'men look down and don't engage, women, once they become more familiar, which happens very quickly, start to chat and gossip with you'. Ex-governors described women's prisons as feeling much more like mental institutions, but with a lot of chatter and friendships, not violent like the men's; on the whole, the most danger the women posed was to themselves. As one ex-governor said, 'You could bring the walls down in a closed prison and the women just wouldn't leave!'

13 MARCH

Up at 7 a.m. again and the same routine as the day before. But it wasn't all doom and gloom, however strange my new environment. It seemed to me that if one was determined there were lots of ways to survive it, at least for someone like me who was fortunate enough not to be coming to prison from the sorts of chaotic, dysfunctional backgrounds that many of the women had endured. Indeed there were also moments of fun in the chaos that seems to be Holloway.

It looked like I might miss the chance to get out of my cell and do my intended induction course for education and the gym this week because planned visits from my legal team and my children were coinciding with the few times that the induction sessions were available – and you weren't allowed to start those courses until you had done the inductions. Nevertheless, with the help of some inmates and a kind guard, I somehow managed to get into the right queue and sneak my way into what looked like a very well-functioning library on the ground floor at the end of the 'movement'. When I was recounting this later to Nick Hardwick he told me that it is these sorts of things, the help given to make life bearable behind bars, that measure how well a prison is functioning – not statistics.

I signed in at the library and picked a couple of books I thought I might borrow – they were crime thrillers, which seemed to be the main genre available there. And then, what luxury, I watched a movie for a couple of hours (the week's showing – I was lucky to have chosen that day). I had already seen the film, *Nowhere Boy*, but it was an unexpected pleasure to sit in a more or less normal setting, surrounded by books rather than my cell walls. The place was packed. But on closer inspection it wasn't because people were keen to watch the movie; the real attraction of the library as far as I could see was that it served as a place for the inmates to spend a few unsupervised hours quietly snogging their girlfriends.

I watched the library staff handle all sorts of requests expertly and it only dawned on me two hours later that they were in fact all inmates. After the film ended and I approached the counter to have my chosen books signed out I was greeted with a 'Hello Vicky' from one library assistant, who turned out to be an ex-senior police officer convicted for talking to a journalist just a few weeks before my case came to court. It was the first time we actually met but many inmates had mentioned her name, Liz, and assumed that I would probably be moving to her landing in D0, which was for 'enhanced' or low-risk prisoners, if I stayed in Holloway. Not knowing what would happen to me and not counting on being moved quickly to an open prison, I enquired how I could get a job in the library. She gave me a form to complete, which I did on the spot and left it for the attention of the external librarian in charge. Soon the library was frantically getting ready for the afternoon event, which consisted of Martina Cole visiting to do a reading and distribute books. The prize was a signed copy of one of her books. She apparently went down very well as the girls felt affinity with a writer who grew up in the East End, seemed like one of them, understood about crime, was streetwise and had done well for herself.

As I left the library women were queuing to attend the reading but only thirty could be accommodated and most were turned away. Liz told me later that given the huge interest, the event could have been staged in the church – in fact, two churches in Holloway were linked and therefore able to provide a large L-shaped meeting room as a result. Unfortunately, because of the way the 'movement' works, every diversion from routine puts an extra strain on security. The movement itself, other inmates told me, can be very intimidating. Processing through the corridors, the movement is stopped at each gate as the guard unlocks it, and the movement continues on through. I was told a story of expert locksmiths/burglars who could look at the keys from a distance and, from memory, draw them and get their mates from the outside to reproduce them. This led to a number of escapes so now the officers no longer walk in front of cells with the keys dangling from their belts but keep them safely hidden in pouches around their waist, and turn away from inmates before unlocking doors and gates. I don't know whether this is true but I was told it on good authority. Anyway, the 'movement' swells as it moves from corridor to corridor with each woman attempting to get to a gym or a class or a health appointment. It is up to each inmate to spot their destination and if they miss the exit they aren't allowed to go back; the movement just keeps going forward. One friend I made had the added problem of trying to avoid an inmate who, for some unknown reason, had singled her out and would heckle her in the most disturbing manner as she passed through her corridor. The result was that this rather experienced and strong person in every other way managed to miss her health appointment twice as she spent most of her time on 'movement' trying to avoid the woman. She finally got to her appointment on her third try.

I luckily had no such problem that day and after lunch made it through the movement to 'visitors' without incident to meet my lawyer, Robert. We spent a couple of hours discussing various matters and Wednesday afternoon was taken care of. Again, it was better than spending it locked up in one's cell. Incidentally, 'time out of cells' is seen as a high priority as far as HM Inspectorate of Prisons is concerned. Their expectation is that prisoners should spend at least ten hours out of their cells each weekday in order to carry out important rehabilitative work and other purposeful activity, although the system as a whole rarely manages this. Particularly bad are local prisons, where 27 per cent of prisoners spend less than two hours per weekday out of their cell. Even resettlement or open prisons only achieve the target just over half of the time.[52]

It was my first meeting with Robert after my sentencing and I think he was pleased to find me calm and composed. He actually arrived late! But the guards gave us extra time, which was really good, and we had a very respectable small private cubicle to ourselves. I have since learned, however, that access to legal advice can vary dramatically from prison to prison. Some prisons only allow legal visits to be arranged on one or two days per week. One has no room for legal visits, thus preventing confidential interviews. According to a recent survey, only 43 per cent of prisoners say they can easily contact their lawyers and a similar number said confidential legal mail had been opened without them being present.[53] And yet legal mail is supposed to be exempt from the usual checks, under measures brought in to protect prisoners against the misuse of authority by prisons. My rather small survey of two prisons showed compliance with that spirit – letters from my solicitor were given to me sealed and then were opened by me in front of the officers, not for them to be read but only to ensure there was nothing forbidden hidden in the envelope among the legal documents. I would then take them away and read them in private. There were also big notices by the phones saying that although all private conversations were being recorded those to approved lawyer numbers were not. I assume they kept to what they promised.

Robert relayed to me the news from the outside, particularly his contact with my family. Obviously there was a lot to discuss – what the press was saying, should we appeal or not – but I was more concerned that he should talk to the kids and ensure that everyone knew that I was OK and accepting my situation calmly. Very importantly he also gave me a list of my contacts, which he'd printed out from my mobile. It wasn't complete but it proved a godsend. On the immediate practical level we agreed that he would urgently post me some stamps and envelopes that very evening.

I showed Robert the note that the guards on my landing had given me detailing my Home Detention Curfew (HDC) date, which was 12 May, and my unconditional release date, which was 11 July. At the time I had no idea whether HDC was granted automatically but soon discovered that it was unless there was a problem with the address you were going to. That was good news and at last gave us something to work towards. We also dwelt on what would happen next and where I might be transferred to. I was until then not fully aware of the various levels of prisons that existed. Places like Holloway for women and Pentonville for men are 'holding' prisons where remand prisoners are held and where sentenced offenders are usually sent until they are classified in terms of their risk of reoffending. They are then sent to specialist 'training prisons', some of them being 'working prisons', around the country to carry out their longer-term sentences. When they near the end of their sentences, men are sent to 'resettlement' prisons, of which there are two: Blantyre House near to East Sutton Park in Kent and Kirklevington Grange in Yarm, near Stockton-on-Tees. If they are perceived as a low risk then they are sent to open prisons. In both cases, they can start to do voluntary and then paid work outside the prison. In the case of women, because of their lower numbers there are no resettlement prisons but only open prisons where most people, including lifers, go to progress towards the end of their sentence. Open prisons for both men and women also house short-sentence prisoners who need not be kept in expensive closed conditions. My lawyer was pleased when I told him that I had been classified as a category D prisoner, low risk, and therefore was in line to move to East Sutton Park, one of two open prisons for women in the country. Robert warned me, however, that in his experience much depended on whether there was space available in the open prisons and more crucially whether they could get the transport to transfer me there – and that could take a few weeks. Lord Taylor, who communicated with me after my release and who had himself recently spent time in prison on the grounds of false accounting, told me that in his view there is very little reason why offenders cannot be classified immediately in terms of risk just as the sentence is passed to avoid the extra cost of closed prisons including that for transferring prisoners and starting many things all over again. I could see the point as it certainly would reduce the overcrowding at Holloway at a stroke.

14 MARCH

In the morning a female guard from a different floor, who had come to see how I was on behalf of the governor two days previously, told me that there had been discussion for me to move to D0, the enhanced wing on the ground floor, but that it probably made no sense if I was going to be moving to an open prison at some stage. I told her I was happy to stay where I was for the time being. Frankly, I had already become friendly with the girls on my landing and had no wish to move and then move again. And I had learned quite a lot of things from them. How to put a pin on the latch door and pull it shut, or almost shut, from the inside if someone had left the hatch open and the lights on in the corridor through the night – and also to cut out noise. It strangely gave you a feeling of being in control, which was welcome. At the same time they showed me what to do if an overzealous guard had locked the hatch door and there was no one there to unlock it – the back of the plastic spoon worked very well as a key.

Girls in different prisons learn different things. Rachel, who had been at Peterborough before transferring to ESP, told me how they used the freely provided tampons to block draughts on the grills of the windows or used a piece of paper, like an envelope, to stop the cold air coming through the vents in the middle of the ceiling. Ways to survive in prison.

I joined the 'movement' again and went to healthcare, which, what with the wait, took the entire morning, just as I had hoped. My luck was in again: the waiting room was showing a movie. This time it was the Jack Nicholson and Morgan Freeman film *The Bucket List*. We were locked in from the outside when one particular officer was in charge and the door was only unlocked to let in a new arrival wanting to see the nurse or doctor or to let one of us out for our appointment. When the officer went for a coffee break, however, strangely the door was left open and a young male assistant slid in and gave me a copy of a tabloid paper which had a story about me going to Holloway with the pictures they had taken of me in the transport van. The room was comfortable with chairs arranged in theatre style and the wait was long but most welcome. I had missed a bit of the beginning of the film but the other girls filled me in. I was able to see the tear-jerking end and noticed that there wasn't a dry eye in the house.

For me another morning spent outside my cell, given the horror stories of very long lock-ups endured by many prisoners, was a relief. When I finally saw the lovely nurse instant friendship developed. She filled in my personal medical history details, checked my blood pressure (which had gone down sharply after a couple of nights in Holloway – I arrived with a blood pressure of 175/100 on the Monday night and by Thursday lunchtime it had gone down to 124/80) and then suggested I should have a hepatitis B injection. I was mystified as to why I would need it and at first refused as I don't much like needles but she explained it was for my protection in case an inmate were to bite me. She pointed out that it made sense given that there are a lot of drug addicts in prison who may be carrying the virus from infected needles. (I was later told by other inmates that it is also to prevent people getting hepatitis B from snogging or through other ways of passing bodily fluids.) After her explanation, I did not hesitate for an instant. And she did it so well and painlessly (other injections, equally painless, followed in ESP to complete the course as my medical records moved efficiently with me when I left Holloway). As I was considered low risk she let me keep aspirin and blood pressure tablets in my cell locker.

And then my children came that Thursday afternoon for an hour. It was a tightly supervised setting, but it was brilliant. We had to sit opposite each other after we kissed and I reassured them that I was OK. There were strict rules about moving around so we had to stay in our seats except for them (I wasn't allowed to do it myself) to get me a much-needed cup of coffee – it was the first I'd had since I went into Holloway, quite a treat for a coffee addict... As we were chatting, suddenly a lovely lady visiting another inmate across the room came over to my chair and gave me a hug – the guards had no time to stop her but soon took the lady back to her place and very firmly told her such behaviour was not allowed. But it was done in good spirit and only to show her solidarity and support.

Actually, support was quite forthcoming. A lady
from the Independent Monitoring Board (IMB), which
is made up of independent unpaid volunteers from the
local area and features in every prison and immigration centre, came to my cell and spoke to me through
the open hatch to check I was OK. What do you say?
I am fine, really, thank you. And someone from the
Christian chaplain's office gave me a Christian diary,
which in fact proved to be very useful throughout
my stay in prison as mobiles and electronic diaries
were not allowed. I am still using it. And then the
letters started arriving. On Wednesday I received
some twenty letters, causing the officer in charge to
profess that in all his time at Holloway he had never
seen anyone receive so much post in one day. The girls
all came to my cell to marvel at the number of letters
on my bed – and also to see whether there were any
unfranked stamps that they could peel off and reuse.
They were all experts and I soon learned how to do it
too. It's amazing, actually, how many letters do arrive
even at my home unfranked. I had never noticed this
before I went to prison and met those girls. If they
noticed any, the prison authorities would draw a line
across the unfranked stamps so they would be worthless to the inmates but I found that rather cruel. For
many girls stamps were the most precious property
they could acquire to keep in touch with the outside,
which was so important.

I soon realised that stamps, at least in women's
prisons, had become the new parallel currency,
functioning like cigarettes used to. There is a lot of
interest in parallel currencies at present and how they
may work – witness the development of an internet 'virtual' currency called 'Bitcoin'. Tim Harford,

the economist and journalist who writes the 'Under-cover Economist' column for the *Financial Times*, recently quoted Robert A. Radford, an economist himself who had studied at Cambridge in the 1930s and who spent half of the war in a POW camp in Germany. Radford had published a paper he wrote in the summer of 1945 in the journal *Economica* enti-tled the 'Economic Organisation of a P.O.W. Camp' on the development of market institutions in that environment. He observed that everyone at the camp started in roughly the same way, i.e. with nothing, and depended on receiving the same-sized rations from the Germans and Red Cross parcels. Given that needs and likes and dislikes differed, a market then developed and trading became rife. Bartering began to take place. Say, for example, I wanted my hair cut in exchange for some coffee or chocolates. I would first need to find the person who combines the character-istics of liking coffee, being short in it and also knowing how to cut hair well. Even if I am able to source the right person, I don't quite know what price I may have to pay for the haircut: how much coffee do they want? A few spoonfuls, half a pack, the whole pack?

What is needed is a currency with as homogenous characteristics as possible – and that is what was developed in the POW camp. Cigarettes fit the bill, as Radford explains: 'Between individuals there was active trading in all consumer goods and in some services. Most trading was for food against cigarettes or other foodstuffs, but cigarettes rose from the status of a normal commodity to that of currency ... they performed all the functions of a metallic currency as a unit of account, as a measure of value and as a store of value, and shared most of its characteristics.

They were homogeneous, reasonably durable, and of convenient size for the smallest or, in packets, for the largest transactions.'

For the women in prison, cigarettes still mattered but obtaining stamps for their letters to family and friends was clearly just as important. And stamps are now expensive. In East Sutton Park, one would have to work for one-and-a-half hours to afford one first-class stamp and a lot more for an overseas stamp. So stamps have developed as a separate currency in women's prisons though the parallel with cigarettes is not so clear cut. Women prisoners, unlike the POWs, do not all start equal. Some come in with lots of money (as I was lucky to have done) and can move some of that to a 'balance', for phone calls and such, to which they can add, depending on what category prisoner they are, an extra £25 a week from their initial cash flow. Some only manage initially on wages from their prison jobs, which is rarely more than £1.25 per morning or afternoon session – in other words, a total of £17.50 a week if you work twice a day every day without a break. At ESP, the same amount is also paid to those who attend accredited courses though prisoners are only allowed a maximum of five sessions a week and most end up doing a lot less. The money earned is then used to buy things from the 'canteen' and/or phone calls (though these were still prohibitive despite BT's reduction of charges that had taken place at the beginning of the year, a notice near the phone informed me). Volunteering or completing training outside the prison earned some women slightly higher prison 'wages' of £20–£30 a week, and while finishing their sentences proper paid employment could see a few women receiving the minimum wage.

Others are forced to obtain a loan on entering prison, which they then have to repay slowly with their wages or on leaving the prison. Some have money on the outside that they can access when they go out on day visits or to see their families under licence or when they go to work. And then you can have money and stamps sent in, assuming you have people on the outside who can afford them and are willing to send them in for you – though one is warned that it is a dangerous thing to do as money tends to get 'lost'.

The result is that a gap easily develops between the 'haves' and 'have nots' and those with money and stamps can end up exploiting those without. Rachel Halford of Women in Prison later told me that they were once specifically asked to stop sending stamps to a particular women's prison as they realised that women were using the stamps for currency and were now identified as a 'trading risk'. Inmates are not allowed to barter but I could see it happens all the time so couldn't quite understand the reason why it should be prohibited – although clearly one would need to make sure it was not abused and prisoners didn't end up owing a lot to others that they couldn't repay. But a parallel currency in these circumstances is a natural development – indeed Radford wrote that the development of a market was 'a response to immediate needs' and that 'the small scale of the transactions and the simple expression of comfort and wants in terms of cigarettes and jam, razor blades and writing paper, make the urgency of those needs difficult to appreciate, even by an ex-prisoner of some three months' standing'.

I would come to understand this perfectly in ESP, as excitement built for the weekly delivery of the 'canteen' goods. Sometimes the whole timing of supper had to be moved to accommodate either the earlier or later than scheduled arrival of the van with its parcels in white plastic labelled with the names of the women who had ordered them. Girls started queuing way before they started distributing the individual purchases. I noticed that the majority of my fellow residents were relying almost entirely on their earnings to buy stamps and it was only natural that if someone was prepared to pay for services in stamps that was fine, as long as their price did not become so exorbitant that it caused a lot of aggravation and pain and put those with stamps in a position of control. Surely it would make sense for the prison service to allow charities to supply stamps. Depriving girls of the ability to communicate with the external world, except through brief but very expensive phone calls, seemed to me to defy logic and to be cruel at the same time.

Back in Holloway I was still oblivious to the value of stamps and continued giving them away if I could. And today it was a feast for them all as forty letters arrived. Like the day before around half were from perfect strangers giving support and half from friends and acquaintances, some from my very distant past, outraged, solicitous, sympathetic and urging optimism for the way ahead. The letters themselves would have been enough to occupy me for the rest of the night if Chelsea, the football team I support, hadn't been playing in the Europa Cup quarter final against Steaua Bucharest that evening. The small portable TV in my cell worked well enough though the image was slightly blurred; there was one problem, however, and that was it blew its fuse each time I used the adjacent plug to boil some water for tea. Each time that happened I had to call a guard to fix it from the individual fuse unit outside each cell. By day three I had learned to use the plugs in the corridor to boil the kettle if I wanted to avoid that happening, so that evening I boiled the kettle outside just before lock-up and settled to watch the match. I had bought tickets and would have been watching it in my usual seats with a couple of my children in Stamford Bridge right then if I hadn't ended up in jail. At least I had arranged to have the family use the tickets even if I wasn't there. Chelsea started off very badly and I was soon groaning and occasionally shouting with frustration at the screen. The night guard heard me alright and came over all the way from his office down the corridor, not to tell me off but to find out how we were doing. We ended up watching some of the game together – me from my cell chair on the inside and him through the hatch he opened for the purpose. What luck to have a guard on duty that night who was a Chelsea fan. And in the end we won. And we also won the final against Benfica a couple of months later, by which time I was out and able to enjoy the game at home with friends.

So far so good. I was pleased with how I was handling such an alien environment but it was only day three and as I was getting ready for bed I wondered how I was going to survive lock-up at 5 p.m. on Friday, Saturday and Sunday. I assumed the earlier time was because of a staff shortage on week-ends. That in itself rankled and didn't seem fair. On weekdays lock-up was around 7 p.m. and after supper one had free 'association' for a couple of hours with no set events. You were allowed to go to each other's cells, chat, watch TV and smoke in the designated smoking cells if you wanted. I had found the practice a welcome diversion and it also got me talking to the other inmates. The idea of a lock-up for sixteen hours till 9 the following morning, three days in a row, was a bit strange to me, so used was I to having people around me. I have since heard that for many prisoners being able to have that time to themselves, watch TV, eat, read, write their letters and rest is a welcome thing. But I wasn't sure how I would react. So for the first time, once the match was over and I managed to boil the kettle and have a cup of tea and a biscuit – even though it blew the TV off – I found myself pacing up and down the cell. I thought this was probably normal as it allowed me to think but fellow prisoners later told me that this is a reaction to the claustrophobia getting to you and a sure sign that you are beginning to go slightly mad as a result of being locked up in a cell. It doesn't take long for people to start talking to themselves and have long conversations with the TV set as there isn't anyone else to hear you. We did later wonder how the girls in the segregation unit could keep sane with no TV, no sink, no reading material as far as I am aware – all as punishment. How is that still possible in this day and age? The girls in D0 who were next to the segregation unit talked of the terrible noise emanating from these cells at night and the inhumane nature of that type of punishment. In Nick Hardwick's view these were mentally disturbed women and the segregation cells did not take account of their specific needs as most facilities in prison are designed with men in mind. Indeed, Lord Ramsbotham expressed his shock that healthcare instructions used in Holloway depicted human organs and the like only on the male body. Though this is astonishing, it's worth remembering that slopping out, i.e. emptying the toilet bucket kept in one's cell, was still the norm as recently as twenty years ago.

15 MARCH

What a funny day. I had for once spent a bit of the night before going to sleep planning my survival for the weekend ahead. Did I have enough books? Yes. As well as the eighteen books I had brought in myself I had received a few magazines, including the latest issue of *Prospect* sent to me kindly by the editor, Bronwen Maddox, with a very nice supporting note. I also had the four crime books from the library. That should keep me going through the weekend, I thought. And there were bound to be more letters, which in fact there were. But when the officers woke me they told I wouldn't be going on 'movement' but I was in fact leaving for East Sutton Park open prison in Maidstone, Kent. I heaved a huge sigh of relief. I wasn't allowed to ring the kids or my solicitor to give them the good news until I got there (the idea, I think, stems from the fear that your associates, if they know where you are travelling to and when, might try and ambush the car and free you) but I packed my things and started saying goodbye to the girls quickly as word spread that I was leaving. I left the girls on the landing a few books of stamps and any food and drinks I had not consumed, took names and prison numbers down and promised I would write to them from ESP, which I duly did and continued to do so throughout my stay there. I had very little time to pack my belongings but as a seasoned traveller it has always been my way to never unpack properly as you never know how quickly you need to leave particular locations. Leaving the room was easy except for the heaviness of my books but the female officer who came to get me helped me carry it all downstairs again and we were soon back at the reception area through which I had entered a few nights earlier.

This time the process was simpler. I had to make sure that all the money I had left could travel with me and that my request for starting a telephone balance would not be lost with my transfer to ESP. My suitcase and handbag were added to my cell belongings. Everyone was very friendly, and there were numerous offers of tea and toast as I waited for my transportation – my main concern was to finish the library book I was reading so that I could leave it behind. I was allowed to take another of my own books with me in the van and a notebook and pen. I then realised that Liz, the very efficient ex-police officer who had handed me the employment application form in the library, was also coming to ESP with me. She had been told the news of her move only the night before and until then had been led to believe that she was going to spend her whole sentence in Holloway. It seemed that my planned move allowed her to leave Holloway without fuss and she insisted throughout our stay at ESP that she owed her move entirely to me.

The transport was late so a couple of cups of tea and biscuits – and a finished Holloway library book – later we waved goodbye and were led into the awaiting van. Once in we were each given some sandwiches and water (it was by now 12 p.m.) and were locked into our respective cubicles. There were no seatbelts that I could see, which was extraordinary in itself. With our nice staff from the security firm Serco – a male driver, a female assistant – we set off for Maidstone, being thrown around the cubicles whenever the van accelerated too much. The sandwiches were inedible – bad even by the standards of Holloway – but looking outside at the streets of London and at life continuing regardless of one's own plight was fun. Soon we were on the A20 and the M20 – and then all went kaput. The vehicle, which I believe costs some £1,000 per transfer, started to have problems accelerating and after about five minutes seemed to give up. Fortunately we manoeuvred out of the driving lanes and came to stop on what is probably the most dangerous place to park in the whole world – the hard shoulder of the M20! There were anxious calls from the driver to control to explain the problem and attempts to get someone to fix it were not getting them anywhere.

I began to calculate our distance from Holloway – surely given that an hour and a bit had already passed we must be over halfway there – and hoped that they would not attempt a slow return back to Holloway, which I didn't really relish. We stayed there for quite some time while the discussions were going on, which we could hear quite clearly. The female officer kept us informed although there wasn't much to say, except that they had finally arranged for another vehicle to come to carry on with the journey. That took quite some time to happen and we waited there for another hour. Unbeknown to me at that stage (Liz told me later to great hilarity in the dining room of ESP) as a fully experienced police officer in traffic duties, Liz was looking out of the window facing the grass and calculating the chances of us surviving. The advice given is that if you need to stop on a motorway hard shoulder, you must always leave the vehicle and stay on the grass as one is at serious risk of being killed by another car crashing in to you from behind. She kept telling our guards that we should be allowed out, but that was flatly refused as they had no authority to let anyone out of the van – though neither of us, given our ages, were likely to attempt to do a runner either through the fields on our left or across a multi-lane motorway. She then asked repeatedly that they should at least call for a police car to come and shield us so that their presence and flashing lights would alert cars from behind that this was an emergency stop and they should be approaching with care. The crew finally agreed to ask headquarters to call the police – headquarters asked them to do it themselves and they duly did.

In the meantime we remained in our cubicles with no seatbelts, and I continued happily reading my book, oblivious to the exchange between my fellow prisoner and the crew outside. Finally a police car arrived, flashing its lights, and parked behind us. Three hours after we had set off from Holloway, the replacement van arrived. But another crisis loomed. The substitute van only had male staff in it and that wasn't right for transporting a female load. So what to do? Why don't you, I suggested to the female guard in the original vehicle, transfer to the new van with us and that way the problem would be solved. Oh no, was the answer, that can't be done. Fortunately, it could and that was exactly what happened, though it took a bit of time for them to negotiate it with head office. Overseen by lots of police, we were finally led out of our van onto a nice piece of grass and into the new van, a bit smaller and rougher than the one before, and we were off again.

And then we got lost. The new discussions between the officers now centred on the uselessness of the satnav and the complete mystification about the address of the prison, which had no numbers, no real road and seemed to be in the middle of nowhere. We stopped at a petrol station for another half an hour while the crew investigated the route we should take, discussed the possibility of buying a map, went and asked the guys at the petrol station for directions, and fretted a bit more. When we finally set off again, we were forced to put up with the starting and stopping that jerked us around our little cubicles for a good further three quarters of an hour as we drove through some rather nice little villages and beautiful Kent countryside. At last we arrived. Four-and-a-half hours since we had set off we were finally at a beautiful Elizabethan house; there were no obvious prison signs, no wire, no fences and only a side entrance opened by a genial reception officer, Nigel. My companion was the first to walk in ahead of me and was greeted with a 'Welcome, Mrs Pryce'. It was a fitting end to a Monty Pythonesque afternoon and the two of us would be confused for each other for the next two months.

CHAPTER 3

EAST SUTTON PARK

So there I was in East Sutton Park, a Grade II-listed Elizabethan mansion set in 84 acres of grounds which couldn't be more different than Holloway, both architecturally and in terms of its regime. William the Conqueror had bequeathed the original estate to Bishop Odo after the Battle of Hastings and East Sutton Park is even mentioned in the Domesday Book. The building itself seems to have been added to over the centuries: there is evidence of an eleventh-century settlement on a moated site which was succeeded by a fourteenth-century building of Kentish rag. The main house where the women are housed is a mixture of Elizabethan and Victorian buildings with a farm attached to it. According to the induction booklet I received on arrival, until 1942 the estate was owned by Lord Filmer Wilson, whose son and heir to the estate was killed in the Second World War. The estate then went to the government, who used it for the remainder of the war as a headquarters for the Tank Regiment. In 1945 the house was opened as the only open borstal in existence before becoming the open female prison it is today. It now houses a hundred residents, comprising ninety women and ten young offenders.

It was clear East Sutton Park set out a very different approach to prison life than I had experienced in
my short period in Holloway. 'East Sutton Park is an
open prison – there are no "Lock-up" times'. But there
were also notes in the induction booklet indicative
of the problems the prison staff often face: an anti-
bullying statement, a decency policy and a comment
that love-bites are classified as self-inflicted injuries,
while tattooing yourself or others is not allowed.

It was a real joy after Holloway to be in a place with
no lock-ups. The reports I received later from the girls
at ESP, who had been transferred from closed prisons around the country, suggested that some prisons
were worse than others. This is supported by the
'Measuring the Quality of Prison Life' survey that
the prison service carries out periodically in all prisons in England and Wales. A report to the select
committee on home affairs in June 2004 detailed how
prisons vary most in terms of treating prisoners with
dignity and respect, as well as offending behaviour
programme and resettlement provisions.[54]

Ex-Holloway girls generally had good memories
of the prison but I realised from talking to those who
came to ESP from other closed prisons that at times
the lock-ups were quite horrific. When there were new
arrivals in ESP you could in fact tell the girls from one
particular prison in the Midlands some two-and-a-half
hours away, as they tended to look more pasty faced
than others and positively cowed in my view – uncertain where to go, huddling very close together in the
groups they arrived in, finding comfort in close prox-
imity with each other in the first few days. I heard one
girl who finally came out to the open area saying to
the others how weird it was to step on grass for the

first time in ages. That was sad. I was told that on many days in that private jail they got no more than ten minutes on the outside and couldn't go out if there was any sign of rain as the guards didn't want to get wet. In the middle of this cold winter we were having, they had a number of instances where the heating didn't work for a few days in a row. I idly speculated whether they had hit their heating budget early and were saving energy to ensure they didn't get over it. On the other hand there were compensating factors, like a better education programme, but the girls all reported being unable to eat the appalling food and a number had lost a huge amount of weight or even arrived with illnesses that had not been treated properly. Interestingly, research so far suggests that private prisons are generally either much worse *or* much better than public sector prisons. There are large differences particularly in levels of staff professionalism, organisation, consistency and staff–prisoner relationships.[55]

As soon as we arrived at ESP I rang all the kids and my lawyer to give them the good news and the first visit on the coming Sunday was booked for me straight away by Les on reception. ESP allowed visits every weekend rather than every fortnight as had been the case in Holloway, and three adults and three children under eighteen could come in either on Saturday or on Sunday. In contrast to Holloway, I was allowed my handbag with all its contents, as well as my toiletries and most of my clothes from my suitcase, which miraculously survived the M20 van transfer. I would be staying in a dormitory room with friendly roommates, a proper carpet and a wooden moveable bed. The other dorm residents immediately helped me find a soft pillow, duvet and duvet cover, and towel and bathrobe, and I was settled in very easily. One of the ladies, over sixty, told me that at her former closed prison she had requested an extra blanket and pillow, as she was entitled to at her age. After three weeks of asking she received the pillow and not the blanket – it may have been the blanket and not the pillow, but either way, frankly, that's shocking. And then another great revelation. The food here was edible – but more than that. As we had arrived so late, we were rushed to the evening meal and discovered battered fish and chips and mushy peas and pudding with custard and fruit – and all this in a wood-panelled dining room with great views of the Kent valleys. It was a far cry from what we had left behind. Of course, as an open prison for low-risk prisoners, East Sutton Park is rather unusual in many ways.

I knew very little – in fact nothing – about East Sutton Park when I arrived. If I had researched it beforehand, I would have seen the November 2012 report by Nick Hardwick, Her Majesty's Chief Inspector of Prisons.[56] He describes East Sutton Park as 'an unusual prison'. He is right of course. It is a Grade II-listed, sixteenth-century country mansion with a farm attached to it, overlooking the rolling Kent countryside. It is also one of only two women's open prisons. As a prison its impact is believed to be a very positive one, providing, as the report concludes, 'unusually good outcomes for both the women it holds and the public as a whole'.

I would also have been reassured by his conclusion that 'East Sutton Park is a very safe place'. There are 'supportive reception and induction arrangements' and 'very little bullying'. The report also states that 'illicit drug use was virtually non-existent'. I never witnessed any on the premises although there were a small number of instances while I was there when residents abused the system on their days out and were generally caught and sent back to closed conditions. Nick Hardwick also found that 'the general environment was impressive but living conditions for most women in small and cramped dormitories were very poor and the lack of privacy caused tension'. I can vouch for that. But on the plus side ESP provided residents with worthwhile external work and lots of training opportunities in the community to help prepare women for release. There were still issues to address, which I discovered and document in the book later, 'but East Sutton Park provides a safe and decent environment for the women it holds'.

First impressions had indeed been good. Very important for me was that I was allowed to make phone calls to thirteen different approved personal numbers and seven solicitor numbers. I still found it restrictive but it was a luxury after Holloway. In some private prisons, such as Lowdham Grange men's prison in Nottingham, enhanced prisoners enjoy landline access in their rooms. Nick Hardwick commented that although 'women were appreciative of the opportunities they had to maintain contact with their families ... it was still not possible to receive incoming calls from their children and the continuing ban on the use of mobile phones in the prison was hard to justify'. I have to say that in discussions with the lifers, some of whom had gone in before the latest mobiles and smartphones became so popular, I found that they had great difficulty adapting to them once they were able to use them out on visits.

Naturally, the media started writing that I had moved to a cushy prison with special privileges like flat screen

TV, Jacuzzis and tennis courts. The other residents found it hilarious and we started searching for all these 'mod cons'. The main issue worrying the women there was their loss of freedom and their separation from their families. That they were treated humanely was in my view just as it should be. But even I was astonished to discover that Friday night was karaoke night in the pool room between 8.30 and 10.30 (which I went to on my first night), Saturday night was bingo night, for which you had to pay a fee (50p block fee from your wages for a number of games if you wanted to take part – practically everyone did – and run by the residents), and bedtime was 11 p.m. on weekdays and midnight on the weekends. It was a far cry from the Holloway, Peterborough and other closed prisons' lock-up time, which forced you to be a hermit and not socialise – an attitude that hardly helps when you are out there again seeking re-employment or trying to reintegrate. The right-wing call for tougher regimes forgets one fact: for these women losing their liberty and their families is the most horrific thing to happen to them.

A lovely girl from Indonesia, who I will call Aanjay, came from Peterborough and immediately threw herself into working life at ESP: she was up at 5.30 to serve breakfast for two-and-a-half hours, then after a short break carried out kitchen duties for three hours, then another three hours in the kitchen before serving supper and finally a very brief break for dinner herself before spending the rest of the evening doing people's hair, nails and eyebrows, giving massages and the like. It wasn't that this was necessarily her métier – she had a sociology degree from the London School of Economics. Yes, it made her popular with all the other residents who queued to have their hair and makeup done before their home visits. It was, as she confessed to me, the only way to stop her thinking about the five children and her (rather handsome) Italian husband she had left behind. On the few occasions she joined us in the drawing room, all talk would be centred on how she could persuade the governor to allow her to go out and see her eldest daughter, aged fifteen, who was due to have a major knee operation just around the time I was leaving ESP. Nothing preys on the mind of these women more than things like this. They didn't tend to classify prisons by the treatment they received but what regimes they could undertake to pass the time faster and push them closer to seeing their loved ones again.

Family relationships and support is recognised as a significant factor in reducing the risk of reoffending by providing a platform for the offender to make positive and valuable changes towards rehabilitation. An investigation by the Ministry of Justice (MoJ) stresses the importance of keeping close contact with the family to reduce reoffending (by as much as 39 per cent), to avoid depression and self-harm, and to improve children's well-being.[57] Maintaining contact with children and families through visits, telephone calls and letters not only ameliorates the painful experience of separation but enables women to adjust more effectively to prison life. Research in America examined the determinants of female prisoner misconduct and found the number of visits and phone calls a prisoner received reduced rule-breaking behaviour, thereby allowing the woman greater opportunities to respond more effectively to rehabilitation and treatment programmes, and offering a greater chance to avoid reoffending on release.[58]

The National Offender Management Service's (NOMS) Reducing Reoffending Delivery Plan identifies seven pathways to reduce reoffending and this includes maintaining prisoners' relationships with children and family.[59] Researchers in the US have gone so far as to say the family 'is probably the most important weapon we have in fighting crime. Prisoners who receive visitors, maintain family ties and are released into a stable home environment are more likely to succeed in leading productive, crime-free lives.'[60] A reduction in reoffending of course has significant costs implications for wider society.

A study undertaken by the New Economics Foundation examined the economic impact of work undertaken with prisoners and their families by the Prison Advice and Care Trust. The Integrated Family Support Programme (IFSP) seeks to support prisoners' relationships with their families by providing assistance with visits (including help with arranging and facilitating visits and intermediary work between prisoners and their families to build bonds), support to families (including emotional support, advice and referrals) and resettlement support. The study 'reviewed the work of the IFSP over a one-year period with 794 prisoners at HMPs Swansea, Wandsworth and Styal, and was based on a proposition derived from analysis by the Ministry of Justice that the odds of reoffending within one year of release from prison were 39 per cent higher for prisoners who had not received visits from a partner or family member while in prison compared to those who had'.[61] The estimated cost-benefit of reducing reoffending over a one-year period through the IFSP work with the 794 offenders and their families was £1,063,529.[62] This was based on a conservative estimate of avoiding the costs of an offender reoffending only once during the year. The costs saved would be significantly higher if cases of multiple reoffending were avoided.

With a stable home and family network so important, the value of being able to return home after serving time cannot be overestimated but, as has been noted, many women lose their homes as a result of imprisonment and are released despite uncertain availability of accommodation or housing. The Wedderburn report in 2000 found that of the women it interviewed, 'half of the mothers nearing release were not expecting to return to their previous accommodation and almost four in ten had lost their homes.'[63] A 2002 report by the Social Exclusion Unit showed that around one third of female prisoners lost their homes and possessions.[64] The Home Office found that 'during the period 2006–08, 44 per cent of female prisoners reported that they would have a problem finding accommodation on release'.[65]

This would suggest that moving prisoners to places where they lose contact with their family because they are too far away makes little sense. This is especially a problem given the small number of women's prisons: there are 118 prisons for men compared to only thirteen women's prisons (and in Wales, there is none of the latter). Data for 2009 showed that the average female prisoner was being held 55 miles away from her home. In 2009, around 753 women were held more than 100 miles away.[66] A 2002 study from the Social Exclusion Unit found that only around half of the women in prison who had lived or were in contact with their children before they were sent to prison received visits from

their families, compared to 75 per cent of men.[67]
That is hardly surprising given that a 2006 study by
the Revolving Doors Agency based in Styal prison
found that 70 per cent of mothers who had been sent
to prison had had their children taken away from
them.[68] Many girls in ESP told me that the visiting
costs were prohibitive for families hoping to visit
them in prison. Fortunately, for those who have
passed their Facility Licence Eligibility Date (known
rather amusingly by the acronym FLED) and are
able to visit their families, the prison covers their
travel costs – at least while the girls are not in paid
employment during their prison sentence.

The practicalities for families of travelling long
distances to remote prison locations by public transport can be challenging, more so with small children
or where there are no visitor centres at the prison to
provide refreshment and facilities after a long journey. At Drake Hall prison in Staffordshire the only
facility for visitors is a waiting cabin outside the
main gate.[69] Where children are being cared for by
family members who have work or other childcare
responsibilities, or where children are in the care of
the local authority, it may be extremely difficult for
these carers to facilitate and support prison visits.
Timings of the visiting schedule can negatively impact
upon the number of visits a prisoner receives.
In Holloway the visits were every fourteen days
and held in the middle of the afternoon – hardly
the best time of the day. I was lucky in ESP as the
visits occurred each weekend and you could pick a
Saturday or Sunday slot. However, in general, evening and weekend visiting slots remain rare across
prisons as this does not coincide with the prison

regime and weekday daytime slots are difficult if family members are at school or work.

Women prisoners have commented that the prison environment is unsuitable for children and some elect not to have their children visit at all.[70] Uniformed officers, routine searches, security measures and visits in large halls where women prisoners are not allowed any physical contact with their children can undoubtedly be bewildering and intimidating for young children. Recent efforts within the prison estate to make prisons more family focused and child friendly, such as the introduction of family days, have reportedly fallen victim to budget cuts.[71]

As a consequence, many women endure their prison sentence isolated and without any familial support. A prison governor recounted the different experiences of men and women upon release. 'Most men were met at the gate by a welcoming party: partner, friends, drink. Almost all women walked alone from the prison gate.'[72]

Some of the latest government proposals for reforming prisons and improving rehabilitation do include recommendations for having special units for women attached to men's prisons. But experts say the drawbacks may offset the benefits, something that will be discussed later.

This problem of being distant from family can also act as a disincentive to go for paid jobs, which are so important for ensuring the move back to the outside world goes smoothly. At times the cost of the fares to and from the job, and the loss of subsidy for home leave (particularly important for those with relatives far away), may be more than the payment the girls receive. The initial excitement at applying and then securing a job with a much better wage than the jobs within the prison quickly dissipates when the girls realise how much of the wage they will actually retain. Income tax is subtracted (though they may be able to claim this back at the end of the financial year) and roughly 40 per cent is retained by the prison, something introduced by the Prisoners Earnings Act, implemented in September 2011, to go towards victim support.

Being able to care for your relatives is, of course, crucial even when inside. I was saddened when I heard that Mandy, a lovely South African girl who also sat at my table and who has four children to care for, was recently sent back to a closed prison and is facing more fraud charges because, possibly in desperation, she did not inform the authorities that her employer on the outside had moved her from a volunteer to a paid member of staff, and she had continued to receive all the benefits while not paying dues to the prison.

Inevitably over the next couple of months I got to know many women reasonably well and most just wanted to tell their stories. I was astonished how many felt they were not guilty and complained that they were given the wrong advice by their solicitor. And many had been remand prisoners or on bail, sometimes for quite an extended period, before they were sentenced. In many instances it seems they had become so depressed by this state of affairs that they had lost all strength to carry on fighting. Using the Freedom of Information Act the BBC asked for and received figures in late May 2013 which showed that there were 57,000 people on bail, with 3,000 or so, a number of them women, on bail for more than six months. As I spoke to people in ESP, a number of the women there were in jail for fraud. Although the violent crimes category for women has the highest number of offenders in it of all categories if looked at individually, the percentage of the total crimes that are violent remains small. Women generally tend to commit non-violent crimes like fraud, and cases take time to be examined properly because they are usually complex.[73] This may go some way to explain why 16 per cent of the female prison population at the end of June 2013 was on remand, in comparison to only 13 per cent of male prisoners.[74]

Aanjay, who was at ESP for fraud, told me how her solicitor had to ring up continually over a period of nine months to find out what the police were going to do after she was first arrested. During that period she had been free to travel but her ability to work and look properly after her five children and her Italian husband was destroyed. And then she was put in jail as they thought that she might instead try to abscond. She was on remand for a further eight months. She pleaded guilty as she was told that at least that way she would be assured of a 30 per cent reduction in her sentence and therefore be reunited quicker with her children, a decision she now apparently regrets. It seemed that this was a pretty common occurrence and that by the time these sorts of women get to trial they have generally lost all their confidence, have maybe seen their children threatened with being taken into care or already in care or are just missing them terribly (as has been noted, the first time in prison is often the first significant period of separation women have from their children) and accept that pleading guilty is their only move.

It is welcome therefore that the Law Society has

recommended that the period of remand should be capped at twenty-eight days to accelerate policing but also to safeguard the right of suspects who find themselves already in limbo and often having lost their livelihoods and who in any case may well be proved innocent at the end. And the state does not compensate for the loss of income and status and family relationships when the case finally collapses or when the woman is finally convicted and the over-all sentencing perhaps fails to take into account the time spent on remand or bail. Remand prisoners are also not eligible for financial help following release if they do not receive a custodial sentence, which they often don't, or help from the Probation Service when returning to the community, even if they have been on remand in prison for more than twelve months. They are forgotten by the resettlement system.[75] The overall impact of such a long and difficult time has serious detrimental effects on the women in question and their families. In Angela Devlin's *Invisible Women*, she quotes statistics that demonstrate remand prison-ers were automatically assessed as being category B, in other words a risk to society, and should be kept under close supervision (my ESP open prison was at the lowest end – a category D prison).[76] They are not risk assessed or assigned to the correct category until sentencing, which only adds to the hardship, particu-larly upon the women's ability to retain contact with their children. Devlin also suggests that this is particu-larly harsh on women in general as only around 40 per cent of the women remanded in custody in 2009 were then sentenced and sent to prison – though they may have received cautions or suspended or community service sentences. Nearly half the women in Holloway in 2006 were on remand. In 2010, the figure was apparently nearer the 60 per cent mark.

What is more, proportionately more women facing a charge than men tend to be remanded in custody; the ten years between 1992 and 2002 saw an increase of 196 per cent in women on remand compared with 52 per cent for men. The numbers continued to increase and although they have reduced slightly in the past couple of years as of end September 2012 women on remand were accounting for 17 per cent of the female prison population.[77] What is particularly disturbing is that women usually receive short custodial services and therefore don't tend to spend a long time in prison. And yet remand prisoners spend an average of around forty days in prison – nearly four fifths of the time I served. What is worse is that for those on remand there are higher rates of self-harm, suicides and mental-health problems, and, worryingly, half of all women on remand receive no visits from their family (compared to only one in four men on remand).[78]

Being on remand can have additional complications. The system of Release on Temporary Licence (ROTL) entitles a prisoner to spend some time at an approved address once every month or so, granted after serving a considerable proportion of the sentence and under-going a risk-assessment. They can spend, at first, two days and one overnight away, then three days and two overnights, then four days and three overnights up to a maximum of five days and four overnights. For Aanjay, however, she was struggling to demonstrate that the prison's calculations of when her first ROTL was due were way off the mark as they should have started from when she first entered prison, not from when she was sentenced. We had to spend a lot of time consoling a very frustrated and tearful woman just trying to see her children and husband, as she was rightly entitled to do. It was not a very clever way to proceed.

Finally the risk-assessment board allowed Aanjay to return home every eight weeks under what is termed the Childcare Resettlement Licence (CRL); this allows mothers who have children under sixteen to go home no more than three nights every two months. It sounds good and it should be. Yet it is exercised in a way that causes resentment because it applies only to women who have 'primary' responsibility for their children, essentially single parents, and remain responsible for them even if the children are staying with relatives. If, however, a woman is still in a loving relationship with a husband, boyfriend or girlfriend and the child stays with them and is looked after by them in the mother's absence, then they are not entitled to CLR. Many mothers could not understand why keeping a relationship with their child was not considered important if their relationship with their partner had not broken up.

Despite appearing calm for the most part, many of the women I met in prison were at breaking point. Some were facing confiscation orders as a result of their crimes and in some cases were losing their homes and their pensions; others were fighting residency orders from their husbands or divorcing or being divorced by them (generally, 45 per cent of all prisoners lose contact with their families while in prison, with many separating from their partners[79]). In some cases the husband, boyfriend or partner was also in prison and that complicated things no end, especially arranging times for supervised phone calls between prisons – a real logistical nightmare.

Being on bail for any length of time seemed to have affected many of the women I met. Another resident who arrived from a closed prison just before I left, Tracy, had been working as an administrator at a school for a long time with a £1m budget and was wrongly, she maintained, fingered for falsifying accounts and fraud. She disputed it, was on bail for a year and when it came to being committed to trial she was already hugely stressed, was eating too much and had put on 2 stone in weight. She was told that if she didn't plead guilty she would get a five- or six-year sentence and be away from her kids for ages. So she pleaded guilty and got three. She bitterly regrets it now. The erratic, inconsistent and arbitrary nature of sentencing is especially hard on women who are primary carers.

Back in ESP, that first evening I made my first acquaintance with my fellow 'residents', as we were called. The term 'resident' was strictly used – the Tannoy messages that were used for both staff and for us always referred to 'residents' announcements' if they were aimed at the girls and 'staff announcements' for the staff. There were only two times when 'prisoner' was used. The first was when one had to fill in the prisoner number in the 'apps' – not some sort of computer programme but rather the ironic abbreviation for the good old-fashioned handwritten application form. The other was on the inside rim of envelopes where the name and prison number needed to be inserted for identification purposes when sending letters out.

In that lovely dining room, I was given a plastic plate, bowl and cup, and a plastic knife, fork and spoon, and told that I could ask my family to bring me proper plates and cutlery at their next visit. In the meantime, I could borrow from what was left behind by departing residents in what was called 'The Butler's Room' – it actually had that inscription on its door. That room was effectively an old scullery for the kitchen, with two big sinks, hot water for teas and coffees, a cold water machine and a fridge, and a place where the coffees, tea bags, sweeteners, whiteners and extra diet sweeteners were kept. But what was interesting was that in addition to all this that same room, where everyone entered constantly either to clear their plates and wash trays after a meal or help themselves to a drink, was also equipped with an ironing board and three hairdressing salon seats (well, I must not exaggerate their quality) with mirrors and three hairdryers and hair straighteners attached to each set. It was actually extraordinary and obviously the place to hang around in if you wanted to chat and know what was going on around the prison. Among the residents there were a number of qualified hairdressers who spent a lot of time doing other people's hair – a sharply worded notice reminded them not to spill hair dye on the floor and if they did to clear it up.

There were occasional mishaps but on the whole it worked rather well. This relatively small space, its only redeeming feature being a nice view to the gardens from a set of big windows, was a hive of activity – girls queuing to throw food away and wash plates; a panicky resident ironing her uniform furiously before dashing to the car to take her to her afternoon shift at a hotel in Maidstone; girls fussing over their hair, girls plucking their eyebrows; black girls putting in the most amazing hair extensions; Aanjay doing pedicures using bowls and I, with hygiene in mind, refusing to let her empty the water

in the sink but making her go to the loo and throw
it there. All the secrets were discussed in the Butler's,
all the conspiring and complaining could take place
there interrupted only when an officer – and sometimes even a governor – would come in to fill their
flask with hot water, whereupon the rest of us either
fell silent or joked with the officer, depending on who
it was.

That first night my plastic plate and bowl were
replaced with proper porcelain ones by a lovely
South American girl, Valeria, who was probably the
most beautiful girl in East Sutton Park. We got on
incredibly well. She explained that she had already
spent some nine years in prison and had been to eight
separate prisons before deciding that she had to tame
her temper so she could be sent to an open and start
rebuilding her life. She was hoping for release within
a year. She was generally keeping herself to herself
but we seemed to click. Liz and I, who were allocated
a seat at the same table next to each other, found
ourselves becoming very friendly with her and went on
to give her advice on her plans for the future, and to
review her business plans that she had put together
to request funding from external organisations so she
could start a fitness training business for women of
a certain age who were recovering from some major
upset. She was in her late thirties herself with a fifteen-
year-old son who lived somewhere in Australia with
his father but with whom she had kept in touch. She
confessed to us that if she hadn't come to prison she
would probably be dead by now from drug use but
she was a very intelligent girl and had learned good
English while serving her time. She was putting her
experience to good use and had been asked by the

governor to go to schools along with other residents and explain her case and why crime does not pay. She had been convicted of importing drugs – clearly the drugs must have been worth a lot of money hence her double-digit sentence (of which one tends to do only half except in exceptional circumstances). She had already started going out on day visits and home leave for a few nights every few weeks and was certainly streetwise already. I marvelled how 'with it' she was and pondered how much she must have gone through to survive so many years in prison already. We always advised her to keep her fiery Latin temper under control but other residents were wary of her and she gave back as good as she got. One learned quickly in prison who not to upset; particular care had to be given to the foreign girls, who might take things too literally or not understand the subtleties of English humour and therefore be offended by simple misunderstandings. But Valeria was clearly capable and determined – and quite a character. As she cheerfully told us: 'See these boobs, they not real. See these eyebrows, they've been done. Everyone does it in my country, it's so cheap. As soon as I get out I'm going back for more!'

While I was at ESP she managed to pass an interview and get a job as a receptionist at a large and busy hotel just outside Maidstone. We agonised about whether it was worth it and our dinners were dominated by the latest twists in the story. The pay was minimum wage, the train fare had to be borne by the resident, and once tax and the contribution to the Victim Support Fund were deducted it didn't leave much. In this case the crucial difference was whether the prison was prepared to drive Valeria and a couple of others who also got jobs in the same place for free to the station and then pick them up at night – sometimes close to midnight – rather than letting them risk returning late at night in a taxi by themselves, something not only costly but also dangerous for these women. It was finally sorted out and though the net earnings were still low, for Valeria the most important thing was gaining experience that might then allow her to get a reasonable job on the outside as she was learning to use her interpersonal skills, work in a team and become familiar with customer service practices.

In my view that was the main benefit of 'open' – the fact that it managed, with all its faults, to move people towards permanent rehabilitation – but ironically you wondered what the purpose of actually staying in prison for people like her was. She was towards the end rarely sharing our dining room table except on the odd rest day; she worked five to six days a week, returning late to sleep at ESP, was up again at 8 a.m. for roll call, then exercise, made her packed lunch and supper and disappeared again for the afternoon – all this interspersed with days out and home leave. And this was the pattern for many. A beautiful girl, who must have been 6 foot tall, very thin and very bright, was doing an open degree in law and found no time to study as she was working on a voluntary basis at a marketing firm in Islington every day, which meant she had to take the car at 6.30 every morning. The bang of the door in the next room as she rushed out in the morning was a sure wake-up call for me in the unlikely event my other roommates managed somehow to sneak out to their jobs on the ESP farm at 5.30 a.m. without me hearing them.

And indeed there is the question of whether people

should be kept in for so long if they are no threat to society, particularly when they have demonstrated that they can hold down a job and get back on time, do not abscond even though they have ample chance to do so (they can access the internet and contact who they want when they are on the outside and also use their mobile phone) and pass the mandatory drug tests if they are asked.

As well as Valeria, we also met Luciana, a Latin American girl, that first evening. I wouldn't see her often during my stay at ESP because she worked a lot of the time but whenever she caught sight of me she would come over for a chat and give me advice on prison life as she had been in custody for very many years already. She told me that while in prison I shouldn't trust anyone. I told her that outside prison the advice also holds. There was a world-weariness about her. I soon realised that her experiences were legendary and I became aware of rumours about what had happened to her while in prison and why she had had to move prisons a number of times. While reading ex-Brixton prison governor John Podmore's excellent book *Out of Sight, Out of Mind* at the hairdressers after leaving prison, I nearly fell off my chair when I read in black and white what had only been whispered in my ears by other ESP residents. A prison governor in a women's prison had taken advantage of a vulnerable prisoner and had himself received a five-year sentence in 2011 for improper relations with her – and from his description it appeared to me it was indeed Luciana who had been thus abused. I was amazed. She had been nothing but kind to me and had taught me more about how to survive in prison than anyone else. I will be forever grateful to her.

After dinner, Liz and I were introduced to the lady in charge of our induction, Barbara. The expectation was that the induction would run for a week or so, maybe more, depending on people's availability. We were each given some nice green folders which had to be filled in and signed by the various instructors as we were going through. It included seeing one of the governors, which I was looking forward to. Back in my dorm, I chatted to my roommates, put my stuff under and around the bed, found space for the many books I had brought in and some pads and pens in the cupboard, put my toiletries in the bedside locker, turned my bed around to face the other way so I could have access to the power point on the wall by the window to light my reading lamp, did my first roll call at 8 p.m. – and then went to karaoke.

Since it was Friday, bedtime was at midnight – by then the main lights and TV should be off. The officers do a further roll check by coming into the bedrooms with a little torch and counting the heads that are in bed – all usually asleep. They do the same at 5.30 in the morning, after which you are allowed to get up. One tried – and managed successfully most times – to sleep through them coming in as they tended to be quiet – except one night when they were clearly train-ing (not very effectively) a new officer, who came in and counted us and then shouted to the officer who was outside in a very loud voice: 'Three.' We woke up. I wondered whether it was deliberate. I had heard a story in Holloway of one particular officer (female) who would turn all lights in cells on from the outside and leave them on all night on the level where she worked – luckily she had different shifts on different days and wasn't always on at night or on the same landing so no one suffered for too long each time, but one does wonder what made people behave this way.

16 MARCH

For a first night in a new environment I managed a good night's sleep. My roommates were very quiet and the only issue was they got up very early: one was a natural early starter, waited always for 5.30 and then went out for her first tea and cigarette; the other worked on the farm and minded the animals, even on weekends. Aside from that, I soon then discovered the joys of a potential lie-in if one were so inclined, as roll call on a Saturday was at 9 a.m. rather than 8 a.m. as on weekdays. Breakfast therefore was also later and more leisurely, though girls were usually preparing for their day visits to family or friends; some could go to London from 8 a.m. until 8 p.m. or anywhere within a fifteen-mile radius of ESP from 10 a.m. to 6 p.m. There was frantic activity the evening before as taxis were organised, agreements entered into, costs calculated. The girls made their applications for travel and cash warrants, as whatever was spent had to be approved by the officers with limits upon how much could be drawn out by the women from their cash balances. In the end, off they went on those weekend mornings, some on their CRL or ROTL; the result was that at times over a weekend the prison was less than half full. In fact, what did amaze me was the sheer number of people who were away most of the time.

During roll call that Saturday morning, I had the opportunity to get rich quick. Anyone who worked in the house during the week always had the week-end off. The staff in the kitchen and farms still needed help during the weekend – mainly to take the animals out, do the laundry and kitchen work – so there were always shifts available. And, to my amazement, women are messy. I thought until then, from my experience at home, that it was only men that made everything untidy. Well, ESP soon changed that. Women ARE messy – in fact, they are unbelievably so. My housewife/mother instincts came to the fore and I would get people to throw things away properly, wash their trays, tell them off when they left mess on the tables – no one got upset with me; they just ignored me!

There was always cleaning to be done. So everyone who was around for roll call on weekend mornings and 'idle' was given a two-penny job which consisted of emptying particular bins, washing showers, cleaning bathrooms, sweeping the smoking area, hoovering particular bits of the building, washing floors. Yes, 2p. No one had any great enthusiasm for these tasks but they were done and we kept the place going, just about until the following morning. I only did it twice as from the following week, once induction was over, I got the job of cleaning the dining room after breakfast and lunch, making sure cereal dispensers were full, trays disinfected for next use, floors cleaned and coffees and the rest filled up. But I actually ended up working every day, including at the weekends, to cover for my co-workers who were often either in education and unable to work or on external visits. They were happy to let me take charge – I must admit I became quite obsessed with cleanliness and tidiness, which apparently is something that happens to many women in prison. The laundry girl told me that she couldn't rest and fretted all day if she hadn't folded a sheet exactly so and someone who was constantly ironing had an obsession with seeing her shirts and sheets with no creases at all.

But after roll call and before cleaning duties on Saturday, a treat. One of the first inductions was to the gym, which was built in a barn originally used for horse displays in the past before the building was turned into a borstal and then a prison. We had two trainers who we also shared with the nearby men's prison Blantyre and we spent some time being taken around the various bits of equipment and told how to use them and how to stretch to avoid any injuries. I had never been to the gym before – actually, that's not strictly true. Twenty years ago, we at KPMG were given subsidised membership of a gym nearby. I had just given birth to my rather large youngest son and as a result I was rather large, too. I knew from experience (he was child number five) that given time that extra weight would go away and I would be back to my rather thin self but I bowed to the pressure from my colleagues and went for an induction. I bought some sports gear and kept it in plain sight. As the weight dropped off, colleagues commented on how right they had been and how successful the gym regime was proving. I would nod wisely and leave it at that – except of course I never went to the gym once!

But I had to try and keep fit; there was no running around as I usually do at work or walking up and down the five flights of stairs in my tall, narrow home. In any case, exercise has been proven to reduce levels of stress, depression and anxiety in low-security prisoners, so it could only be a good thing.[80] Also, nice music was played, which was worth attending the gym sessions for alone, and I had company from girls

I got to rather like. Of course, being a hater of gyms I had to find something that was relatively easy and relaxing, so I took up rowing, which I am told is the best thing. I would row gently for half an hour – nothing intense, so horrified was I by reports that the journalist and newscaster Andrew Marr had incurred his stroke while rowing rather fiercely. And I came to depend on this gentle exercise. We would beg the trainers to come as often as possible so that we could open the gym as it was obvious that exercise was making a big difference to our mental well-being. The girls were also all conscious of their figures and there was constant weighing going on while the gym was open. But it was open only a few times a week and increasingly less often as the weeks wore on due to cuts in that area (something occurring across the prison service) and the retirement of one gym instructor who was now part-time and wasn't being properly replaced. We had hoped for a risk assessment that would allow the gym, like the IT room, to stay open all the time as there was very little harm that could be done by the use of the equipment except for the machines with weights, which we were all happy to see disappear if we at least had the rest of the equipment available to us for longer. But despite hopes that this would indeed be granted and a number of discussions with the governor, it still had not been implemented by the time I left.

After the gym induction, we went for a walk – there was always meant to be one at 9.45 on Saturday mornings, for which I hurried my obsessive dining room cleaning to ensure I could always take part. That soon became the highlight of my week. A number of us would gather (too few in my view) outside the gym and borrow boots from the farm changing room

– the first week I was lent the governor's boots, so wet was it outside, but usually we would borrow boots left by the farm workers who were only at the farm for an hour on weekend mornings. The walk was just marvellous. Come rain or shine, we would leave the big house behind, and walk through a gate that said 'out of bounds' (itself a great pleasure), then climb over gates and ramble through a series of fields full of horses, then sheep with their young lambs (which took a great interest in us to the great concern of their mothers), then over a few more fences until we arrived by the side of a rather big lake, all belonging to ESP. Then we'd trek up towards a little woodland, with the big house in the distance on the left, spotting some pigs higher up along the way. Fairly exhausted, we'd walk round to the yard at the back of the house and stop to look at the view of where we had just walked. It made you feel human, being allowed 'out', and the journey was quite a magical one, or so it seemed to me. We'd walk in rain and snow in the first few weeks and then as the weather improved towards the very end of my time there, in brilliant sunshine. I truly believe that those walks kept me sane and still united with the outside world. I tried to encourage as many people as possible to come but there were far too many girls, probably exhausted from a week's work, who if they were not going out went back to bed after roll call and the 2p jobs. But some were as inspired as I was. One of the girls who always came had started a degree in horticultural landscaping and was just finishing year one of her course at a local college. I only saw her at the weekends and during those walks as she was out at college all week and working for her studies every other moment while in ESP.

Saturday lunch at ESP is called brunch – and it was cholesterol-raising stuff: eggs, bacon, sausages and what I thought were called hush browns. This was the first time I'd come across them and when the kitchen lady mentioned them I said that the only hush something I knew were Hush Puppies, to the great amusement of everyone. But they were delicious and I always took the maximum two you were allowed, I enjoyed them so much. You'd also get mushrooms, baked beans and fried bread. I'm surprised we didn't all die of heart attacks after eating such a meal. Porridge was on offer too and though I gave it a miss on that first day I soon started ordering it and taking it back to the dorm for my roommate, who would often miss brunch because of her morning activities. The truth is that I grew to like it, too, and often ended up having it myself as late night pudding cold on Saturday evenings – this while we were all watching *The Voice* on TV, which was definitely the most eagerly awaited programme of the week by my roommates, who preferred it to *Britain's Got Talent* on the rival channel, which most of the rest of the residents preferred.

Some people argue that you only understand prison if you have been in for a long time. I don't agree. It seems to me you get the feeling and the ensuing claustrophobia after being in prison for just one night – and you become institutionalised very quickly. I found the change of regime in ESP after just four days in Holloway astonishing. For me it was all very welcome. But there were a number of people I spoke to who had come from closed prisons and for whom the transition was a difficult one as they had forgotten how to share (room sharing was just not popular) or how to interact with others. Frankly, for some it was also hard to start making decisions on their own in an environment which leaves you to get up on time, attend the early morning roll call downstairs, show up for work, get out of the prison if allowed and get back on time through your own efforts and manage to fill your time with your own initiatives. It transpired that a number of girls who had been in closed conditions for some time had on arrival asked to go straight back to closed prisons because they couldn't cope with the albeit limited freedom.

For me those were the very reasons why places like ESP are absolutely essential. I find it hard to understand how people can be put straight back into the community and expect to survive and find jobs that they can keep when they come out, even after short periods, from closed conditions and find that there isn't anyone to tell them exactly what they should do at every minute of their lives. One ex-prison governor is adamant that the resettlement process is an absolute must with prisoners beginning voluntary work first, and then paid work while still in prison, all in preparation for the outside world. Some offenders may never have held a job before but the educational opportunities in prison would have made them more employable. Being able to get up in the morning and keep a daily schedule of work was very beneficial. In the town housing one of the prisons the governor had been working in, the local private buses were mainly driven by offenders. And I doubt whether many of the thousands of passengers they were transporting knew this – would they have objected if they had? Boycotted the bus route? Possibly, although that would be sad if it were true.

The retired governor also pointed out that in a number of prisons, as I discovered was also the case in ESP, offenders could have their own cars parked outside and use them for transport to and from work. The challenge of course was to obtain car insurance and that in itself was another way of encouraging offenders to take responsibility for their own lives and their own future. I did point out that the meagre salaries, usually just minimum wage and with the prisons keeping up to 40 per cent of whatever was earned, would not leave them with enough cash to do all that, but anyway, the idea was clear: offenders should interact with the community before their release for more positive results.

I could see how constructive this regime was for the women; it gave them a sense of responsibility, belonging and self-confidence which they needed. I also realised as I was writing to my friends and family that no one on the outside realised what goes on in open prisons. For me, though by no means perfect, what open prisons did to reintegrate people in the community was an eye-opener. And yet there are only 228 open places for women in the whole of England: 100 at ESP and 128 at Askham Grange in Yorkshire. What is more, even those places seemed to be under threat from the review of the women's prison estate taking place in the summer of 2013. ESP was to be subject to an official review visit the week after I left but it was then postponed to early June.

At the time of writing, we are still awaiting the publication of the government's review of the female custodial estate. Yet, both Juliet Lyon of the Prison Reform Trust and Frances Crook of the Howard League for Penal Reform have expressed concern about how effective any proposed changes may be. They raise as a particular concern the distance that women are held away from their home or release area, and argue for a radical transformation of both the sizes and locations of custodial estates to meet women's needs. As noted earlier, the distance of prisons from family and communities is more acute for women, who are on average 57 miles from their home, more for the Welsh women who must come to an English prison to serve their sentence. Larger prisons, holding offenders from many different locations, also face difficulties coping with the women's transition to probation and release; they must coordinate with services from numerous different areas. The House of Commons justice committee gave an example: 'HMP Eastwood Park works with eight probations trusts, seventy-two local authority areas, fifty-two drug and alcohol teams, and a complex network of healthcare trusts, social services departments, and third sector organisations.'[81] The committee also emphasised that the scope of the government's probation services review is particularly limited in that it takes the size of the women's prison population as a given, when other strategies could be used to reduce this population vastly, thereby affecting the relevance and validity of any proposals the government may produce.

Within the generally positive move to place greater emphasis on rehabilitation services, there is some concern about what this means for the work being done inside prisons and with offenders on long-term sentences. Giving evidence to the justice select committee, which reported in July 2013, Nick Hardwick felt that 'giving responsibility for through-the-gate services to reduce reoffending to new providers under the Transforming Rehabilitation proposals had the potential to neglect the role of prisons themselves'.[82] This is on top of a service which is already falling far short of its obligations: 'A prisons inspectorate survey found that 38 per cent of women in prison did not have accommodation arranged on release, and that only a third of women who wanted help and advice about benefits received it.'[83]

The concern therefore for me remains what will happen to ESP. A number of organisations that deal with both of the open prisons have, overall, a positive view of them. A former senior probation officer who worked in Holloway for many years and had dealings with the two open prisons agreed that they are a good thing. In her view Askham Grange in Yorkshire has had an excellent reputation for many years, particularly in relation to improving family contacts in planning for release. However, it is true that both Askham and East Sutton Park have struggled a bit because of their 'remote' locations and she reported that when she was at Holloway many women on longer sentences resisted moving on to ESP, mainly because they were Londoners who had never ventured out of London and whose resettlement plans remained focused on London.

Both the ex-probation officer and I encountered some young women at ESP who had never seen a cow before arriving there and who found life in the depths of the countryside quite 'spooky'. Others complained that the costs of visits were prohibitive for their families and they had moved with great reluctance. Some in fact resisted a move but that only results in a negative on their prison record. One girl I met halfway through my stay at ESP moved from Peterborough to

us for the last three weeks of her sentence and was
very upset as her family was in Scotland.

The ex-probation officer wondered whether
the open prisons would survive the Transforming
Rehabilitation plans for resettlement prisons located
in the 'right' places where supervision of offenders' 'resettling' would be outsourced to firms under
contracts that would reward them by how successful they were in reducing reoffending – the so-called
'Payment by Results', tantamount in the eyes of
some critics to 'privatisation through the back door'.
Whatever happens there will be real challenges
for those currently undertaking the review of the
women's estate to come up with appropriate regimes
and prisons for women who may have received
quite lengthy sentences but need to progress to
settings with lower security. It will be important of
course when looking at alternatives to see whether
they might make open prisons less important in the
structure of the women's estate. But with regard to
alternatives to custody such as women's community
centres (which seek to address the complex needs
of isolated women in particular, and to enable them
to comply with community-based sentences and
treatment programmes), the general belief of those
I spoke to seems to be that these should not pose a
threat to the concept of open prisons – even if those
who may have received short sentences get sent elsewhere. It is also worth noting that reoffending rates
for those given community orders in 2009 were 7 per
cent lower than those given short prison sentences.[84]
In addition the former official suggested that there
will still always be a need for those serving sentences
of longer than four years and who progress through

various programmes and are deemed to have become 'lower risk' to be 'tested' in more open settings for parole or other purposes.

The former probation officer told me that often women's prisons are viewed by the system as being too expensive – they do indeed cost more because of the complex needs of the women sent to prison but there can be a tendency to almost 'blame' women for being difficult and costly compared to men, rather than looking at their specific needs and designing prisons to fit those needs. And there could be savings if that is true, as many believe there is a strong argument that women just don't need such high-level or very expensive security as men do. But people I spoke to think that it is possible that the MoJ and the NOMS will see reconfigured 'resettlement' prisons as fulfilling the purpose of open prisons. There is some talk about prisoners staying put in one prison throughout their sentence, being (relatively) near to home and undergoing a more open regime towards the end of their sentence. If they do go down that route, one might guess that it would be tempting to 'sell off' the nice bit of 'real estate' that an open prison like ESP represents – 'realising' assets to pay for the 'new' approach. I was told that this might indeed be in the minds of the reviewers, who may subscribe to the view that for some reason open prisons are always thought as too expensive. They should not be, given the much lower staffing and regime requirements on the security front. While I was there all the work was done by the residents and the staffing was minimal. The farm seemed to be self-financing though of course relying on rather cheap labour. And I'm sure a lot could be done to improve the revenue of the estate.

Of course ESP is housed in a rather old building that needs constant attention. There were workmen there most of the time fixing things and also dealing with the lighting, fuses blown because of the bad wiring of hairdryers, floors falling under the strain of extra heavy office furniture, repairs to the roof, you name it. Repairing the rather splendid but yellowing Spanish ceiling in the pool room, which seemed to have been ruined during its smoking room days, would cost near £100,000: it would have to be dismantled, brought down, cleaned and then put back together again. Those assessing it didn't think that the prison was ready at that point for the extra expense.

That Saturday evening at ESP, after the 'grab bag', which contained our takeaway dinner products, was distributed at 5 p.m. and roll call was taken, the dining room got ready for bingo. I had never played bingo before. Even though so many girls went out on the weekend a large number would make a special effort to get back to ESP and through security by 6 p.m. on Saturdays so that they could take part in the game. Various tables were very competitive and when there were wins people often shared the rewards – though I don't want to exaggerate the extent to which people really wanted to give part of their hard earned Kit Kat prize away. I won a Cadbury's Flake the second time I played and made it last a week. I only won once more and this time it was a Kit Kat. To my shame I just don't like Kit Kats and couldn't bring myself to eat it despite its novelty value – I had to give it away!

17 MARCH

Roast lunch today. Lovely parsnips and pork. I shuddered to think what my previous inmates in Holloway must be having for their lunchtime meal and determined to start writing to them. Straight after lunch, we had our visits. For me, it was the first visit in the new place; no one had questioned the names I'd put down for visits and even the grandchildren were coming, which was so exciting. Girls 'dressed up', put make-up on and jewellery, which was freely allowed, to see their loved ones and we waited in the drawing room to be called one by one as our visitors arrived. In contrast to what happened in Holloway, we were able to walk by ourselves, through the grounds to a visitors' centre, which was like a large cricket shed with round tables, a bar, children's toys and a good view of the house. We were then left alone. If the weather was nice we could sit out in the garden at tables. Visitors were checked when they arrived and we were checked when we went back into the house in case we had been handed anything which was still not allowed. But they could bring clothes and toiletries and books and plates and other things one needed, particularly in the first twenty-eight days of getting there – thereafter clothes could be exchanged every three months but you still had to keep to the upper limit of items allowed at all times, which the women found too restrictive. You were also entitled to five toiletry items a month (women's sanitary needs were met for free inside ESP) and, if you had money on your account, purchases of up to £20 a month were allowed from the monthly Avon catalogue or Pak Cosmetics company, which specialises in products for Afro-Caribbean women. This was all in addition to weekly purchases from a 'canteen' sheet which contained some 100 items from which residents could buy extra products using their weekly wages

and up to £25 from their 'float' if they had one. The
list of items ranged from cigarettes to hair dyes. Most
of the girls spent their money on phone calls and the
rest on sweets and cereals though a number of us used
'canteen' to buy some healthier items to eat each week
such as fruit and olive oil.

My family duly brought me lots of things I needed
and that was great – more items arrived with each
visit over the next month: books, stamps and station-
ery were allowed but had to go through reception
first. I couldn't understand why stamps had to be
sent separately rather than handed out to us when
we met our families. I later discovered that there was
a concern traces of LSD or other drugs may have
been pasted on the sticky bit by whoever was sending them. Similarly magazines were considered to be
dangerous as there could be other drug substances
smeared on the pages. I had no idea! As a result,
during my entire time inside I thought it was some
bureaucratic rule to frustrate everyone for the sake
of it – no one had explained to me why the system
was as it was. This lack of communication is not a
trivial point – academic research into experiences
of imprisonment shows that rules without explanation serve to fuel anger, frustration and a sense of
injustice among prisoners. Worse, these experiences
will likely be reinforcing the inequality or unfairness
many have encountered prior to their time inside.[85]

I was thrilled to see my visitors and they were
so pleased to see me in a much more pleasant environment compared to Holloway. The two hours
passed very quickly and the treat for me was also
being able to have a drink of Blantyre apple juice,
which was made with local apples and bottled by

the Blantyre inmates. Having compared the juice in these bottles with other apple juice available on the outside I would vouch that it was brilliant – and my children and other visitors thought so, too. For some reason it was not available in ESP except through the coffee shop in the visitors' building although it was also sold to the general public in the farm shop that sold the produce from the ESP farm, meat factory and gardens. But they never made enough of it and for some of the weekend visits we were left disappointed with no juice available. There is some business opportunity being missed here, it seemed to me. Also for some incomprehensible reason the farm shop closed at 12 on Saturdays when it could have sold a lot to the visitors who arrived at 1.30 p.m. if it stayed open a bit later. Many of us suggested this while I was there but never got a proper answer. In this rather tight fiscal environment, with cuts across the MoJ's budgets requiring the service to 'sweat' the assets, this seemed to many of us to be another lost opportunity to increase revenues.

Come the end of visiting time, we women hugged our children, parents, partners; waved our desperate goodbyes as cars departed and returned to the house, with many often in tears. In fact, some women I met deliberately chose to limit their visits to avoid heartache. Most would spend the rest of the day like zombies, sorely missing their loved ones. We tended to huddle around, try and chat and read the papers, do whatever one could to cheer each other up. Not easy.

On that first day, as photographers had camped around ESP having got word I was now housed there, it was decided I wouldn't walk to the visitors' centre but instead be driven there to avoid the press. There was space in the car so we took two others along. One was a woman in her very early thirties with a number of children including a very young baby. She was having trouble adjusting to it all and on the way back, after seeing her youngest child, she sobbed uncontrollably. A few weeks later she tried to commit suicide, though somewhat half-heartedly, and a week later she was sent back to a closed prison.

18 MARCH

As part of our induction course, we met with the prison chaplain, who ensured that ESP covered all faiths and who took service himself in a makeshift way in the multi-faith room, which happened to be next to my dorm room. There were plenty of bibles and hymn books for whoever may want to read them and clergy came to look after any Catholics, for whom the occasional mass was held, especially at Easter, and also any Muslims. At the invitation of the chaplain under the Prison Fellowship scheme, we also had visits from various groups, including a group of evangelist and New Testament folk, who had an interesting way of portraying the 'facts' and argued strongly in favour of the creationist view of the world. A Pentecostal group from Brixton visited a couple of times while I was there and ran services that were quite jolly with the level of singing and clapping rising substantially on those occasions. I knew what to expect as my daughter-in-law's father is a Pentecostal bishop who preaches both in Brixton, near my home, and in Ghana, where he is from originally, and I had been to a number of services he had held.

I started attending service after meeting the chaplain as he seemed to be serious about providing help to the girls in ESP, who he believed had special needs that were quite different to those of the men in Blantyre, who he also looked after. For the benefit of killing any rumours to the contrary, I must say that I did not discover God like some famous male prisoners seem to have done. I have to confess also that I am not particularly religious but as a Greek Orthodox I attend church on special occasions such as for weddings (including the two that involved me), christenings, the odd funeral (to be avoided) and the Easter celebrations in Greece, which are quite spectacular as they involve open air mass, candle processions, a lot of noise and fireworks at midnight when Christ is resurrected, even though they are supposedly banned. What is more, I had to explain to the congregation that audience participation is not encouraged in my church. You have to sit or stand still while the priest and the male criers sing psalms in a strangely nasal way, leaving the end of the psalm hanging in the air for quite some time for special effect. The congregation sits there getting slightly nauseous on the incense that wafts up as the priest waves around a holder he is dangling from his fingers while singing and walking about holding the gold-leaf-covered Gospel. The women all found this terribly intriguing but I felt I had something to prove so became an enthusiastic attendee of the various church services. I don't think that in the eight weeks there I missed a single Tuesday evangelical meeting, a Thursday Bible-reading session (taken by the second chaplain, who came from the Free Church movement, which as far as I understand it is an interdenominational national Christian organisation separated from any government endorsement or funding), or the Sunday service with communion (which I sadly had to turn down each time even though the bread and 'wine' – which I suspect was Ribena – looked quite appetising). And there were always branded biscuits, a few classes higher than the little 'basic value' packs we were given in our 'grab bag'. What is more – and definitely an extra attraction for me, being very conscious of needing to keep up my vitamin C intake – the prison fellowship guys brought with them the most delicious mango and pineapple juice for us all each time. A real luxury.

Depending on the time of the service, some girls would arrive a little late from their kitchen duties, others would have just got back from their jobs outside, some would even turn up in their bathrobes and slippers. Not, in other words, the usual type of church attendees in my local Holy Trinity church in Clapham. But the chaplain and preachers were very flexible and understanding. There was a routine. Bible and hymns: books and the CDs and CD player would come out of the cupboard and the person conducting the service or session would also bring CDs with them. We would then shout out the hymns we wanted and if lucky the CDs did have the music needed to accompany them and we would sing along. But at times the hymn would be too obscure and there was no music to go with it, in which case we relied on someone, not necessarily always the chaplain, to give us a lead. We were terrible at singing and the combined cacophony at times brought out giggles but for me it was such fun to be able to sing along. Belonging to a slightly different religion and not knowing the hymns from childhood I had always kept quiet during singing in the Church of England but loved the way in which people participated. With my son being at school at

Westminster, the abbey was his local church and I had gone many times to special church and thanksgiving-type services for the school, including his own confirmation when he was a teenager by the Bishop of London. I'd loved it all. But the words sung by everyone on those occasions still escaped me.

Now I can proudly say that I have become familiar with many hymns – the girls had their own favourites which were chosen again and again, week after week, and they were mainly uplifting ones. Every now and then we would choose one that not many knew and the one I chose floored them, a 'pop song' called 'Tell It on the Mountain'. It had been popularised by the group Peter, Paul and Mary in the 1960s and selecting it showed my age! No one else had a clue how to sing it and my one attempt to lead the way and gain some clout among my fellow churchgoers fell horribly flat. We abandoned it after the second verse.

There were not very many of us but most were regulars, augmented periodically by short-termers like me. Some did not use the books provided but seemed to be able to sing the songs nevertheless but I was never able to ascertain whether this was because they knew most of those hundreds of hymns by heart, having been in prison a long time, or in fact because they just couldn't read and therefore had to memorise them. Research has shown that women prisoners in particular are likely to have, or be bordering upon having, a learning disability – roughly 40 per cent, compared to 27–30 per cent of male prisoners.[86] Generally, 7 per cent of prisoners have an IQ below 70, with another 25 per cent having an IQ between 70 and 80.[87] Some 48 per cent of prisoners have a reading age of eleven or lower.[88] I had at times come across girls who would ask me to read what was on the notices for them and even add their names to lists and there were certainly a couple of them in the church group.

The girls also liked to participate wholeheartedly in the debating sessions that we had once a week where we would take a passage from the Bible and analyse it. One of the most interesting debates was about forgiveness, which caused many a problem given the feelings many of the girls had about the people who they believed had got them there. The stories they told as they expressed their feelings were often heartbreaking. One 'lifer' explained how in her moment of deepest despair she had found God and was able to function from then on; her story brought tears to all our eyes.

The most attendees I counted one day was ten, the girls enjoying the clapping and loud singing the Pentecostal team encouraged. The first time the team came while I was there, their leader was unable to come in as she had forgotten to bring any identification with her. She had to stay in her car while the rest of the group tried to keep us half-heartedly and very apologetically entertained. The small congregation was very disappointed but fortunately the leader managed to arrive with full identification papers next time they tried and great fun was had by all. I had to close the door of the room to muffle some of the sound as my roommates next door were trying to watch TV and I wouldn't have been very popular on my return at the end of the session, but never have I heard such enthusiastic singing from my fellow residents. The way I managed to keep my roommates on side was by always bringing them back the biscuits on offer; on their return from their evening cigarette they would find them on their beds neatly put on napkins like offerings before the evening roll call at 8 p.m.

Those sessions became part of life there and I became strangely dependent on them. My period there was punctuated by a number of religious events going on in the national and global stage. First of all was Easter, which brought us all together quite a lot, but then we also had the news of the resignation of the Pope and the vote for the new one – I had no idea that the residents were so interested in the process, the anticipation, the waiting, the endless camera shots of presenters at the Vatican like Jon Snow trying to guess when the white smoke would blow out, the endless interviews with the UK head of the Catholic church, who was there and willing to give interviews, speculation about the way any new Pope would go. There were endless discussions among the residents about who the new Pope might be and what the consequences would be – it was almost outdoing *Casualty* for popularity. I had not realised that we had a number of Catholics among us but there was genuine interest by many residents no matter their religion.

Then there was the ordination of the new Archbishop of Canterbury on 21 March, all happening not that far away from ESP in Kent. Our chaplain was invited to be there – and was clearly very pleased to be going and had warned us (a number of times lest we forgot) that he would have to miss the session we were due to have mid-week as a result. The 'congregation' was very excited about it. I had only a passing interest except for the fact that the new Archbishop, Justin Welby, used to work in the oil industry, which I had also done for a while, though for different companies.

But what interested me was that these religious organisations were filling the gap the social services were leaving in the rehabilitation process. The community chaplaincy helps people integrate and connect with faith communities outside which give continuing mentoring and other support and also puts them in touch with other specialised organisations that may be able to provide further help. The chaplain explained to me that although the Christian faith generally encouraged forgiveness and reintegration, some of the other faiths didn't necessarily as they considered committing an offence an act against their religion; some women often found themselves shamed and ostracised and unable to return to their communities. There had been some cases of girls changing faith and starting new lives but needing extra help to do so which the community chaplaincy tried to provide.

My research assistant, Nicola Clay, currently based at the Institute of Criminology in Cambridge, had previously carried out a study looking at the significant role faith played in the experience of imprisonment. Through a number of in-depth interviews with male prisoners at HMP Littlehey, she found that Christian teachings about God's love and forgiveness helped the men to take responsibility for their offences, and for their rehabilitation, as did the support of the chaplaincy team. Indeed for some, it had been their faith that had led them to handing themselves in, realising that they needed to own up and seek help so that they could break free from their offending behaviour. Many also felt that imprisonment provided them with an opportunity to show love and support to their fellow prisoners, often transforming the meanings they gave to their time inside.

This sense of purpose was echoed in the way they saw their faith as a way towards their own rehabilitation, providing them with an alternative lifestyle, a moral framework to live by and a way of working through the difficult experiences from their pasts that had led to them offending in the first place.

More broadly, many of those interviewed spoke of how the chaplaincy provided a place of respite from the dehumanising effects of imprisonment, and allowed them to 'feel like a human being again'. They also gained a sense of peace from the idea that God, rather than the prison authorities, was in ultimate control of their lives.[89]

Much of this mirrored what I saw at ESP. In our airy and light multi-faith room we were all treated with respect, there was discussion and debate and we were listened to as we voiced our various opinions and thoughts and discussed things, like the meaning of various passages from the Bible, in such a way that allowed us all to lift ourselves from our human conditions and move to a different level of understanding and feeling. There was also compassion and willingness to share experiences and listen to other people's feelings and as such it was very liberating. I did not discover God, or at least I didn't discover anything spiritual over and above what I already believed in, but I now think that these sessions were seriously therapeutic – I was not aware of the real difference they were making at the time but I always left with a feeling of well-being, and not just because of the excellent mango juice and chocolate biscuits.

There is a long tradition of the church helping women in prison. It started in earnest with Elizabeth Fry, the great Christian philanthropist and prison reformer, who

did a lot to highlight the conditions of women in prisons at the beginning of the nineteenth century. In 1818
she gave evidence to the House of Commons committee
on the conditions in women's prisons – the first woman
ever to present evidence in Parliament. She had been
instrumental in encouraging women to read the Bible
as a way of getting them to help themselves, something
that continues to this day under the stewardship of the
chaplains in each prison. It seemed rather sad when
I discovered soon after my release that the Bank of
England had announced plans to replace the image
of Elizabeth Fry on the £5 note with one of Winston
Churchill. It was worrying that the departing Bank of
England governor, Sir Mervyn King, admirable in many
other ways, should leave behind him on his retirement
a monetary policy committee (MPC) and a financial
policy committee consisting of only men and banknotes
which, although all featuring the Queen, should have
no other female in the long history of Britain worthy
of mention on them. His successor, Mark Carney, later
announced that the £10 note will now feature Jane
Austen. That is good in itself but I can't see why, just
as the issue of women in prison has risen up on the
agenda, we can't have more than one woman on our
banknotes – or a female on the MPC again.

19 MARCH

There is now proof beyond reasonable doubt that I
have achieved universal name recognition, for better
or worse. Denise, a mature lady convicted of trying to
defraud her mother-in-law, showed me a long interview printed in the *Telegraph* with Nancy Dell'Olio,
who mentioned my name casually during her interview without needing to explain who I was. For the

uninitiated, Nancy is an accomplished Italian lawyer who came to fame in the UK as the girlfriend for a period of Sven-Göran Eriksson, once manager of the English football team. At the time of her interview she was in the process, I believe, of moving out of the £2.5m home belonging to Sven which she had refused to vacate all those years since their breakup. Fun to read. I like football and she is a feisty lady. Not the type my judge would like, said my fellow residents. Aanjay suggested I should get in touch with Nancy when I got out as she is probably a great woman. I fantasised for a while about us meeting up and going out to supper together one day. That would be sure to put the paparazzi in a real spin. But then again maybe it wouldn't be such a good idea after all. But fun, yes... So if Nancy is reading this and fancies a cup of coffee, by all means get in touch.

The girls insisted that it was certain, now, that I would be asked to go on *Celebrity Big Brother* or *I'm a Celebrity, Get Me Out of Here!* They fantasised about how we could all go as a team once they were out and they would come as my assistants. I ridiculed the idea that this would ever happen but how wrong can you be. After I left ESP and the invitation to appear on *Celebrity Big Brother* was sent to my publishers I realised how much more with it the girls in ESP were. I laughed, wrote to the girls to say they had indeed been correct in their expectations but that I had declined. Nevertheless one of them later wrote to me to say that the *Daily Mirror* in mid-August was still carrying a story saying that I was listed as a possible *Celebrity Big Brother* contestant... Oh well...

My lawyer visited today with his assistant Sarah, who had helped me through the trial and with whom

I had walked in front of the photographers every day. Robert had not brought her with her last time in Holloway but decided to do so in his first visit to ESP. And the meeting was great. We were allowed to use the so-called 'quiet room', also known as the 'listening room', a tiny little cubicle near my bedroom but with very comfortable armchairs with one of the officers taking orders for tea and coffee and then bringing it to us. Very civilised. More news from the outside, some instructions from me and then I escorted them to the door by noon, in time for my roll call and lunch at 12.15. I have to say that for such an experienced lawyer it was clear that he didn't know what to expect. I suspect that Robert's clients commit more dangerous crimes and I didn't get the impression that he had ever had a female client before or that he had visited a women's prison. I think the nearest he has come to representing someone in my position again was when he was hired to give advice during the marriage break up between Charles Saatchi and Nigella Lawson, which resulted in lots of articles in the press about the abuse of women and which ended with a caution for Saatchi and divorce for the two of them. I have never discovered which side Robert had been on.

That afternoon we had more inductions and when the time came to visit the education department in the purpose-built building at the end of the garden we had a real emergency. The photographers, it seemed, were still there, having failed to take a picture the previous Sunday. They were now camping behind the trees on the wall that surrounded the lovely church of St Peter and St Paul, which dates back to the thirteenth century and which was just at the edge of the garden. You could walk by the side of it, as the girls did, admittedly the small number who took their exercise seriously and who went outside for reasons other than just to smoke and chat, which is what most others did – except sunbathing in the summer.

At times there would be weddings or christenings and the bells that rang frequently to the annoyance of anyone trying to take a nap would ring even more joyfully. And that would seriously excite most of the residents, who would all come out and stand as close they could without being intrusive and look and admire the bridesmaids, groom and guests who were walking around the church in full view of us before the ceremony. Lovely bride, they would say, lovely beautiful bridesmaids – and their eyes would water.

The church was so close that there was an 'out of bounds' sign serving as a warning that we were normally not allowed to go the extra 3 feet and through the little gate into the cemetery and then the church. These 'out of bounds' notices were, I understood, put up relatively recently after a resident had been told off for going 'out' and then successfully argued that as she hadn't been there long enough she had not learned yet what was 'in' and what was 'out'. For me those discreet signs were very useful as you had to be licensed or have permission normally to leave the area within the confined grounds of the prison – though some of the girls who were already past their FLED were allowed to go to church with the chaplain at Christmas and Easter. I wouldn't reach my date until I was discharged on Home Detention Curfew (HDC) so I would have to make my own way independently if I wanted to visit it. I vouched I would. But in the meantime the lovely grey church was so close to us I could just about touch it with my arms outstretched.

The officers assured me that they would try and get rid of the photographers but it was best that I not go out that way. We decided to stick with the inductions that were either in the house or those that could be accessed from the back door such as the health centre, the drugs rehabilitation unit, probation and the governor's office. Education would have to wait as it required walking across the pathway and up some stairs into the garden, which was perfectly visible from the church wall. I was concerned that I was creating extra work for everyone but most were hugely excited by all this attention. There was an announcement for the girls to be mindful of the fact that if they were in rooms on the side of the house overlooking the garden and the cemetery they should watch what they were doing and how they were dressed as they stood by their windows as the photographers were likely to have long lenses that they would use to take pictures. That caused huge hilarity and a lot of excitable discussions. They would often update me on the photographers' status as they kept watch from their rooms. The officers behaved impeccably, their main interest being to protect me from unwanted publicity, which was my right, so I followed their advice and avoided that day's induction. A number of the girls walked up to the photographers, asked them what they were waiting for and then told them that I wasn't there at all but was instead in Askham Grange in York. Since they hadn't seen me and there hadn't been any confirmation of my transfer by the prison service some of them believed the girls and went off to check with their papers. But they soon returned. Given that we were enjoying one of the coldest winters in living memory I hoped that at least they were being paid enough to make hanging around a bitterly windy and sleety cemetery worthwhile and we fully expected that those poor chaps – it seems they were mainly male – would soon disappear in search of somewhere warmer to shelter.

And indeed they did – there was no sign of them in the following few hours so we assumed they had gone for good. But it was then that I realised that the room I was put in when I arrived looked onto the internal courtyard. The windows were covered with that semi-white stuck-on covering, of the type people have in their houses when their front room is overlooking a busy street. This blocked anyone's full view into the room even if they had managed to sneak in and trespass into the prison area. And it was also as far away from the church from which one could be seen as possible. Clearly the prison officers had enough experience of the system or had been warned by PR in headquarters, which they seemed to be in contact with constantly about me, that this made sense. It was also why it seemed right for me not to do any external jobs which were 'out of bounds' and where anyone could approach me. In the meantime I had to take my exercise either in the back courtyard or after 6 p.m. as it was assumed that in this Arctic weather no journalists would stay past their newspaper deadlines.

20 MARCH

It was agreed that I would today finally venture out and go to the education building to have my IT induction, which I was really looking forward to as I am useless at it and was determined to learn to touch-type and improve on my Outlook, Excel spreadsheet and PowerPoint skills, which to my shame are non-existent except for sending basic e-mails. It was suggested that just in case there was still someone hanging around and wanting to photograph me, I should be shielded by staff who would walk with me there on the direct normal route to prevent a clear view for the camera and on the way back we would take the roundabout way back through 'out of bounds' terrain which would be well out of shot anyway. Well, there was someone still there. According to the girls who were threatening to go and shake him down, he was hiding in a tree! He managed to take a couple of pictures after all, which made it into all the national newspapers, me dressed warmly in my winter clothes clutching some books and looking studious. I thought I looked OK – not harassed, in my own clothes, doing something useful. My children complained to the Press Complaints Commission and all my friends were horrified at the intrusion. I read what they had written after I was released on tag and was really touched that they felt so strongly about it. I am a lucky mother. But I personally felt at the time that the journalists were just doing their job and that in many ways it was better to get it over and done with; once they had taken the first picture of me in open prison they would surely leave me alone. And so it proved; despite some false alarms they didn't come back until near the end.

Even so, so paranoid was everyone that we once chased a group of perfectly innocent, rather bewildered, Dutch tourists away – wonder what they thought of a prison governor coming to ask them what they were doing taking pictures of the house and gardens. Being a Grade II-listed Elizabethan house with a great history, tourists could often be seen stalking the grounds. But the staff seemed to worry about me more than I worried about myself. I made it clear that having been constantly followed around by journalists in the last few months I was unfazed by it although I worried about the inconvenience to everyone else, residents and staff. But they rose to the occasion with good humour. It is not every day they have to handle the press and they also had to take good care of the other prisoners who didn't want their pictures to appear in the national press while they were in prison. Many of the women had been more traumatised by the lurid coverage of their cases in the press than the sentence itself and by the damning comments of the judge that had humiliated them and in their minds made a return to their community that much more difficult. In some cases their acquaintances had been told that they were simply away – studying, travelling or whatever. I came across this a lot. A lovely Indian lady never told her parents, who had moved back to India, that she had gone to prison and was calling them weekly from the ESP phone box keeping up the pretence that she and her husband – also in prison, like her, for benefit fraud – were just fine and leading a normal life. Having their pictures taken and then broadcast just wasn't going to be something they would welcome.

This was generally respected by the press so, apart from me, all other faces in the published pictures were obscured. Prison officers apparently often don't tell others what they do for a living though the lady senior officer next to me was very pleased to be identified by her friends and acquaintances by her shoes. It became quite a topic of conversation in the centre office and she and I joked about it again on the day she retired a couple of weeks before I left East Sutton Park. To this day I am convinced no one in ESP held any of this against me and they were much more solicitous towards me than I should have expected.

21 MARCH

I met with the nurse today at the immaculate if small healthcare unit between the two medieval towers and next to the gym and the huge laundry room. She checked my weight (I'm losing some), took blood for tests and gave me a second hepatitis B injection. Again for someone who hates needles this was completely painless. I ordered my extra blood pressure pills and 'Viscotears' for dry eyes as well as headache pills and was told to collect them on the next delivery day, which was next Tuesday when the blood results would also be ready. I was treated like a real human being. I had wondered why many of the residents were popping in and out of healthcare all the time. It probably did a lot for them psychologically especially since I discovered that there was no longer a counsellor available to deal with mental issues and the girls had to be given special licences to go outside and get treatment if they needed it, a cumbersome task and occasionally one that seemed to sink beneath the weight of bureaucracy.

I had been completing my inductions for three days already and the session that really made me think hard and reflect about the situation I was in was the 'pathways' induction with the head of education. What we did was discuss in quite a lot of helpful detail what we intended to do to respond to what had happened to us, what were our concerns and how we were going to address them between now and when we came out

– and beyond. This would then form part of a plan that would be considered by the first risk-assessment board we would attend in the following few days.

Two of us did it together and we had been assured that everything we talked about would all be kept confidential. We both seemed to care deeply about the impact our actions may have had on our family and our reputations, which is fairly typical for women. But we were both amazed to find out the trainers' experience regarding the differences between men offenders and women offenders doing their 'pathways' for the future. The administration of East Sutton Park, the only female open prison in the south of England, had been amalgamated with the nearby male open resettlement prison Blantyre in 2007. This allowed staff to make comparisons – albeit anecdotal ones – and patterns had emerged. Women were preoccupied first and foremost with the impact of their imprisonment on their families in general and their children in particular. Their concerns were heightened by a feeling of helplessness because they were away from them and an inability to exercise control over events. Making amends and re-engaging properly with family was priority number one for women. Men in general (and it is a generality but very much from the experience of these prison officers) took it for granted that their children would be looked after by the mother and so were less concerned about the impact on them and much more interested in finding ways to negotiate a reasonable path through prison and then making money once out. When offenders in both prisons were asked what had prevented them from achieving their potential in life the women's answer was children and family and the men's was a lack of money. It seemed to me that judging from the controlled experiment of that session as the other resident and I discussed our plans during prison and thereafter, our concerns and worries seemed to fit perfectly into the female pattern of behaviour and improved the statistical significance of the 'survey' results based on the two prisons by two.

22 MARCH

A very important day as I had my first meeting with my probation officer at ESP, Dee. They have these really sweet offices on top of one of the two towers that formed part of the medieval building and you have to take a spiral staircase that you enter from the courtyard to get there. As you sit talking about your issues, people wander in, assuming they are fit enough to come up the stairs, usually out of breath but asking for appointments to see the staff and for information on the progress of their cases with external probation, which is where a lot of the problems emerge. The girls complained of frequent changes of personnel in external probation and of slow and cumbersome processes. They found the concerns that external probation often raised over the suitability of the accommodation on the outside frustrating and at times petty and inconsistent (they would frequently make comments like: 'my probation officer really hates me'). The general feeling about in-house probation, however, was positive but all the new girls worried hugely about the first meeting and some had a better experience with one officer rather than the other. I had heard a lot of that being discussed in the Butler's Room as it was probation that often determined where and when the girls could go out, which addresses on the outside the women were allowed to visit or stay at, and how quickly they progressed towards release. In the case of one girl I got to know well, there was an issue concerning whether she could visit her mother at her mother's address on her day release and home visits once she started being entitled to them because her mother had also been convicted, for a short period, for her alleged small part in her daughter's offence, for which the daughter had been sentenced to four years' imprisonment. I saw what distress this caused her. She was very close to her mother and spoke to her a number of times a day on the phone. But the whole day's mood would be ruined by yet another sign that her home visits that she was so looking forward to and her eventual return to normality might be in jeopardy. In addition the company she had worked for and defrauded wanted the money back that she had taken from them. In the end, while I was there, she was coming to the conclusion that given her lack of assets the best way forward was to hand her pension entitlement back to her former employer. It was a neat solution but not one that bodes well for her future security. And in that it resembled the case of a public servant who was in ESP with me and who not only had the ignominy of losing her job and the bad publicity that would make it difficult for her to return to any decent standard of living when she got out, but had to fight through lawyers the threat made by the public institution that had employed her to take her pension away because of the nature of her offence'. Whatever the rights or wrongs, such extra knocks reduce so hugely the chances of a smooth and fast rehabilitation that I wondered what, if any, protection there is for prisoners who basically face being destitute on leaving prison.

Many of the negative by-products of having a conviction when one returns to outside life, however trivial, victimless or non-threatening the offence may have been, are not widely understood. They can make life rather more expensive as well as being a constant reminder of one's 'criminality' in the eyes of others. When my friend Rachel, convicted of fraud, rang to tell her building insurance that covered her mortgage that she had a conviction, the chap at the other end of the phone apparently said something like 'sorry, we are stopping insuring you as of this minute' and hung up without any further explanation. She was rather shocked. It was a similar story with her car insurance. Fortunately she got help from Leanne, a fellow ESP resident working for a company called Unlock while finishing her sentence, who put her in touch with providers who don't exclude offenders and ex-offenders and managed to get her cheaper insurance than before for both her house and her car. The Unlock charity, founded and run for a number of years by ex-offender and commentator Mark Leech, gives advice on its website to prisoners wanting insurance, but experiencing difficulties because of their convictions. There is even a chart to let prisoners know when their convictions are actually spent and no longer need to be mentioned and it also offers advice on when and how convictions have to be disclosed. But the point still is that seemingly small hurdles like these are in reality major obstacles to rebuilding a fully functioning life in society for prisoners and their families. It is a 'brick wall' moment when you realise your conviction could stop you being able to insure

your possessions, your car, your health or your home.
Given the very large number of people with criminal
convictions you wonder how many are keeping mum.

Anyway, the girls were right. My case with probation was much more straightforward although the
various interruptions from girls and staff entering
the probation office through our open 'interview
room' just by the entrance door meant that we had to
stop frequently and the meeting took quite some time.
But the space, however idiosyncratic, was delightful.
It was great to be high up looking across Kent and the
actual meeting was professional and thorough – the
right noises were made, the preparation and conditions for release well explained and the unconditional
release date all in the system – it was something to
look forward to. The first thing was to go through the
risk-assessment board that was due to meet at some
stage – not sure yet when – with the notes I needed for
that board. By the time I left I felt that I had been given
all the facts, fairly, had been treated like everyone
else, had made progress and knew that someone was
going to further things for me. All that was needed
was for social services in my area to check that the
house was OK, that the daughter and son who lived
in it agreed to have me back (what a joke, I thought,
little terrors, wonder whether they would object and
enjoy possession of the house while I have to go to
a hostel!) and since there would be no probation
officer assigned to look after me while outside as my
sentence was under twelve months (Justice Minister
Chris Grayling's potentially very costly proposals
extending supervision to all released offenders including those who have served short sentences having not
yet been implemented) the only control would be my

curfew from Serco, who would come on the day of release to fit a tag, which would work for two months until my unconditional release day on 11 July. All was clear. The path ahead was fine but I sensed that being fully engaged in the prison activities (as I was) was something expected and that it was being monitored. When I left, my probation officer Dee exclaimed once more about the odd office space and I understand they are trying now to move back to the main building with an extra secure interview room and not too many flights of stairs up so that people are not put off by the effort required to get to them.

23 MARCH

And suddenly in the news something very much up my street. Cyprus, as widely expected, was in economic trouble and the solution seemed to be a particularly destabilising one requiring ordinary savers to be the first to take a hit. Although Cyprus represents only 0.2 per cent of the total EU economy a mishandling of its debt problem threatened to spiral into a major Eurozone crisis. It was all very odd and of course sent shivers down the spine of all countries in debt as trust in banks would be shattered if people who had a few thousand euros of savings suddenly found they were not safe. And indeed that is precisely what happened. Long queues formed outside the Cypriot banks as word spread that everyone would have to lose up to 10 per cent of their savings in a levy to satisfy the demands of the IMF and the EU and allow a bailout to be fashioned. The banks had to close to prevent a run. There were shades of the queues forming outside Northern Rock in 2007 as depositors feared the bank would close and all money would be lost. The European Central Bank and the European Commission seemed to have forgotten that protecting small savers was a sine qua non for confidence in the banking system. It seemed crazy to me that anyone in Cyprus would agree to this but newly elected politicians were unlikely to be thrown out overnight. The public made clear there were limits to what could be done to their savings. Finally, the Troika (IMF-ECB-EU Commission) agreed to limit the size of the deposits beyond which the depositors had to take a cut to over €100,000. But the damage had been done. Once again the EU politicians had shown themselves to be out of touch and by establishing the practice that depositors have to be forced to 'bail in' to rescue banks they changed the terms of the game. It was obvious to me but even more obvious to my fellow residents, who had a clear understanding of the potty logic behind the handling in Brussels, Frankfurt and Washington of the Cyprus crisis. So we watched the riots and just waited for things to calm down. Wherever I went in the open prison people would raise the Cyprus issue with me. I am not Cypriot but for some reason they lumped me together with all those southern Europeans, I had to tell them and all the friends who wrote to me saying they missed my commentary on this that I was dumbfounded. Was there a logic in this madness? Or was it all lost? I still can't decide. The Cyprus events made me determined to update my book on the euro crisis and try and make some sense of it. But I was impressed by how switched on my fellow residents were on the matter and how they were able to instantly see the craziness of the originally proposed solution.

This weekend I realised that out of some 100 residents

there were only about forty left behind during the
day – and many of us were there because our FLED
had not started yet. It had the advantage that we each
were able to have an extra sausage or double portion
of scrambled eggs with our brunch on Saturday and
my job cleaning the dining room and looking after
the cleanliness of the trays after they had been washed
and ensuring teas and coffees were plentiful was
much easier. But it raised the issue in my mind that
this is precisely how it should be; many more prisoners should be able to enjoy open prison conditions
on the inside and more establishments on the outside
should offer offenders voluntary or paid employment
to help re-engage offenders with the community in the
hope of reducing reoffending levels. In the meantime
the weekend allowed for a lot of catching up once the
walk (in the snow) and time in the gym (warmest
place in ESP, run today by the second gym instructor, Pete) were completed. And I got my first haircut
by Debbie – scissors being allowed in ESP – and
had a much more expert bingo session that evening.
The newspapers somehow heard of this and had a
story the following day about how I was taught to
play bingo, which I had never played before, by my
fellow residents and that apparently I loved it. Who
can possibly be interested in that story? But the girls
seemed to think it was as it should be so I supposed
I might as well get used to the fact that nothing is
sacred while in prison.

24 MARCH

Getting into the swing of things. Amazingly our main
gym instructor, Craig, is here today and the gym would
open in the morning and again after lunch. More

rowing. Becoming slowly addicted. I row between levels two and three to replicate rowing on water and therefore prevent doing any harm to myself by an overenergetic rowing regime. Some of the girls were practising some dance tunes and asked me to participate. Obviously I would make a fool of myself but who cares. No cameras are allowed inside prison so there was no chance that my attempts to stay upright would make it onto YouTube, so I obliged. Cue much hilarity. 'You dance really well, Vicky!' Yeah, right.

And then my second family visit since I got to ESP. What bliss. Three grandchildren visited up with their parents. How lucky I am! The nephew of my room-mate discovered that he has a new best friend in my two-and-a-half-year-old grandson and they terrorised the place. Then it was back to the house, slightly shaken as normal but as it was Palm Sunday we had a 6.30 p.m. service with the chaplain, which raised the spirits of us all.

Just before the evening service and after the family visit the chaplain sought me out and found me reading the papers in the drawing room. The enthronement of the new Archbishop of Canterbury had indeed been a great event but interestingly our chaplain had bumped into the Greek Orthodox Archbishop of London and had helped him find his way around. They had started talking and amazingly our chaplain had a message for me from him as the Greek Archbishop apparently knew me and remembered me fondly. I racked my brain in a bit of shock as I couldn't remember whether I had ever met him but soon decided that the only possible explanation must be that he was around when I got married some thirty years ago in the Greek Orthodox cathedral on Moscow Road, in London. He

may even have been the bishop who conducted the
rites of my second marriage. I explained to the chaplain that a great advantage of the Greek Orthodox
church is that it is happy to allow you to divorce and
marry in church a number of times (four, as far as I
recall) as long as you have a good excuse for divorcing your previous husband and are prepared to pay a
certain sum to grant you a religious divorce which is
accepted by the Greek state. The trick is to negotiate
the appropriate amount for your wedding for things
to go smoothly. In my case, after the arrangements
were made and cheques changed hands, I drove myself
to church on the Saturday afternoon of my wedding
only to be greeted by my brother on the steps of the
cathedral. He instructed me to go and park my white
BMW round the corner, out of sight, and hide there
for a while. Apparently the church officials took one
look at the assembled congregation and decided they
had seriously underpriced the wedding. It took half
an hour of wrangling between the church on the one
hand and my mother, my brother and my best man,
the *Guardian* journalist Patrick Wintour, on the other
before the priest agreed to proceed with the ceremony
on the production of an extra modest cash sum and I
was then summoned to enter the church to get married.

25 MARCH

People have started sending me e-mails! I was very
surprised to get printed copies of e-mails written by
a handful of friends who had realised that a system
existed to get news to me more quickly, or so they
thought, using my unique prison name and number and
subscribing for a modest monthly fee to the 'emaila-
prisoner' service, started by serial offender Derek Jones

some ten years earlier, apparently frustrated that his girlfriend was not getting in touch. You don't receive them while sitting by your computer as the internet is bizarrely not allowed – more on that later. The e-mails are printed off by officers and given to prisoners to read with the normal mail. But since they have to be printed, then read and then handed out to you if they pass the test, sometimes, especially if they were sent in the early evening, they do not get delivered to you until post is given out at 4.30 p.m. the following day. You don't save much although it is slightly cheaper than a first-class stamp. Well, good ideas are rewarded and Jones has sold his Bath-based Prison Technology Services for a six-figure sum to Unilink Software, apparently. There is hope for all of us.

With working and replenishing the coffees and teas for the girls in the dining room one of my daily tasks, I was astonished to discover that there was such a thing as 'prison salt', which arrived in specially labelled boxes, 'prison sugar', 'prison coffee' and the like but none carried any real indication of who was making it. On some weeks we even got 'prison shreddies' and 'prison bran flakes', which were a real hit with the residents – I made sure the chefs who were doing the ordering knew when we were running low so we were never left without the 'bowel-opening' cereals for long. They were not Kellogg's quality, so the girls added to their order from the canteen the cereal they particularly liked every week, but it was understandable when I looked at the figures in more detail what pressures the kitchens were under. Ministry of Justice figures suggest that in 2009/10 the overall food costs in prisons were £59,959,424. This was up from £33,900,093 in 2000/01, rising somewhat faster than the prison population over that period, but it still leaves very little to be spent per prisoner.[90] The annual report on ESP by the Independent Monitoring Board (IMB) for the year to October 2012 calculates that there was still only £1.95 a day allocated per resident in that period, pretty much the average elsewhere. Admittedly we occasionally received help from the farm shop – left over home-grown vegetables (most produce, including the meat from the farm that the residents looked after and then processed in the meat factory, was sold externally) and occasionally sausages that were reaching their sell by-date. We didn't let the date worry us as they were delicious and no one to my knowledge while I was there suffered from serious belly problems – although that could have had more to do with my obsessive disinfecting of everything in and around the kitchen and dining room area.

The tight budget the prison service has to work with probably explained the bulk buying of the rather insipid Vietnamese fish we were served on numerous occasions, which must be very cheap indeed despite the transport cost. Some of the girls boycotted the fish because it was so tasteless but I knew that fish, however horrid, must be good for you so ate it diligently – particularly when it had spices on it that added some flavour. Indeed, when I began bringing my tiny bottle of spray olive oil into the dining room each day and my 30p lemon bought from the canteen, which I made last a whole week, to put on the fish others soon brought ketchup and chilli sauce to obscure the taste as much as they could. But overall I think the ESP chefs did wonders with the tiny budgets they were given. The IMB in its report praised ESP's catering team 'for

their hard work and ingenuity in providing nutrition-
ally balanced meals that are well cooked and varied'
– including halal and vegan food sourced from 3663,
the food wholesalers – but expressed surprise and
concern that the excellent lamb and pork produced in
the farm and sold at the prison's farm shop or by the
shop in farmers' markets at Headcorn and elsewhere
cannot be used in the kitchens.

Still, ESP is lucky in that regard. It still has a working farm. There is a dedicated space for the farm
animals and 5 acres are used to grow vegetables and
plants, some of which are sold through the farm shop
and some used in the kitchen. Similarly the plants are
either sold or used for the house and gardens, which
are very well looked after – all by the women residents
under some supervision by the manager of the farm
and the farm shop. The girls are able to study for their
NVQs in agriculture and horticulture, and progress
if they stay there long enough, though few seemed to
be doing so while I was there aside from the woman
I would meet each weekend on our walk around
the grounds. Those doing garden and farm duty or
manning the shop are all licensed to be outside the
formal prison grounds and take great pride in how
many sausages they have made in the week – very
high quality with lots of varieties, traditional country
sausages and those with hops being the most popular – or how much they may have made that week in
sales. It being a female establishment there was fierce
competition going on between different groups of
meat and farm workers – I witnessed many a heated
conversation where girls would guard proudly the
information on their takings from the other set that
manned the stand in the farmers' market the previous

week (there are four different markets that the shop goes to in towns in Kent in the vicinity of the prison).

The farm breeds pigs, keeps sheep and lambs in season and has a livery for twenty-one retired horses for which it charges just £170 a month, which is a reasonable fee. Not surprisingly therefore there is always a long waiting list from local farmers who want their horses to be looked after. So there was demand, limited supply and yet all the time I was there people were talking about how to increase revenue by 'sweating the assets' but doing very little about it as the investment for more capacity was not forthcoming.

According to the girls working there the farm shop and meat shop were run excellently by Mr and Mrs C, as they were known. I still to this day have no idea what Mr and Mrs C's full names are and I suspect this was the case with quite a lot of the people working there. Even the staff referred to them that way. The IMB report duly praises the existence of the farm and farm shop and the gardens and how they are run. It believes that for many women working with animals or in the gardens is therapeutic as it gives them the chance to experience rural life for the first time in their lives and allows them time to reflect outdoors, which can be beneficial. Working in the farm shop serving customers and handling cash also brings back a bit of normality to their lives and allows for many, particularly lifers, their first interaction with the community for years. And as working in the shop is classified as 'volunteering' it also gives lifers and those on indeterminate sentences incentive to do it well as this could count positively towards their hoped-for parole. But it goes further than that. All the girls who work outdoors or in the shop seemed to have a much more positive attitude to the job they are doing to the point of driving the rest of us mad. The number of times I had to hear all the details of the births of the latest little lambs or piglets; the sick mothers who were abandoning their little ones which then had to be bottle fed by my roommates; the latest horse that escaped and ran through the fields because someone had AGAIN not closed its stable door; similarly with sows – enormous things that were difficult to catch and carry back. For my sins I was sharing a room with girls who worked in the farm and the shop and they cared deeply for their animals, and, though the work was tiring, never complained about having to get up even at the weekends at the crack of dawn to let the animals out into the field.

So doing these tasks had a major impact on everyone involved – a sure sign of developing individual responsibility, getting up on time entirely by themselves, caring about the outcomes of their work and the professionalism they displayed, moaning about laggards and generally behaving as team members, helping each other and working together and keeping Mr and Mrs C happy. Perfect preparation, it seemed to me, for employability in the outside world. I must admit that although I love looking at animals and used to ride horses I am not one to want to actively look after them if I can avoid it and my kitchen job, especially in the Arctic conditions we were experiencing at the time, suited me fine. So I moaned a bit at the thought of early morning wake-ups but they were so solicitous not to wake me that they got up in the dark and left half dressed, putting on the rest of their clothes outside the room once they went through the door.

A Home Office civil servant in charge of the prison farms some twenty years ago told me that farms, apart from providing fresh and healthy food to prisons at low cost, were also tremendously valuable at getting people to overcome many of their problems as they cared for animals, worked as teams and took responsibility for growing plants, looked after horses, delivered new lambs and worked in the meat shops. The interesting thing is that as a result of the farms in existence the prison service used to be self-sufficient in pork, bacon, potatoes and some other vegetables, but this is no longer the case as most of those farms have been dispensed with – either sold for development, taken over for expansion of other prison facilities or abandoned as the cost of extra supervision of prisoners during their time out was prohibitive. The Royal Society of Arts project Transitions in Wells prison is aimed to try to reverse this. But for the moment the general lack of fresh produce, with some notable exceptions, was easily evident to me as I worked in the kitchen.

Given those constraints, trying to keep the residents in ESP happy was an unenviable task. The poor girls who cooked there were always anxious to find out what people thought. Many had never worked in kitchens before but after a while became interested in becoming chefs themselves. There used to be an NVQ you could get in catering while in ESP but that didn't seem to be offered anymore, though the girls still learned a lot. In fact, they were experimenting with puddings, fatal for those trying to avoid putting on weight as they ended up often being the best thing on the menu. There were shrieks

of enthusiasm when one chef who was retiring came
back to ESP for a few days just before the end of his
term with the prison service to cook for three days –
he was apparently the best pudding maker ESP had
ever seen. I watched him make a series of cakes that
he was then leaving behind to be served on different nights – he proudly took me round and showed
me what he was making and then we went together
to each of the ovens where trays full of chocolate
sponge, raspberry cheesecake and apricot tarts were
proudly displayed. He explained that he had been a
chef for the prison service for a long time, and had
also experienced big prisons where it was impossible
to keep anything warm when you mass-produced
food as by the time the food was delivered to and
served in the different units around the prison it
had inevitably already gone cold and lost a lot of its
taste. Cooking for ESP was bliss for him especially as
the girls seemed to appreciate it. Reaching retirement
age some time ago, he had finally hung up his apron
after years of working part-time.

As a result of his skills the enthusiasm for puddings
had caught on. I recall being followed around by one
of the girls, Helen, who on a number of occasions
wanted me to taste the mixture for the apple crumble or the cream that she was intending to use for the
cheesecake, which in fact got better and better during
the period I was there. Indeed, by the time I was leaving, the apple cake and the apricot sponge served with
a huge dollop of packet custard were in my view near
perfect. But the girls moaned – as girls do – and they
filled in the comments book with negative comments.
The poor trainee cooks would pore over them at
night – true, sometimes they forgot to add sugar or

used the wrong kind of flour, which made a pudding inedible, but I suppose that happens everywhere. They needed encouragement though and one day, looking through the book of comments myself, I found an entry allegedly from me which I had never written. It said: 'Soup was yummy – Vicky Pryce'! That, at least, was true – in fact, most days the lunchtime soup was freshly made with vegetables left over from the garden and whatever bits of chicken may have been left from the supper the day before. I'm sure I must have said something like that because I genuinely enjoyed it – of course it always helps to have the alternative in mind i.e. Holloway, the new 'Bowani test' for me in terms of food. Compared with that everything else was a big improvement. Happiness, I think, is being able to adjust your expectations (a long way) downwards and to be prepared to be pleasantly surprised. From then onwards I was always given extra helpings when I arrived at the food counter...

The positive feedback had its drawbacks, however. A week later I had been lovingly given a larger than normal portion of brown, slightly unappetising-looking, soup with a dumpling at the bottom by a rather fierce girl, Hannah, who worked in the kitchens and whose wrong side you had learned to generally avoid. On arriving at my designated place in the dining room I discovered that my table companions had already ditched it saying it was inedible so I gave it up too before I even started. Once you've finished lunch or supper you take your tray into the Butler's Room and empty everything you haven't eaten or any rubbish into one of the three bins that are there before washing plates, cutlery and tray, which of course I then disinfected. So we entered the Butler's with trays still full of soup. The first person we encountered was Hannah. 'Oh,' she said, 'did you not eat your soup after all?' Before I was able to say I was a bit full actually, so couldn't finish it, Liz, my straight-talking ex-police officer friend, butted in: 'It was rubbish really, truly awful soup. Who made it?' 'I did,' was the reply. I hid from Hannah for days thereafter.

26 MARCH
A number of girls told me that my name was on a notice board outside centre office, with an appointment for my risk-assessment today at 10.30. I had a talk with Miss Callaghan, the prison officer assigned to me as my personal officer, who told me it should all be fine but she couldn't be there herself as she was doing something for charity outside the prison that day. I went in for my appointment just after Liz, who came out of it looking OK, I thought. I walked in carrying my pathway papers – according to Mo, the education lady, I was the only one to ever do so even though all the girls are asked to bring them to the board. I confirmed that I was intending to do as much education and mentoring of girls as possible and work in the kitchens, which I had already started to do. They seemed to think that my intentions to look at various studies on release was a 'good thing' and were pleased that I was having regular family visits, which to them was a positive sign.

I was assessed as very low risk – the probability of reoffending was estimated at 2 per cent for the first year after release and the probability in the second year was strangely put at 4 per cent following some statistical average. Puzzling, as I don't think I intend to allow anyone to pass their points onto my driving licence in the future, but who was I to argue? I was told that my HDC date when I could leave prison and go home to serve the rest of my time at home on a 'tag' was confirmed for 13 May but that it still depended on the governor signing my release on tag, though it rarely gets refused. I was also apparently now able to go unescorted for an emergency visit to a doctor or dentist or optician, probably in Maidstone. I thought that might be fun but in the event I couldn't think of a reason to pay any of those people a visit. I began to wonder how I could possibly leave without having visited Maidstone while in ESP, the destination of choice for those girls going out on day visits at the weekend. I suspect they spent most of their time out eating. I asked one girl one Saturday evening when she returned whether she had had a nice day and she described how she had first been at a curry house where you can eat as much as you want for a fixed price, then a couple of hours later had a McDonald's and then feasted on Nando's at 5 p.m. before coming back – she was recounting this while complaining with a straight face of a belly ache as if the actions of the day had nothing to do with that. I thought I should go and repeat just that culinary trip on my last day, 11 May, as that was my FLED, i.e. when I could go out on visits and also have employment. Alas, there is a (I think unwritten) rule that says that before release you must spend the previous twenty-four hours in ESP and I wasn't going to jeopardise my departure. So no Maidstone for me.

27 MARCH

Time for my manual handling course – yes, you haven't misread it. Three of us, Liz, Anya and I, went to the visitors' centre (out of bounds, by permission) to have a course with Craig on how to lift a parcel without hurting ourselves. I would say it was the most relaxed two hours spent in ESP. The course is there, I guess, to ensure that one is not injured if one can avoid it doing the work around the prison but more importantly, if the cynic in me can be allowed occasionally to surface, to ensure that there are no claims against the prison for any injuries suffered while working. It is true that I did meet a number of girls who had managed to do serious damage to themselves by lifting heavy pans around the kitchen several hours a day and some whose work on the farm or the meat shop had left them with pain in their arms and back. Some of them had to have healthcare sign them off these tiring jobs and switch to other, less physically demanding, activities but the process wasn't easy and relied on an ESP labour board providing approval. But in general they loved to do their jobs and took pride in what they did. I was lucky in a way – my dining room duties were not back-breaking, though I can't explain how it was possible that out of four of us doing dining room and Butler's Room duties and tray cleaning and, my favourite pastime, disinfecting everything, I was the only one who seemed not to have a bad back. It was me and me only who went on my hands and knees twice a day and cleaned the floor with a dustpan and brush. I must admit I still can't decide whether those ladies were having me on.

We were taught what was good for our bodies: apparently sleeping on your back was the best in terms of putting as little pressure as you can on your body and staying healthy and free of back problems for longer; on your side a bit worse; and sleeping on your front with face down against pillow was by far the worst. I had no idea. Hilarity soon stemmed from two things. First, Craig demonstrated all of this with the use of a plastic male skeleton called Eric – an odd name to use and for some of us who knew an 'Eric' doubly hilarious to see the skeleton practise all sorts of movements that, if done in real life, would be back-destroying. We also wondered why it had to be a male or why, since we probably wouldn't have noticed, not call it Erica. And second, causing many laughs were our attempts to lift the packet we were practising on without in real life injuring our backs or tripping or falling. In the end we were just women having fun; the best therapy for three grown-up women finding themselves in prison. Finally we were all presented with A4-size certificates to say we had completed the manual handling course – mine is now framed and proudly displayed on the hallway wall outside my study.

28 MARCH

Today the professional hairdresser came to cut and colour hair. It was a real scramble to book a place and though Liz and I managed to both get one, the visit ended up coinciding with the gym for me and a knitting class for Liz, so we gave our places away. We had had to pay out of our wages to get the appointments: £1.50 for a cut, £2.50 for a colour. It must be the cheapest place in the UK to have your hair done. One of our appointments went to Anya, who had just arrived and who had not had her hair cut since she had gone to closed prison many weeks before. She insisted on giving Liz, whose appointment she took over, a Kit Kat after she managed to make her first purchase on canteen a few weeks later. Liz later told me that in Holloway, despite having a hairdressing salon, haircuts were impossible while she was there. There was at times only one hairdresser for 500 women and she was often apparently sick. Sharp objects were not allowed in Holloway so no scissors were available for the inmates to cut each other's hair and many prisoners had unkempt hair as a result.

30 MARCH

The girls mentioned an article in the *Mail on Sunday* by a lawyer who had herself been an ESP resident a few years earlier when she was convicted of fraud. It was only then I realised that the girls were scouring the papers every day and tearing out any pieces they thought might upset me. We agreed they would stop doing so even though I was grateful for their protective solicitude. This lawyer, called Kate Johns, had apparently argued that 'for an educated, middle-class woman such as Pryce the regime at an open prison – where the walls are psychological, the competitive atmosphere suffocating and the rules petty and patronising – may prove unbearable'. She also argued in her piece that I would be challenged by 'humiliating menial roles' such as taking rubbish out and cleaning toilets and that I would be asked to do 'back-breaking' manual tasks that would be hard for a woman like me who is apparently used to 'firing off e-mails'. Talking of her experience there she wrote: 'For the first time in my sentence I became conscious of being scrutinised, to an extent that felt obsessively intrusive. Staff listened to my telephone calls and discipline was dished out for the pettiest reasons.'

We read the piece together in the old drawing room

and we did not recognise the description that she gave of East Sutton Park or how I would be able to cope. Things may have changed since she was there and she may have been justified in her description of the conditions I should expect based on her time there. But again it all seemed far removed from what I was experiencing in ESP at the time. And my fellow residents agreed. And frankly, as a mother of five children I find nothing humiliating in cleaning toilets or taking out rubbish; in fact, as at home, I felt good having contributed to keeping the place clean and hygienic for all. And I felt very little intrusion from staff. Kate Johns's conclusion that I would be 'longing for the monotony of Holloway' could not be further from my mind. I became a real fan of open prisons and I vowed to defend them as best I could.

31 MARCH

Easter Sunday service was followed that afternoon by a visit from George, my brother, over from Greece, accompanied by some of my children. It took a bit of time for him to cheer up at all despite the glorious surroundings. After all, according to him what I was convicted for does not seem to constitute an offence at all in Greece (i.e. doing something for your husband as a wife) and he was still coming to terms with his sister being in jail. So I spent a lot of the time when he came trying to cheer him up by showing him the house and the beautiful countryside, introducing him to the nice residents – including my grandchildren's new best pal, my roommate's nephew. In fact, the young boy quite fell in love with my granddaughter and they spent one Sunday afternoon, both all of three years, walking around holding hands and kissing each other. After long, serious chats with my brother I felt exhausted after he left but I was told that he was much more cheerful about it all during the return journey. Because it was Easter Sunday and there was a bank holiday on Easter Monday there was another bingo night – and I won my Flake!

1 APRIL

After lunch we had a session with the lady governor and we were invited to watch a video sent by head office in which Michael Spurr, the current director general for prisons in the MoJ, outlined the new plans for the prison estate and the strategy for the future. I saw his face in the video but didn't recognise him from my time in government even though we were both at the same level. Maybe he became a DG after I left. I was very keen to see what he would say. Because the meeting was held at the exact same time that Chelsea were playing Man United in the FA Cup quarter final, we switched the big TV on in the dining room opposite the pool room and Miss Carruthers, a senior officer, and I had to take it in turn to rush from the pool room into the dining room across the landing that separated them to check the score and then rush back again.

The DG was doing his best to present what was a further cut in budgets by using the usual civil service mantra of 'doing more with less' – I must admit I still don't understand exactly how but everyone seems to outwardly believe that by just saying it you can convince people that you can do 'more with less'. Try saying that to someone who has to feed a family and suddenly has less money to do so. We all wondered whether in fact that might simply mean fewer staff

and more lock-up in prisons and less time therefore
to be out doing other things. And the girls noted that
the word 'rehabilitation' only made it once into his
speech and women were not mentioned at all, and
everyone worried what it all meant for open prisons
as the video seemed to focus on closed prisons. But
what impressed me was that the governor encouraged
discussion which widened to include the culture in
prisons, how to deal with bullying, the right attitude
to staff if the girls felt put upon and many other areas.
I felt that this attempt at inclusion was good. But
there was still this uncertainty regarding the review
that was coming up of the women's estate and the
governor was keen to ensure that we were all prepared
for the review meeting that was coming up in May –
later postponed to June.

By the end of the meeting Chelsea had won 1–0
and progressed to the semi-final. Blue is the colour
– strangely I had brought not a single item of blue
clothing with me to prison.

2 APRIL

My South American friend had come to find me the
night before with a message from Debbie, one of
the residents who lived in the workers' area down
on the ground-floor corridor. I had noticed her looking smart just before the 8 p.m. roll call eating late
supper in the dining room along with other workers
who were returning too late for the regular evening
meal. Talking to Debbie I discovered that, like others,
she worked during the week for Working Chance, the
charity whose main aim it is to act as a recruitment
consultancy for current and ex-offenders. Her chief
executive wanted to get in touch and see how I could

help. I, of course, agreed. So this morning I was called into the activities office to be told that they had an e-mail for me from Jocelyn Hillman from Working Chance explaining what they did and asking whether I wanted to be a patron of theirs and meet up as soon as I came out. The charity seemed to be very well known and in a few days' time they were due to visit my old hunting grounds in Whitehall and were going, Debbie too, to the Treasury for a breakfast event with potential company supporters hosted by Nick Macpherson, the Treasury's permanent secretary. I spent some time talking to the activities manager, who explained the links they had with Working Chance and the crucial role the company played in rehabilitation of offenders, and then tried to understand better from Debbie that evening what her work entailed.

It was obvious that getting women back to work was not an easy task. There is no doubt that carrying a conviction can have profoundly negative effects on someone's ability to get a job on release. For women in particular who display the characteristics of low self-esteem and confidence and have a lot of educational gaps to fill, a daunting task in itself, it is a mammoth undertaking. As far as I can see, Working Chance is the only agency that focuses just on women offenders. Many of the permanent staff have come from other agencies and have strong views about the negative impact that imprisonment can have on women's employment prospects.

I started talking to the ESP girls that afternoon about the issues facing women seeking employment while in prison and on their release. One rather bright lady in her forties, who had been a manager in a housing unit of a council before coming to prison and was in for fraud, told me that she had intended to go to the business enterprise course, which was highly rated by everyone in ESP and ran over seven weeks. Having always had a passion for jewellery she was thinking of starting a jewellery design business on leaving prison. One could imagine her distress when at her risk-assessment board on arrival at ESP, she was apparently told by a senior officer chairing the board that there was no point in thinking about going down that route as no one would be prepared to fund her because of her offence. My fellow resident was devastated.

After I was released I visited Working Chance. When I arrived, the staff were trying to coach a lady who had gone to prison on a highly publicised case, though not for long, and who had been able to secure interviews in the City on her release but was not getting the jobs. Working Chance believed that she had lost all her confidence as she was told by officers in prison that she had no chance of getting a job of the sort she had left and needed to lower her sights because of her conviction.

And indeed in an interview workshop I attended later the greatest worry the women all had was how to approach the issue of conviction and what to say if they were asked. Most had written a disclosure letter while in prison which was usually perceived to be quite inadequate but fortunately Working Chance had usually already dealt with that issue with the prospective employer when arranging the interview so the likelihood was that it wouldn't come up during it and the girls wouldn't have the embarrassment of having to answer the question. Interestingly disclosure in many types of jobs was not in fact obligatory. But

Working Chance gave the example of an offender who had been tangentially involved in and then convicted of an armed robbery but after release didn't tell her new employers because she wasn't asked. She was a model employee but unfortunately for her there was an armed robbery in her place of work, the police were called and they checked on the backgrounds of all the employees who worked there and discovered her past. She was sacked on the spot on the grounds of gross misconduct even though she hadn't been obliged to inform them of her conviction. Working Chance suggested therefore that the girls should not take any chances and always disclose their convictions in the future.

All this justifiably worries the girls. The Department for Work and Pensions estimates that in the year following release, about half the year is spent claiming Jobseeker's Allowance, Incapacity Benefit or Employment Support Allowance. Overall, 49 per cent of ex-offenders were on benefits at the twelve-month point after release.[91] What is particularly worrying is that this is in part related to a lack of good education and training programmes (which I discuss elsewhere), but more significantly related to the stigma attached to ex-offenders. In an investigation conducted by the charity Working Links, almost three quarters of employers said they would use a disclosed conviction to reject an applicant outright or would discriminate against them compared to an equally qualified candidate with no conviction. Only 20 per cent of employers (in their sample) have knowingly recruited an offender.[92]

The general belief that ex-offenders lack honesty and reliability is also unfounded, since the same investigation revealed that over 60 per cent of employers

of ex-offenders found that they worked as hard, if
not harder, than those with no convictions. This is
supported by the fact that 97 per cent of offenders
say they want to stop offending, and 68 per cent say
the biggest factor in helping them to do so would be
having a job.[93] For women prisoners, employment is
an even more significant issue. Only 33 per cent of
women were in employment before entering prison,
compared to 54 per cent of men.[94] This is very nearly
half the national employment rate for women.[95] What
is more, it is unclear how many of the 51 per cent not
claiming benefits at twelve months after release are in
employment, and how many are reliant on partners
or families.

The services provided by organisations like
Working Chance, acting much like a recruitment
agency but specifically for women released from
prison, are vitally important. As well as training and
mentoring, the charity liaises directly with employers, helping them develop appropriate policies, and
deals with probation services to facilitate a transition
into employment. They argue that this not only deals
with financial problems experienced by unemploy-
ment, but helps instil a sense of pride and self-worth.
This would concur with the arguments put forward
by what is known as 'Desistance Theory', in which
women are able to associate themselves with new and
positive identities rather than the labels of 'offender'
or 'criminal'.

I looked at data provided for me by Working Chance.
Of the women going through their programme into
employment, 70 per cent are still in work six months
after getting a paid job, with each earning an average
of £17,425 per annum.[96] Furthermore, there is only a

3 per cent reconviction rate for people using Working Chance services, and none of those crimes took place in the workplace.[97] Although it could be argued that the people who ask to go through the charity to get jobs are a self-selecting group, committed to finding and keeping a job and therefore naturally less likely to want to reoffend, they are nevertheless disproving many of the myths about ex-offenders. It is obvious that having the right employability skills makes a big difference. Overall, the evidence suggests that in-prison education and vocational programmes bring a lifetime net saving to society of approximately £69,000 per offender (ranging somewhere between £10,500 at the low end, to a potential of £97,000 just for one person when victim's costs are included). Even if such a measure were put in place for just half the women who enter prison in a year (approximately 6,500, who we can safely say will be released again within twelve months), this would generate a lifetime saving of £448.5m.[98]

The difficulty in getting any ex-offender facing prejudice back into work is compounded by girls having lost their self-belief and many in fact end up for years in low-paid, low-quality jobs which often provide them with little training to allow them to progress. Of course I generalise and there are many exceptions and some great companies around who make it clear that people with convictions should have the same opportunities as anyone else.

What is often forgotten is that in many cases, particularly for residents in open prisons as I have already described, people work on licence often on a daily basis commuting to jobs outside the prison and when they come out on tag in many cases they are encouraged to secure jobs as soon as they can. That way they cost the economy less and the offending and reoffending rates reduce markedly. And yet the negative perception remains. It would be useful here to bring the difficulties that these girls are facing into sharper focus by looking at the overall jobs market for women. Not only has the recession affected women more than men in terms of job losses, as women are disproportionately represented in the public sector workforce, which has been most affected by the cuts, but the difficulties faced in rejoining the labour force by women who leave for a while to start a family have recently been highlighted. In general they go back, if they do at all, to jobs that are well below their skills level and earn a lot less than before because they have lost their confidence and also because things have moved on – they are older, there is a new genera-tion that makes decisions since they left and (with some small exceptions) they find it hard to get back to the senior positions they had before. Their confidence is shattered and even their language is affected – more baby talk rather than business talk. What is more, competition out there is intense. Imagine the extra difficulties when the interruption from the labour market is even longer. Advice given at a Mumsnet conference was apparently to go back to work part-time and take advantage of greater opportunities for working flexibility.

I agree with that – I had always advocated that there should be more part-time work at higher levels and more job sharing; though the public sector does offer the latter and it has been seen to work effec-tively in practice, it is still rare in businesses. The loss of women's productive capacity as they are stuck in low-skilled jobs is obvious to me. Until shortly after the coalition came to power in 2010 I was director general and chief economist at the Department for Business, Innovation and Skills (previously the DTI) and while Labour had been in power had been appointed as the unfortunate senior official responsible for attempting to convince departments across Whitehall to think in terms of what their policies would do to productivity in the UK economy before enacting them. The lost productivity of women has always been a problem as many exit the workforce or quit well-paid full-time jobs for lower-paid, generally lower-level, part-time employment when they hit what they perceive to be the 'glass ceiling' and their chances of promotion become more limited. Skills are then lost, earnings remain below what they should otherwise have been and the economy and society suffer. This will be even more pronounced if one has spent a lot of time in prison, receiving little in terms of useful education and training, losing social skills and the ability to successfully interact with others, and therefore becoming effectively unemployable or confined permanently to less rewarding and less challenging work, even for those with high skills who would otherwise have had the potential to contribute positively to society and to the upkeep of their family. Permanently earning less than one's potential means more need for public sector support and very little to show in return for a period in jail in terms of any discernible benefit to the community except of course the satisfaction of having someone punished, which is transitory and serves very little purpose, particularly when there are children involved.

The United Nations Rules for the Treatment of

Women Prisoners and Non-custodial Measures for Women Offenders (also known as the Bangkok Rules) and the Human Rights Act, which the Conservative Party have said they will abolish if they win the next election, both dictate that the courts should take dependent children into account when sentencing. The various pressure groups claim that this is rarely done and the evidence I collected while in ESP would seem to confirm that – I couldn't check up what the girls were telling me, of course, so the conclusion from my sample may not be definitive but the only case I found where this was taken into account in halving the sentence of a female prisoner was because the mother was in the process of adopting a child from an unusual background and the social services which had worked so hard to get the child adopted feared that the whole thing would fall through. Sadly for the mother, who felt strongly that she was innocent of the charge that got her into prison, the adoption process also meant that thoughts of appealing against the sentence were abandoned as that would have prolonged or even scuppered the adoption process. It could also have led to hers and her husband's first names, which was all the natural mother knew, being made public as the case re-emerged, increasing the chances of their identity being discovered and preventing the adoption from going through.

3 APRIL

A lovely Caribbean girl, Abi, asked me to help her with a question, as part of her course, on how to take account of environmental damage when conferences are organised. She wants eventually to go into event organising and this is a good way of getting there. I agreed to meet her in the morning but she didn't show up. At lunchtime, since we were both working, we agreed to reschedule for 3 p.m. When she didn't show up again I went looking for her and found her asleep in her room! We rescheduled and finally met in IT before they closed down at 8. Well, eventually she got through the course with a good mark and I hear she has been hired by some event organisers in London. Maybe if all else fails when I get out I will ask her for a job.

As it happens I spent the late afternoon with Lesley, who managed the Vision office in ESP (the link between the residents and the outside education and employment worlds), discussing employment issues and what options there were for women in general to prepare for work on the outside again. She thought that in my case and on account of my specialism there was no point in thinking of anything other than using my specialism to good effect, which was oddly reassuring in a way. We discussed teaching, too, and she gave me some brochures and further information.

4 APRIL

During supper we sat with Kirsty, a twenty-year-old newly converted Muslim and vegetarian with a heart of gold, who was in prison for the fourth time. She insisted that this time around she'd done nothing wrong except protect her sister. They had been on a night out when two Pakistani men had tried, she said, to pull her sister into a car masquerading as a taxi. Both she and her sister, who had never before been in front of the courts, were charged and convicted with grievous bodily harm and attempted robbery. Kirsty claimed that they were only trying to protect themselves but that her previous brushes with the law hadn't helped.

The good thing is that this latest episode in prison seems to have taught her that she needs to stop getting into trouble. Due to be released in a couple of weeks, she has a job lined up with a supermarket at just over minimum wage, which she intends to keep. And in the meantime, despite her streetwise behaviour, she is known as the governor's pet, who uses her openly to find out what girls think about various aspects of the prison regime – not a bad thing at all as it does her confidence a lot of good and she tells it straight. We all love her directness.

I told Kirsty and the others at the table how odd it was that a number of women I came across in Holloway and even in ESP seemed to think I was an MP before I went to prison and always ask me what it had been like. I am just an ex-MP's ex-wife! 'What's an MP?' asks Kirsty.

5 APRIL

How do you have a shower without scalding yourself? You would think the answer is simple. Make sure the tap is not too hot. Not so simple if you have no control. The shower room in East Sutton Park was a revelation. It was a big white, light room overlooking the back courtyard down the stairs past reception and near the back door, where the girls often congregated just outside to have their first cigarette of the day. It was clean and airy, with six shower cubicles on each side shielded by curtains that were changed each Sunday during those famous 2p job sessions. These apparently were put in relatively recently after

persistent complaints that there was no privacy for
the women who were obliged to expose themselves
in unprotected cubicles. And in you went, all precious
toiletries at the ready and hoping that there would be
plenty of others there running showers. This wasn't so
much for the companionship but mainly to ensure that
the temperature of the water was manageable if lots of
you were running it. The problem was that you had no
control. You pushed a button and the water came out
for about 30 seconds, coldish for the first few seconds
then piping hot if there was just you or even just a
couple of you. So a ritual had to be had. If no one else
was there, which was usual, or just a couple of you,
one had to do two things. First, turn the hot tap on full
in the one wash basin that existed so that some of the
hot water was diverted there. Then you had to use a
cubicle as close as possible to that tap so that you got
the maximum effect of the hot water diversion. Then
you went on this funny run. You had to start pushing
buttons for the water to run in one shower, run out,
then dash into the one next to it, run out again then go
into yours and enjoy a few seconds of relatively tepid
water while the other showers were on full blast. As
soon as the water in your cubicle stopped running, as
it was timed to do after a very short burst of water,
you had to repeat the process, often five times, rushing from cubicle to cubicle like a madwoman pressing
buttons if you wanted to complete the shower thor-
oughly washed but with your skin intact. Otherwise
having a shower was impossible. Baths did not
exist. One finished the washing process cleaner but
absolutely exhausted, as if one had also completed a
marathon run at the same time.

6 APRIL

I have clearly settled into my weekend routine. Am I becoming institutionalised? Tomorrow, Sunday, is visitors' day and I am expecting Sir Brian Bender, a previous permanent secretary at the Department of Business, Innovation and Skills (BIS) and my boss while I was there. Wonderfully, he's also going to bring some of my children with him.

Saturday, therefore, was relatively relaxed and I enjoyed the much-cherished long walk around the grounds. In the evening, while queuing for our 'grab bags', Liz was picked on (again) for coming down to supper with open-toed shoes and was sent back up to her room to change. Odd bureaucratic rule, I thought, why does it matter what shoes you are wearing? And what was the point of having a woman in her fifties with grown-up children, formerly in a position of power, sent up to her room for wearing the wrong shoes? I was later told that it was meant to avoid anything hot scalding your feet while you were being served dinner and then it being recorded as an injury inflicted upon you by the prison. I suspect though that the original rationale had long been forgotten and officers liked to apply rules wherever they could. Fortunately it never happened to me (I was too cold not to be wearing socks and proper shoes all the time I was in ESP).

8 APRIL

The day I had been looking forward to: ICT day. I enlisted to do Microsoft NVQ 1, also PowerPoint and Excel. The IT course went well – a week later I managed to pass my NVQ for the basic Microsoft and discovered all these things I used to ask my PA to do for me. I am determined to manage better in the future. I was really excited about learning to touch-type. Having been married to a journalist who had been taught to touch-type I had always marvelled at the ability to type almost as fast as you speak. The prison had available a program called 'Maeve's Friend' which taught you how to do it online (on the prison intranet) and once logged on allowed you to practise as much as you wanted at all times of the day and get better each time through repetition. Or so it proves with most people. I was useless at it. Every now and then the program would say: 'You are doing well. Let's repeat the exercise.' It used to bring my blood pressure up as it was clear my brain and fingers were simply not coordinating the way they should. So I conceded defeat. As I am typing this I use the same old techniques as always – bad typing and then long sessions with the spell check function.

I returned to the dorm to discover that the fourth bed in our little room, which was usually given over to just three of us because of its size, had a new person on it with bags of belongings strewn all round. Just arrived from a closed prison, Alison was in her early sixties, tall and thin and with a hairdo that reminded me a bit of Rod Stewart in terms of style, though she was much better looking. She had tight jeans, longish hair, a husky voice from smoking, and was really cool in a million ways. I had no idea what she was in for. I, having been there all of three weeks, was now an 'old hand' and started telling her about the place. I told her a bit about the IT course in ESP and how I was due to do Excel next week, which I hadn't done for decades. She paused to think for a few seconds and then said: 'Yes, Excel, good thing really, but when you are running a dope factory you try not to put things in Excel but do all the figure work in your head.' It left me speechless.

Sadly she eventually decided that our room was too claustrophobic with four of us in it and moved out some time later but her story fascinated me throughout my stay. I now look at police helicopters flying at night over the houses near Brixton in south London where I live and realise that they are not trying to track down people running away from robberies as I had always fondly thought but instead are using thermal imaging cameras to capture any glowing houses among the dark ones, which is a way of detecting those that hide cannabis factories in their lofts.

9 APRIL

And then it was family day. There had been such interest in this extra day of fun from women who had not reached their FLED yet and had to rely on their family coming to visit. There had been a rumour circulating the previous week that those going to the family day would be having it instead of a weekend visit and there were many worried faces around but the rumour proved, like many other things, to be unfounded. The girls who had been in before me talked of a brilliant Christmas family day arranged by Mrs Beck, a wonderful and very energetic senior officer who was also organising such days – in fact, because of popular demand they arranged two of them, on Monday the 8th and Tuesday the 9th. I went on day two so as not to miss the beginning of the IT course; given I only had a few weeks remaining until my HDC date I wouldn't have had time to complete the course if I started a week later.

I finished breakfast dining room duties that morning in a hurry, arranged for my fellow workers to cover for me at lunchtime and got ready for a day starting at 11.30 and finishing at 3.30 – the longest I would have been with the children and grandchildren for a while. The excitement from all sides was palpable as the cars started arriving. On those occasions family can come and spend most of the day with the residents, kids play pass the parcel, draw pictures, and visit the farm and play with the piglets and lambs, see the horses and also the gardens and the flowers that the residents were growing and selling. My grandchildren loved it. We all felt like we were not in a prison at all but were able to wander around the entire estate like a normal family. One of my roommates, who was serving two years of a four-year sentence, helped the little ones feed the horses. And we all went to the shop. My other roommate, the lifer, served us. I wasn't allowed to have any cash while in ESP but my daughter paid and took a joint of roast pork and some sausages home for me. And as it happens the pork loin and brilliant sausages that my fellow residents at ESP helped make spent a couple of months in my freezer and were eaten with my friends as celebration on the day my tag came off on 11 July. Incidentally, that was the same day that the main tag providers, Serco and G4S, were castigated in the press for over-charging the MoJ some £50m over a number of years, apparently still billing the taxpayer for tagging people who had already been released and even ex-offenders who had long since died![99] My friends admitted they had never eaten nicer pork in their entire lives and they were not exaggerating.

The family day had another perk attached to it.

It the only day that relatives could bring in a picnic for us, which was not allowed on any other normal visit. I had made my request in advance – prawns, smoked salmon, Parma ham, Gruyère cheese, all of which I ate with abandon. And then the pièce de résistance – strawberries and cream. Strawberries were not in season at the time and the imported fruit in the plastic container my children brought was a bit hard but no matter, I scoffed them down and then annoyed everyone back at ESP by frequent mentions of how delicious they were. And for me, not having tasted them for about a month, they were. The simple fact that I had had what I had wished for was enough and stopped me missing them at all for the rest of my stay. To this day I do not understand the policy that does not allow visitors to bring in treats. And I also do not understand why a commercial outfit like the farm shop does not capitalise on the influx of people coming to see their loved ones on Saturdays and Sundays by keeping the shop open. I know for a fact the residents would love to staff the shop themselves and would sell more produce this way. Oh well. At times I felt inclined to offer to write them a proper business plan but I knew my place.

10 APRIL

I received an envelope containing the menu of an event I should have been at organised by my ex-KPMG colleagues. They all used to work for me but were now dispersed in all sorts of organisations. More than a decade ago we had formed something called the Bath Club, which got its name because the first event was, for some reason we have now all forgotten, held in the city of Bath; the club has since met annually for supper at the Farmers Club in Whitehall Court, in Westminster.

The dinner was held on 13 March, just after I had entered Holloway. They all apparently drank my health and sent me the menu signed by all with individual messages, some absolutely hilarious, all very moving. If I believe the menu, which I read out loud to my roommates Sarah and Amy, they ate celeriac and tarragon soup followed by seared bass fillet with roast fennel, smoked tomato sauce and fresh seasonal vegetables and then almond and pear tart with clotted cream for pudding. The meal, accompanied by the club's own wine, was finished with coffee and chocolate mints. Honestly, what did they think they were doing sending me this? We were salivating even though I know from experience that the menus in 'gentlemen's clubs' often read better than they actually taste. My friends at KPMG determined that we would have a welcoming drink and indeed when I got out I sat with them on a hot balmy July evening on the terrace of the Farmers Club, and a lot of champagne was drunk – not by me who hates bubbles, but by my colleagues, pleased to have the group intact and together again. I will be forever grateful to them all.

CHAPTER 4

HALFWAY THERE

There is a ghost in East Sutton Park. She is called Arabella, a little girl long dead but who keeps making appearances, apparently. According to a booklet in the visitors' centre, Arabella lives – and has lived for a good few hundred years – under the stairs leading to a loft. Rumour has it that Arabella walks up and down the stairs on her way to and from the room in the loft which as far as I understand it, not being a believer in ghosts, is blocked off until the money is found to refurbish it as a room for the governor, as that side of the house has great views over the valley. But the women in ESP believe it is sealed off because no one wants to go into it, it being haunted. There are numerous tales of people having seen the little girl, dressed in white, walking up and down, and of hearing her making noises in the night but while I was there I never met anyone who had actually seen the ghost though many were prepared to swear that they knew of someone who had – but they had all left ESP already. New girls who heard about the little ghost as they arrived fully believed in its existence and it always caused a lot of hilarity for the non-believers among us. But then again, who knows?

12 APRIL

A Tannoy 'residents' announcement just before lunch warned us all that our rooms would be inspected to see if there was any food left on the windowsills, which was not allowed, and that if found it would be confiscated. Panic stations. Everyone, including me, kept fruit, butter, milk, cheese and anything perishable as near the window as possible as contrary to what the newspapers may think there were no fridges in the rooms – the one communal fridge in the Butler's Room had not worked properly for ages and was a health hazard. I was on dining room duty in and out of Butler's when the workmen came and finally took that smelly fridge away – and didn't replace it with another. As I was rushing to clear my belongings from the windowsill after the announcement I was told that in a previous inspection everything went, including the biscuits, which apparently you were not allowed to hoard. The logic of that defeated me: how was keeping biscuits for a rainy day a problem? And how could I continue swapping my custard creams for the digestives I preferred? I had stacks of them there including a few bars of chocolate which would melt if I put them anywhere else but I went to try and hide it all for a while.

Well, no one came to look at our room; it seems there was a culprit somewhere else. It turned out to be my friend Liz, whose window had no window sill on the inside, only on the outside. She, like many others with a similar window configuration, would regularly put everything outside overnight and at times not just on the sill but also in a hanging makeshift contraption they had devised. As her room was at the front of the house, the whole thing was visible to any casual observer – and to make matters worse her large carton of milk bought on canteen had been toppled over by strong winds and had just missed, on its downward journey, the head of an officer walking past. It was all a warning to her and the occupants of her room. We were much more careful from then on to ensure that our curtains, even when opened, were strategically positioned in such a way that they hid the bananas, milk and chocolates that absolutely needed to stay by the window to remain fresh and edible. It became a bit more difficult to balance it all hiding against one corner of the windowsill when I started buying bulky grapefruit and lemons from canteen but they somehow managed to survive my stay there and the regular residents of my room didn't have anything forcibly taken away.

13 APRIL

Visitors' day again – hurray! When I was arranging for this week's visit, I rang one of the friends who was coming to see me to make sure I had all the right details for him in my 'app', such as his address. I caught him just as he was in a coffee shop in Kensington High Street and as we were talking he interrupted me to say that someone I knew well had just walked in – and he passed the phone to her. It was Patricia Hewitt, who, when a Cabinet minister in the early to mid-2000s, was the reason I entered the civil service. She had wanted someone completely different to the traditional civil servant to replace her departing chief economists in what was then the Department of Trade and Industry (DTI). Although I had seen her since she left the government and since I rejoined the private sector, it was so great to reconnect, me on the prison payphone and her in a sandwich bar. How weird life is. We made arrangements to meet as soon as I got out.

My colleagues duly came to visit, two of my directors in the company I used to work for, Alison Sprague and Mark Conaty, and my ex-PA, Ava Alleyne, all of them great friends. I cannot describe how happy I felt seeing them. They were like a breath of fresh air, breezing in and bringing me their stories from the outside, their optimism about my future, and pen and paper on which we proceeded over the next couple of hours to draw up my 'recovery plan'. I don't know what I would have done without their support and guidance. And funnily, our plan has worked according to the letter ever since, even down to expecting and preparing for the occasional knocks to come (though they have come from unexpected corners) and how to survive them and bounce back. Alison sent me both at ESP and at home PowerPoint-type slides, like a strategic review one might put together for a client – we weren't management consultants for nothing. Every conversation we have had since includes a brief rundown on where exactly we are on the plan and a reminder of the next steps. There's just one thing I haven't done yet but am working on – hiring a proper PA again so that there is at least someone who can say no to the things I am asked to do.

14 APRIL

Since my visitors came unusually on Saturday this week I had the whole of Sunday to myself, which gave me plenty of time to agonise and worry about the Chelsea 4 p.m. semi-final kick-off against Man City at Wembley, which was shown on ITV. As I was watching it in the dining room, I became the target for friendly abuse mocking the image of Chelsea as the millionaire players' club. Luckily there were two staff members who were keen Chelsea supporters including Nigel, whose daughter attends games regularly. At least I had someone to commiserate with after we lost 2–1 – undeservedly in my view.

15 APRIL

We were all horrified to see on the news that a bomb had exploded during the Boston marathon, killing three people. Footage was shown again and again, and it looked horrific, the bomb exploding just in the coffee shops behind the runners and onlookers. I panicked as my niece, Melina Georgantas, lives and works in Boston and has run the marathon a number of times. It was difficult to find out whether she was hurt but frantic calls to my daughters finally elicited that she was fine. She had been sitting in a bar away from the main impact and when the incendiary devices blew up so powerful was the blast that her drink flew out of her hand and the glass was smashed. She was OK though it all left her rather shaken. I saw her later after my release and she described how she was just 100 yards from the finishing line and if the glass doors of the café had not been wide open to ensure a good view, the glass would have been blown into her face and body. She had had the presence of mind to march her fellow drinkers in the café down into the basement and through the back door to the street behind from where they quickly left for home.

16 APRIL

As we cleaned the dining room today, one female governor entered through the corridor landing and

stood at the top of the stairs leading from the dining
room to the main hallway. We have a number of
governors: a No. 1 governor, a male, who we share
with the nearby male prison Blantyre, and at least two
if not three governors who haven't tended to stay very
long but who at least are there most of the time and
know the workings of the prison well.

The governor pointed to dust on the banisters and
called upon me. It was not the bit I was responsible
for so as soon as my co-workers arrived I read them
the riot act – they had to get up earlier and really pull
their socks up. They all agreed they would. At lunch
time the governor reappeared and called us over to
her. Oh dear. I could sense an IEP coming (not that
I was sure what the Incentives and Earned Privileges
scheme really was; it is, I believe, basically points
for or against you, usually the latter, though I had
never come across them myself and doubt they ever
applied in ESP). But no, she wanted to know how
we thought we should prepare for the forthcoming
inspection and meeting which would be part of the
review of the women's estate. We all wanted ESP to
do well so we sat down with her for a good hour,
looked at the terms of reference for the review and
told her what we thought ESP's unique selling point
(USP) was. Cutting out the management consultancy
speak, we said what we thought ESP excelled in and
what it contributed that other establishments, apart
from Askham Grange, the only other women's open
prison, could not provide. It was great to spend an
hour thinking strategically, a bit like the old days at
KPMG where I used to work – though this time I was
alongside a drug importer who was serving fourteen
years for bringing cocaine into the country in food

drums in the back of her car; a girl who was a mule, bringing drugs from the Caribbean; and a young offender convicted for violent attack and robbery – all, apart from the Caribbean lady, proclaiming their innocence. And they did a great job, sensibly debating rather than arguing and clearly caring for their fellow residents but also for the survival of ESP, which they thought added a lot to rehabilitation despite some glaring faults.

17 APRIL

Today was Margaret Thatcher's funeral. When the news of her death was announced, I was on the phone to one of my children (it must be obvious by now that I ended up with a huge phone bill). Everyone started talking about it even though many of my fellow residents were hardly alive when she was Prime Minister. There was so much in the news that one couldn't avoid it. Over lunch and supper in the ensuing days there was a lot of debate about her funeral: Would it be a state funeral? What would it cost? Was it worth it? All the things that I suspect were being discussed around many tables throughout the land. The foreign girls were rather indifferent but amazingly no one thought Mrs Thatcher was a role model for women. There was no doubt that everyone liked the pomp and ceremony of such state occasions but the cynicism shone through. Of course, on the day, the funeral procession was watched by all, if not at the time it took place when many were working but during the endless repeats. But the most heated discussion in the end was on costs. Here we are, said the girls, our chances of getting legal support if we need it are under serious threat from the cuts in legal aid being introduced to save a few million pounds, in the process raising the feeling of helplessness and hurt at being singled out as non-deserving of support, and yet all this money is being spent on this funeral.

It's easy to see what such comparisons of costs say to people in prison. After I was released it was reported on 5 June that more than 600 senior judges warned that cuts to legal aid would cause rioting in prisons, as prisoners, they said, would be left with no recourse other than 'mutiny'.[100] Indeed, in 2011, in Ford open prison a riot over prisoners and officers' relations caused £5m worth of damage to buildings, in addition to staff overtime and all the follow-up costs involved. It turns out that the girls, however unsophisticated their economics, had a point. Justice Secretary Chris Grayling later stated that the changes would save just £4m a year in prisoners' legal aid costs[101] – in fact lawyers argue that this saving is likely in practice to be even less than that as cuts implemented already under the previous government had reduced the number of legal aid-supported cases for prisoners dramatically.

The Thatcher funeral was eventually estimated to have incurred direct costs of £1.2m and costs for staff who would have been used elsewhere of £2m.[102] From a purely economic point, and despite being an admirer of Thatcher, it still seemed perverse that while support for people who needed legal aid was being cut by £4m the government could find more than £3m to give a dead Prime Minister a grandiose send off.

18 APRIL

The sandwich and coffee company Pret a Manger came and spoke to residents today, arranged by the

recruitment charity Working Chance in association
with Vision at ESP, about the opportunities it had for
current and ex-offenders. Girls took a break from the
kitchen still wearing white uniforms and caps on their
hair to listen. I attended to learn what was on offer
for the residents and watched a video of the company
and its ethos and then the manager talked to a number
of girls who were looking for positions. They all got
rather excited about the opportunities on offer.

At the beginning, once the offenders are allowed
to be in paid employment, Pret pays its apprentices
a training salary and travel costs as well as a clothes
allowance. The girls also receive an additional £1
an hour as a bonus (like all the other employees) if
the shop they are working in passes a mystery shop-
per test. After the three-month training period, they
receive a rise and Pret often gives out free food and
arranges lots of events and prizes – the company
promotional film even showed the chaos of Pret's
Christmas party in a nightclub.

So the girls were very enthusiastic about it all
and there was a disorderly queue to talk to the HR
manager and put in an application form. It was clear
to me that the company would be doing well out
of people to whom it would have to pay the bare
minimum, but at least it provided opportunities and
the company seemed to be genuinely positive about
employing offenders.

I arranged an interview with the Pret representative
afterwards and asked why the company was interested
in offenders, apart, perhaps, because of the cheaper
labour. She said that they were harder-working than
the norm, punctual, and tended to stay on after their
release except when they were released to locations

where there were no Pret branches – a rare occurrence these days. As they stayed in the job longer, retention rates were improved and the costs of rehiring and retraining were reduced, making a real difference to the company. In my view, it should be widely publicised that companies such as Pret are making a real business case for hiring offenders and those who are still squeamish about employing people with convictions need not be. I am convinced that companies like Virgin, who put a policy of hiring offenders and ex-offenders in their corporate social responsibility policy documents for all to see, know what they are doing.

A lovely Indian girl of just twenty-two, who was convicted during her first job since finishing her studies for allegedly helping her boss profit from false insurance claims, has secured a position through the charity in the HR department of one such company, with help from Working Chance. At first she'll be employed on a voluntary basis but then she'll move to a paid job. To me she was the girl from the kitchens who gave me second helpings whenever she could, and I was very proud of her.

21 APRIL

Each evening while in ESP I used to don walking shoes, hat and gloves, and go for a brisk walk (I called it my power walk though it was anything but) just round the garden at the back of the building to get some fresh air, however cold, and a bit of exercise after an enormous supper. The walk always had to be completed before 8 p.m., which was when the back door to the garden was locked closed and one was no longer able to smoke out the back (I don't smoke)

but had to use the side exit into the courtyard by the
kitchen. It was usually a bit of a rush to get out before
the door shut as I used to spend the time after supper
writing letters to catch the collection time of 9 p.m.;
I'd often have to interrupt the letter writing for my
evening walk. I would occasionally walk with another
resident if *Coronation Street* did not intervene but
more often than not I ventured out on my own
just after 7.30 for half an hour. Everyone thought
I was mad going out in that weather, which indeed
was freezing for much of the time I was there. But
it did me a lot of good; walking round and round,
avoiding the out of bounds areas which were clearly
though discreetly marked, but still having enough
ground to cover and absorb the beauty of the Kent
countryside rolling out in the valleys below.

That evening I started a bit earlier but still had to
hurry as I wanted to spend some time as I always
did on a Sunday in the library returning books and
borrowing others. Even when no one is in charge,
the library opens from 8 a.m. until 8 p.m. over the
weekend, which is great, and there is a system where
one can record on a piece of paper books returned
and those taken out. You can take out a maximum
of eight books at any one time but the librarian is
very lax about this as long as we record what we've
borrowed. At times there are also 'free books' donated
by authors and a book club which meets every few
weeks to discuss a single book. The club also sets a
'six book challenge', which rewards residents who can
demonstrate they have read six books over a given
period with an award and free books for them to
take home, often donated and signed by an author. If
lucky, the library is also visited by a renowned writer,

such as Martina Cole, who came to Holloway while I was there.

The resident librarian, who had some difficulty walking, had left a big notice asking that if anyone came in could they please take the pile of the main prison newspapers, which after being delivered had remained in the library, back into the big house and into the drawing room so that everyone could read them. So I did – it took me a few goes, running against the clock, as the witching hour of 8 p.m. approached. There are two main papers: *Converse*, edited by Mark Leech, and *Inside Time*. They are very well presented with many articles, comments and letters from inmates from prisons all around the country, and provide prisoners with a lot of the information they need about legal developments that might affect them, given the lack of internet access. I noticed that the issue they were majoring on was indeed the proposed cut in legal aid for prisoners, which had already become a major discussion point at ESP. Of course the legal aid budget may indeed be too big and needs rationalising but prisoners were singled out as the group likely to lose this 'privilege' of free advice from lawyers. With no one to explain what it all meant in practice within ESP, people had started using their precious phone money to ring their lawyers and try to understand its implications. Many expressed the view that it was already very hard to get any solicitor interested in helping them with legal aid and a number who spoke to me at length were concerned about the ability to pursue their appeals against sentences or lodge complaints against the prison service. Others worried about how to defend themselves in confiscation orders and also in residency hearings by their ex-partners, who they held responsible for being there in prison in the first place, and others.

Becky, a forty-year-old with a beautiful family that always came to visit, panicked about the implications of the cut in legal aid for her as she was instigating divorce proceedings against her husband. She blamed him for her being sent to prison in the first place and feared that with no proper representation she would lose her house, which was so important if she needed to find a job and look properly after her son, who was having serious difficulties coping with her being away and was being looked after by her father, who himself wasn't well. She had not been allowed to visit her son as she wasn't on her Facility Licence Eligibility Date yet for Release on Temporary Licence to kick in and couldn't get a Childcare Resettlement Licence as her son was seventeen – just above the cut-off age of sixteen. So she tried and tried to get some leave to visit him; the boy was in a bad way and the school was writing to her to encourage her to visit. She was constantly refused leave by the governor and didn't know who to turn to. The anxiety and concern caused was immense. I hadn't seen her smile in ages and yet she had often in the past been the soul of the party. We had long discussions about what could be done and her misery was increasing with every rejection she received to make the visit. I wondered whether perhaps she just wasn't expressing herself properly when making her case. And then I saw her chatting in the drawing room with a lady from the Independent Monitoring Board who then took up her case. Three weeks before I left, Becky was finally able to visit her son and she returned much happier. The visit had been so important for him. He then came to see his mother a week later on visitors' day with some other members of the family – something he had refused to do before – and we all commented on how handsome and how well he looked, smiling and confident. It was extraordinary to see how important keeping the connection with the family was for all concerned and it confirmed all that the literature says about the therapeutic effect that keeping families in contact as much as possible has.

Once Becky got over that problem the worries about being able to prevent her husband from walking off with her assets continued as she was not at all clear whether she was allowed any legal aid. I couldn't help her but the confusion and heartache it has created for people who feel that they have once again been singled out as villains who don't deserve legal representation is incalculable. Since my release this portrayal of prisoners as undeserving of any representation has been reinforced by the fuss over the legal costs associated with the failed attempt of Ian Brady to be moved from a mental hospital to a normal prison. In a written parliamentary question the Ministry of Justice gave the figure of 43,780 inmates who used legal aid to the tune of £23m in 2011/12 to complain about sentences, disciplinary matters, their treatment and issues to do with the parole board.[103] The tabloids used this as background to the Brady story and majored on the £250,000 cost to the taxpayer of his case being brought to court. Interestingly the Ian Brady costs are not part of what the government intends to cut as his legal aid was, as I understand it, part of anyone's entitlement under the Mental Health Act, which allows a periodic review, paid for centrally, of whether people need to remain in mental institutions.

There have been comments from lawyers that in no other area are the basic human rights that allow people to complain about the way they are being treated taken away so easily without an outcry. For women, in particular, these types of complaints may result in better treatment, parole and early release or better access to their children, and can only help them to reintegrate with the community and their families. Without them, these women lose all self-confidence and the ability to have some control over their life because they cannot afford to hire someone to advise them. To me, this is a dangerous move. Mark Leech, ex-offender and now editor of *Converse*, one of the main prison newspapers, has been reported as saying that the government should stop focusing on vulnerable prisoners, who are a soft political target, and warned that if 'you remove a prisoner's right to challenge their treatment legitimately ... you'll have them parading complaints on prison roofs'.[104] Lord Ramsbotham says that although men do protest and occasionally get results in this way if all else fails, women just get depressed. And one ex-prison governor said: 'When did you ever hear or see pictures of women throwing tiles from prison rooftops? Never – they just internalise it and self-harm.'

In the media frenzy that accompanied the Ian Brady judgement, Chris Grayling said: 'It's unacceptable for taxpayers to fork out millions for prisoners to bring legal cases that just shouldn't be going to court.'[105] It is easy to attack a part of society that cannot easily defend itself. Robert Brown of solicitors Corker Binning says that most costs in cases like this are incurred when they do go to court as the solicitor advising a prisoner on legal aid will not want to spend a lot of time and effort on a worthless case. And he argues that there shouldn't be a presumption by the CPS, which makes the ultimate decision, that those cases shouldn't go to court even before the decision is made. The cost to the taxpayer of just giving advice on complaints is in fact very small, as Chris Grayling has himself acknowledged. Interestingly, *The Observer* on 28 July 2013 pointed out that some '1,210 crown court trials collapsed because of problems with court administration' and that in 2012, 'the CPS was forced to pay compensation for costs in nearly 400 criminal trials'. Whatever the rights or wrongs and the reasons for it, which *The Observer* attributed to the 27 per cent cuts in the CPS budget, the sad fact remains that the costs of wasted cases are substantial and the prisoners' figure pales into insignificance by comparison. Providing yet another comparison, the same article, quoting figures provided from Freedom of Information requests carried out by the Bureau of Investigative Journalism for *The Observer*, suggested that between 2011 and 2013 the ministry spent some £230m on making people redundant.[106]

22 APRIL

Today was Liz's birthday. We made her birthday cards and her sister-in-law sent her some jewellery, which Liz managed to get through reception without a problem, and her husband bought her a nice shirt and a suit for the jobs fair that was due to be held shortly. She also managed to get through security some high heels and a box of perfume from her sister. I gave her two Kit Kats from the canteen, her favourites. She worked all day in the farm shop and when we met for a celebratory tea in the drawing room after roll call, most of the girls sat in their pyjamas and bathrobes. I hadn't thought to bring my own bathrobe and had been given a spare one from the laundry room, but it wasn't one to parade around in and I resolutely stuck to my trousers and tops.

Liz was on good form. She recounted how since we got to ESP we were constantly confused for each other. We are both tall with short brownish hair and both of us wear black-rimmed glasses. Apparently the last time she was in the farm shop a woman had come in, smiled at Liz and said: 'Did you make these sausages yourself, Mrs Huhne?' Liz, quick as a flash, answered: 'First of all it is Mrs Pryce, not Mrs Huhne. And second, I am neither of those women.'

It did happen to us a lot. Just two evenings before I was due to leave ESP a relatively new male officer sidled up to Liz and told her that as he would be on night duty for the next two weeks he might not see her before she went, so he just wanted to wish her all the best, adding, 'Do be kind to us in your book!' Liz was too shocked to correct him before he shook her hand and left the room.

23 APRIL

I had a big task to do today. A friend had recorded a reading for a 'story book' for her daughter with the aid of the library; you read a story aloud into a tape and then a service adds the noise of the forest, birds, cars or whatever works for what you have decided to read. It is then assembled and sent off as a CD to your child at the address you give them. And you could read more than one book if you asked nicely. I saw it as a wonderful way of encouraging the links between children and their mothers, and was so impressed that the facility was available.

Soon I was told that I too could make a recording for my grandchildren. I had to wait a few weeks as the post of librarian changed hands and then for the new librarian to practise the recording process. I must admit I hadn't thought very hard about it but knew that tastes had changed since my children were small. My two-year-old grandson seemed to be rather keen on *The Gruffalo*; my eldest daughter had recently sent me a picture of him in a gruffalo suit and I had seen him watching the television films of the books. I still wasn't sure what a gruffalo was but I thought maybe choosing *The Gruffalo's Child* to read was the way to find out. And I was hooked.

I dedicated it to my grandson and read as well as I could; I was really chuffed that I had been able to do it. I even stayed behind to read the first book to understand its origins. I gave the librarian the address to send the CD and was told it would take a couple of weeks. It really filled me with great pleasure doing it. I had visions of little Alfred listening to the CD and marvelling about his *Yaya*, as grandmothers are called in Greece, reading the *Gruffalo* story to him.

Alas, two months later and at home, now rather keen on gruffalos, nothing had arrived. Then the day before my tag was removed, a packet was delivered accompanied by a letter from the librarian saying that due to an administrative error, for which she apologised profusely, the company had sent four copies rather than one but that she hoped the grandchildren would like them. I wrote back thanking her and said that I hoped these types of administrative errors are not corrected. I was a very happy grandmother.

24 APRIL

Aanjay and others are determined to pluck my eyebrows, paint my nails and dye my hair pink. I keep refusing but with everyone else agreeing to makeovers, I'm running out of excuses. I almost had nightmares of being forcibly picked up by Antoinette, gagged and manacled to a chair in the Butler's Room, and Aanjay being let loose to turn me into her ideal woman. I have had to tell everyone I intend to effect a complete transformation just before I am released – red hair, red fingernails, and I'll take up smoking with a long holder so when I come out to face the throng of the waiting photographers I can pass them incognito. It caught on – they all fantasised about how I might look and as it isn't meant to happen until the very end of my stay in ESP they have left me well alone.

25 APRIL

Finally came the day of resident Meera's release. She was a smiley lady in her late forties, still quietly pretty and very quiet. She and I had chatted when we found ourselves outside, her for a smoke and me for my usual attempt at 'power walking' to keep down the impact of too much custard. Half Pakistani and half English of origin, with a grown-up daughter, she volunteered during the day at a coffee shop run by a charity and was out of the prison a lot of the time. Meera didn't associate with many people but she was always smiling.

It was difficult to make sense of her situation though and she didn't seem to be sure why she was in prison. After some time she told me how she had met another Pakistani in the park. They started going out together but he soon wanted to introduce her to some others for sex. She had said no. There was then apparently a burglary in his house and he accused her of letting burglars in and stealing his TV and other possessions. What other things, I don't know. What happened to him? Nothing. Did you take his TV? No, she said, she only went to his house twice. Of course I had no way of knowing whether her story was true but her lack of self-esteem and confidence were very evident. She was also having a bit of a hard time. Her HDC date had passed but she was homeless and had nowhere to go. Finally a hostel place was found in Milton Keynes where she would have to stay for a while but that was miles away from her daughter and also from her work. How will you cope, Meera? 'I don't know' was the by now usual answer.

Soon to great excitement a date was set for her release at the early part of the week. She wanted some time off work for the last few days to get her clothes and possessions together and prepare for her release but the prison insisted she should work at the charity shop practically until the last minute. She was too weak to resist and although she told a few of us of her frustration she duly went, smiling a little submissive smile. Her release day came round and it transpired that another new boyfriend, who she had met on one of her days off and who used to pick her up on her day visits in a car, drive her around and bring her back, would be picking her up again. Alarm bells went off in my head; would she fall foul to the same problems as before?

As I was completing my tray-disinfecting duties and placing them neatly on the windowsill in the narrow corridor opposite the hatch for kitchen service, there was Meera, looking really smart, running past me to reception to have her possessions checked and crossed off. But then disaster! She couldn't find her laundry bag to return it to the central office. Then worse luck. Her laundry number, by which the girls in the laundry knew whose clothes they were washing and what day they had been handed in, was missing. By that time poor Meera was crying. The senior officer on duty was not letting her leave until the laminated card with her laundry number on it was found. An hour later, with it not found but with one brave resident complaining to someone else about the harsh treatment of this girl who had already waited so long to be allowed to leave, Meera was finally released. I'm not sure to this day whether that little card, so easy to replace, was ever found. I made sure from then on that I didn't mislay the one I was given but when I left no one checked whether I still had it.

When I was in ESP, I marvelled at the fact that rather than absconding the women all came back every day from their work outside where there was no supervision of what they were doing except by their employer. If they were so reliable and only came back to ESP mainly to eat and sleep, what was the point of them being there rather than closer to their families? The girls all made it clear that they wanted to be as clean and as blameless as possible so they would pass probation and their eventual HDC or release board. But apparently while all goes well for a long time, the riskiest period for absconding was the one nearest to release, which is perverse. This just demonstrates the tension that develops. Women seemed to be able to spend years in prisons, sometimes over a decade behind bars for a life sentence or an IPPS (serving an indeterminate public protection sentence, which, following a European Court of Justice ruling, will be illegal in future). When they finally pass the parole board and are sent to open prison with a real date of release looming, they apparently become increasingly tense and emotional. And then if something goes slightly wrong they flip and can take it no longer. To any logical person this might seem madness but it's really not surprising seeing how long they have spent in prison and how much they must yearn for a return to normality.

A lifer who had already spent twenty-one years in prison for the murder of a lady she had been carer of – something she apparently denied at her trial and during her whole period in prison – absconded on the day I got to ESP, according to fellow residents, because something went wrong with her parole and she was not going to get an answer for a few more months. She was found a few days later trying to board a plane and was sent back to a closed prison with more time added to her sentence. After I got out I heard that the very same thing happened to another lifer I had been with in ESP, who absconded in June with just seven months to parole. Maybe it also happens to men but women are particularly sensitive and emotional and I can't fail to think that surely what they need is extra attention during those very tricky periods when the light at the end of the tunnel seems so near and yet so far.

It makes me think of a short story by Kafka, who wrote vividly about trials and prisons, called *The Tunnel*. In it a group of people board a train to go from A to B and at some stage during their journey they enter a tunnel. They carry on doing what one normally does, discussing this and that, drinking, talking, reading, thinking and waiting, in full anticipation, to exit the tunnel at some stage. But it remains dark outside and as they are getting deeper and deeper into it they eventually realise that they are never going to get out of it. This is the stuff that nightmares are made of.

26 APRIL

Many of us attended a jobs fair today, organised by Vision. We met at 10.15 inside the front gate and then all walked together to the visitors' room at the end of the garden. Everyone looked very smart. Liz wore her new suit and blouse, and looked very professional. The organisations that came were pretty widespread. Some were public sector – notably Kent County Council – and some were private – such as Timpson, which employs a large number of current and ex-offenders; in fact, the proportion is near 10 per cent if you include its training academies inside or attached to various prisons. Timpson doesn't really advertise its work with the prisons and I have since been telling my friends that the next time they have their shoes fixed or keys cut or dry cleaning done, it could well be that the manager or the person that serves them is a current or ex-offender – or, in the parlance of the tabloid press, a criminal.

After my interview with Pret a Manger the previous week, I found that the other companies and organisations represented at the fair that day had only positive things to say about employing offenders. In fact the Unlock representative, the Clean Break representative and one of the three representing Timpson were ex-offenders currently working for those groups and now in senior positions. Clean Break is a very interesting charity that puts on theatrical productions in prisons using a mix of trained offenders and external

actors. Clean Break strongly advocates the benefits
of this type of activity for prisoners as they improved
their self-worth, became proud of their achievements
and learned to work in teams. Some had become
actors once on the outside. There is a lot of evidence
of the therapeutic but also professional development
benefits of acting and other artistic endeavours for
prisoners and such things can transform their lives.
Sadly these types of activities are just the ones that
seem to always be in danger of being cut to satisfy
occasional conservative-with-a-small-c indignation if
the prisoners are seen to be having fun – and in the
process ignoring the benefits to the community as a
whole in both the short and the long term.

Timpson was well represented though it was
already well known in the prison with a number of
girls working at the academy Timpson had set up
at the nearby Blantyre prison. James Timpson, with
whom I met after my release, explained that having
had many foster brothers and sisters who his parents
took care of as he was growing up he had found
himself at times helping some of them with scrapes
with the law and even visiting some of them in prison
if they got into trouble. He quoted statistics that show
that among offenders some 31 per cent of women
and 24 per cent of men had been taken into care as
a child, a huge percentage when compared with just
2 per cent for the general population.[107] He recounted
how on one visit to one of his foster siblings, who
had received a custodial sentence, he had met an
offender whose personality he liked and he hired him
on the quiet after his release. He went on to employ
more ex-offenders without telling his colleagues. He
eventually owned up and found to his astonishment

that a number of his colleagues confessed to being 'offenders' themselves – not just guilty of motoring offences but things they had done when young that may have resulted, and in a number of cases had resulted, in a suspended sentence, community service or a caution or fine. And that is a point he now reiterates: many of the people who serve us in a number of well-known establishments are in fact offenders. Most supermarket chains are probably, in his view, the largest employers of ex-offenders than any other organisation but don't know it because they don't ask that question on recruitment – and offenders do not have to volunteer it unless it is specified in the company recruitment policy. Even if it is specified, companies don't necessarily check up on it or let it affect the recruitment process. And what is more people do come out of jail and need employment; if they don't achieve it they become a burden on the economy and often reoffend so employment is a main contributor to low offending and reoffending rates.

James chairs the Employers' Forum for Reducing Reoffending, which shows how significant it is for companies to employ offenders as the cost of reoffending to society is somewhere between £9.5bn and £11bn a year.[108] For James, it makes sense to recruit offenders and train them. It is true that during the early training stages in the academies and in some of the so-called 'prison industries' run by One3one Solutions on behalf of the government, such as the Timpson shoe repair factory in Forest Bank prison in Salford, the company only pays the prisoners enhanced wages of just £20–£30 a week, but it offers opportunities for a trial in one of its shops on release. Timpson points out that it makes a big investment in providing the equipment, supervision and training, and that the prisoners end up with a skill they can use on the outside. I would guess that with the increase in unpaid internships at present, where thousands of well-qualified graduates work in companies for nothing, often for long periods of time as they move from one unpaid internship to another, the Timpson approach may in fact be paradoxically preferable and more equitable.

Timpson's figures backed up what other companies had told me about why it made business sense to hire offenders and ex-offenders: James Timpson told me that in his company's case some 80 per cent of ex-offenders employed lasted for more than twelve months, which is very good going. Apparently, many of the ex-offenders were also better at their work than the ones they recruited from the outside, though stories were recalled of ex-offenders flipping out in spectacular fashion, being aggressive and causing damage to property. But James insists that on the whole they are great to have on board and if you pick a good one he or she tends to be way above the average; indeed, some have become managers. Timpson's recent acquisition of the photo chain Snappy Snaps may well result in more opportunities for offenders. And indeed one of the girls in ESP with senior executive experience has just been recruited by James to assist, as I understand it, with this acquisition.

The most important characteristic looked for by the employers I talked to at the jobs fair was an engaging personality, as the jobs on offer often include a lot of customer interaction. But Timpson's recruitment is selective as the company deliberately excludes sex offenders and prisoners with health problems as they are too difficult to handle. Timpson does fire those that don't fit or cause trouble or disrupt the normal flow of business; one of the ESP girls had lost her job and when I enquired what had happened I discovered that current offenders working either as volunteers while training or as paid employees have no employment rights. This does cause distress to the employee, who often does not receive a full explanation for why they are no longer employed, but for the employer the ability to cut their losses without threat of retribution or tribunals reduces the risk of employing people who may not adapt well to the working environment.

Timpson is not the only company to link academies to prisons. Another example is the Clink charity. Founded in 2009, the Clink is sponsored by a group of philanthropists, including Edwina Grosvenor, and a number of trusts and foundations. Edwina volunteered in prisons abroad when still a teenager and her interest in these issues was enhanced by her degree in criminology and sociology, which led to a spell working in Styal, a women's prison in Cheshire. The main aim of the charity is to achieve a permanent reduction in reoffending by training serving prisoners in catering skills, helping them to find work in the catering industry and then providing support for ex-offenders for six months upon their release. The Clink manages training restaurants open to members of the public, who can enjoy meals cooked and served by prison inmates. For the moment there are just two restaurants, one just outside High Down prison and one inside Cardiff prison. Wherever possible, they use high-quality food and local produce.

Edwina has seen during the eight-month training process how employees have grown in confidence and alertness, are able to interact with the customers and work as a team. She also mentioned to me that in her view there are also a number of unintended beneficial consequences; interaction between the offenders and the community helps to avoid future reoffending. And she believes that it also leads to a culture change among the prison officers; at first hostile, they come to see the benefits of the business when reflected in the better behaviour of inmates. The Clink's review of its activities shows that among its graduates there is a recidivism rate of just 12.4 per cent as against the average 47 per cent for all offenders,[109] and the charity is planning more restaurants, the next one hopefully in Brixton. I will have to go and try it for myself when it finally opens.

CHAPTER 5

PREPARING FOR THE EXIT

27 APRIL

I am clearly losing it. It must be because the day of my release on Home Detention Curfew (HDC) is approaching.

After returning from my shower to an empty dorm I realised to my horror I couldn't find my glasses anywhere. Not being able to see much, I frantically fumbled around with my hands but found nothing. Fortunately Sarah came back from her morning cigarette and instantly took pity on me, and we spent the next half an hour looking desperately under the bed and all around it for my lost glasses. Quite frankly, under my bed is rather a mess and Sarah told me off for having too much down there. It's true: I have been using the area underneath my bed as a makeshift filing cabinet, using plastic baskets – two big ones, one small one. There were often periodic searches by the staff to ensure no one had pinched anyone else's basket or taken any of the spare ones. Mine were not used for clothes but for my papers, notebooks, diaries and letters. One big basket held letters I hadn't answered and the smaller one, to my shame, contained those I had answered (I must do better). The other big basket held magazines and newspaper cuttings, and any other material I was beginning to hoard: notices from the officers, general applications (the famous 'apps'), approval notices for past and forthcoming visits, pens, post-its, pins and paperclips, as well as the various magazines and books I was trying to read all at the same time.

Defeated, Sarah insisted I had to have a clear out. Breakfast was nearing and I was soon to miss my morning orange juice if I didn't find my glasses. Entering the dorm with disbelief at the sight of Sarah and me on our knees, having taken all of the contents of my 'office' out from under the bed and scattered them across the room, Amy asked us if we'd tried moving the bed. We hadn't... As soon as we did, we heard the glasses clatter to the floor; they had been entangled in my bedding the whole time.

28 APRIL

My great friend George Houpis came to visit today and brought my daughter with him, who wasn't able to come the following weekend, her birthday, because she was due to be rehearsing for a play on that day. We were lucky to have such brilliant weather as it had rained much of the weekend. My daughter looked gorgeous. It was so nice to sit outside in the glorious weather and have a long chat about everything. Aanjay, who tried to work continuously, had volunteered for visitors' duty again and was moving around serving and collecting cups and I introduced her to my little group. The time was nearing for me to return home and they were all looking forward to having me back, so the usual post-visit separation was much more bearable than usual.

29 APRIL

We said goodbye to Anya today and her two sisters came to collect her. Having stopped wearing her hijab in prison to avoid being singled out, she was back wearing it again, though we saw her sisters didn't.

Anya had spent one night in the room I shared with Amy and Sarah. She had arrived looking quite disoriented and missing the closed prison, where she had been on a short sentence like me. She was serving two months of an eight-month sentence (assuming HDC came through) for benefit fraud but did not like sharing or being out of a closed environment. She also told us she had heard that Indian and Pakistani women in ESP were picked upon by the guards. She was scared and had no idea what to expect.

We tried to reassure her and told her not to listen to rumour or gossip and she calmed down a bit. She then announced that she had to get up at sunrise to pray – the multi-faith room was next door to us but Amy, Sarah and I had difficulty adjusting to the idea that we would be woken up at 4.30 from then on. Fortunately, for us, she forgot to set her alarm the next morning – hurray! As we wondered how we were going to cope with the early mornings if her alarm worked from then on, she decided to ask to move with some other girls she knew from before. 'We will miss you,' we said, and we would; she had already become a good friend. But the idea of an extra uninterrupted hour in the morning was too good to miss. We eagerly helped her carry her stuff over to her new room.

30 APRIL

Jacquie, who was finishing a sentence for dangerous

driving, having caused the deaths of two people, sought me out as I was queuing for roll call this evening, to ask my advice on a personal matter. Her boyfriend was also in prison and his previous partner would not bring his son to see him, even though he was convinced that the boy missed him terribly. He would ring the boy's mother, who he believed was on drugs, and could hear his son begging to be allowed to talk to him but she wouldn't put him through. He was getting desperate.

It is clear that a large percentage of men also want to ensure they keep in touch with their kids and I wondered how it was that he was not getting the right advice from the prison service. All I could suggest was for Jacquie to somehow contact an organisation that helped to try and keep families connected, particularly fathers. There was genuine concern in Jacquie's voice which conveyed well the helplessness her male friend obviously felt stuck inside and unable to control events or prevent the probability, if the stats are to be believed, that his son would end up a troubled young man himself because of this separation.

1 MAY

In a meeting with Dee, my probation officer, she told me that the checks to my house have been completed and my daughter has said that she is happy to have me back. Do I ring and thank her for her kindness? The only other thing remaining is for the social services in Lambeth to find out whether the house address is known for any disturbance or child protection issues. I was fairly sure there was nothing of the sort but who knows what may have occurred before I moved there? Though I knew my worries were unfounded, I

couldn't help but feel a little anxious. I could understand even better now the concerns of many of my
fellow residents whose living arrangements were
not as straightforward as mine and whose planned
departure was often fraught with uncertainty as they
often had to move to a different house than the one
they had left.

I had seen girls so worried about whether tag day
would be met, concerns from probation about the
address they were going to if there had been an incidence of violence – and this was frequently the case as
it was common for the girls to have been in an abusive
relationship. It was also a problem if the address had
been known to the police because of crime committed
on the premises – and of course that was also often
the case. One girl told me how her brother had hidden
a gun in her house unbeknown to her and the police
that night raided all the possible addresses where
her brother might have been and found the gun. She
was sentenced as an accomplice despite the fact she
had nothing to do with it. She intended to 'get him'
when she got out – I hope for her sake she doesn't
but somehow manages to get justice properly after all
this time. But all these things cut the chances of being
able to return home, assuming you still had one after
your conviction.

In many instances, the girls had been renting their
homes and had lost them while in prison; others
were struck off the council house lists – in some cases
because they were deemed to have made themselves
'intentionally' homeless. Painful divorces finalised
during prison sentences meant some marital homes
were lost during the separation of assets. And in some
cases, particularly when the girls were convicted of

fraud, court orders meant houses were confiscated to cover the repayments of proceeds gained by the crime committed.

Many girls, therefore, had nowhere to go. So, there was terrible depression and agony in the weeks just before HDC and in some instances long negotiations with external probation so the girls could clear their return address – often staying with parents or daughters (where were the sons?) or in a hostel, depending on availability, which was the next best thing. It was not surprising, therefore, that in a number of cases the HDC date wasn't kept.

Eventually the girls would leave and often practically penniless, despite the £46 allocated to each offender on their release and, depending on circumstances, a small travel and clothing allowance. It is not surprising that according to probation officers some women didn't want to leave the prison because it was the only time someone took care of them.

A good case in point is Sharon, who I met in ESP, convicted for fraud, and who came out on HDC about a month before me. She was a jolly girl, very helpful, someone who often performed extra tea and coffee duty during family visits at the weekends. She was clearly well educated. We were all involved in lots of discussions in the drawing room about the problems she was having with an address to go to as probation were not allowing her to go home as there had been one incident reporting domestic violence at her house some fifteen years ago, since when there had not been an incident at all. She seemed to be very fond of her husband but it was finally agreed that, as a condition for her HDC, she would live at her sister's house, situated quite close to her family home. I remember waving her goodbye and we all missed her and her laughter which was frequent and infectious. We then heard that she had managed to get a job but either probation or the governors had not allowed her to take it because it involved dealing with accounts, which was what her conviction had been related to. That was sad in itself as it makes little sense to prevent someone from doing a job in case they reoffend if someone is prepared to take them on being fully aware of the offence they had committed. But I presume there may have been a reputational issue for ESP if she had committed an offence while still serving her sentence.

When I enquired after Sharon a couple of weeks after she left ESP, I was shocked to hear that she had been forced to go to a women's refuge in Southampton. Because she had left her designated address and had no other safe place to replace it and serve her probation period, she was recalled to finish the rest of her sentence in custody and was sent back to a closed prison for eight weeks. It makes no sense. And just goes to show how important housing is for women on their release. The question for Sharon will be what permanent solution can be found given so many housing options are unavailable to her.

Indeed, work by Nicola Padfield on recalled prisoners based on a survey she conducted in 2011 argued that recall is a costly process to offenders, to their families and to the taxpaying public and there was indeed a belief among the prisoners she interviewed that the certain licence conditions in fact increased the risk of reoffending rather than reducing it. Being recalled and spending more time in prison actually increased the risks of reoffending in the future due to the impact on them and their families.

2 MAY

It is getting warmer. I had been wandering around the entire period since I got to East Sutton Park in a 'uniform' of T-shirt, polo-neck, another V-neck jumper on top and a blazer on top of that – that is how cold it felt inside the house. For going outside, even for the short distances between buildings, I would often wear a coat, hat and gloves. For me there was no other way with the cold winds hitting the old house and its grounds, standing as they do at the top of a hill with nothing but open space around them. When the sun finally appeared I ditched the coat during the day (but not in the evenings). Multiple jumpers remained. I am, after all, a Mediterranean and feel the cold. When the English see the sun after such a ridiculously cold winter, however, they are straight out in their sleeveless tops lying in the sunshine at the first opportunity. Well, it was no different at East Sutton Park. And I soon discovered that I must be the only resident in East Sutton Park without a tattoo. As the layers came off they were all proudly displaying some wonderful, often wild, often beautifully crafted images and words, and began recommending to me the places where I could go and have one done when I got out – clearly they all thought I was missing out on something. Even my more buttoned-up friends had one, even if it was just their husband's or boyfriend's name. When I enquired whether these things come off at some point they all assured me with pride that they were permanent. Where have I lived all this time?

I remained resolutely tattoo free but also pale faced and shivering. My fellow residents on the other hand started to go pink and some even burned. And then panic ensued; letting yourself burn is apparently tantamount to self-harm and that means you could in theory get penalty points under the IEPS (Incentives and Earned Privileges Scheme) and may be grounded. Everyone tried to cover themselves up in the house so the extent of their burns could not be seen by the officers but their red faces gave them away. The women working on the farm and in the gardens were particularly annoyed as they claimed they had no choice but to wear the vests given as standard uniform for working when it is hot. Fortunately it was a false rumour – no one was given an IEP for having sunburn, at least not to my knowledge. Nevertheless sun cream was miraculously found and the women started being a bit more careful. Since my release, the weather has been so hot this summer that I have been trying to visualise how red my fellow residents must now be. I hope they are covering up but somehow doubt it. They are nothing if not risk takers...

There is, though, a serious side to this. Women are seen as an easy target for disciplinary procedures. A recently retired senior probation officer told me how she was amazed at the waste of money involved in disciplinary procedures when it was common to see women being put 'on report' for things like 'talking in church'. In her view that would never happen in a male prison, where attempts to do so would probably result in a revolt. Women just accept it and become (even more) depressed and maybe then self-harm. The same former probation officer was sad to see that some of her experiences from back in the 1990s still had resonance with my recent experience. It was yet another example of how slowly institutions change.

3 MAY

Last night everyone watched the results of the elections for the twenty-seven English county councils and seven unitary authorities, as well as those in Anglesey. In all, about 2,300 seats were being fought and there was a lot of discussion in our room about the fact that UKIP won over 140 of the seats, averaging some 25 per cent of the vote in the wards where it was standing. The issue for most of the women there was not the attitude towards Europe but whether this would force a toughening up of immigration rules – there were foreign girls in ESP who had served a long time, were just about to start rehabilitating themselves and getting jobs on the outside but their main fear was that they might just get shipped back to their home country on release, which they didn't want. It didn't look like anyone was giving them the type of information and support that would help them plan ahead and ease these concerns.

There was much less discussion and concern about voting rights for prisoners, which surprised me as there had been quite a lot of publicity about these issues. The law in the UK at the moment says that only prisoners on remand are entitled to vote, although the European Court of Human Rights ruled in 2005 that a blanket ban for convicted prisoners was unlawful. Since then, whether or not the UK should ignore the court's ruling has been the subject of much heated debate in Parliament. The delay attracted criticism from the Council of Europe in December 2012, who formally reminded the UK government of its obligation to implement the court's decisions and asked the UK to continue its role as a leader in protecting human rights. Frankly a lot of that debate had passed most of the women by. But it remained a live issue throughout my time in ESP and following release. Indeed six weeks later, when I was released on a tag and at home watching TV, it was reported that Nick Gibb, the Conservative chair of the Draft Voting Eligibility (Prisoners) Bill, had said that Parliament will never back votes for all prisoners, despite the court's ruling.

There are three options for Parliament to consider: allowing convicted prisoners serving up to six months to vote, extending it to all serving up to four years, or keeping the blanket ban as is. Juliet Lyon, director of the Prison Reform Trust, has been quoted as saying that the only prisoners who shouldn't be allowed to vote are those who have been convicted for electoral fraud but also said that in reality there wasn't very much evidence of prisoners really wanting to vote. That very much agreed with my own observation but I fear this was more that they felt removed from society and that they didn't really belong. I agree with Juliet Lyon's other comment that in fact just taking that right away further separated the prisoners from society and made reintegration more difficult.[110] Indeed, there seems to be wider acceptance of this point and during the debates on the issue the Lib Dem MP Lorely Burt, a former prison governor herself, said that the right to vote ought to be linked to rehabilitation.[111] Interestingly Dr Peter Selby, former Bishop to HM Prisons and now president of the National Council for Independent Monitoring Boards for Prisons, said in written evidence submitted to the political and constitutional reform committee that 'denying convicted prisoners the right to vote serves no purpose of deterrence or reform. What it does is to state in the clearest terms society's belief that once convicted you are a non-person, one who should have no say in how our society is to develop, whose opinion is to count for nothing. It is making someone an "outlaw", and as such has no place in expressing a civilised attitude towards those in prison.'[112]

For what it's worth, in France judges can add a penalty of suspension of civic rights to a prison sentence, which seems to keep the ECHR happy. As the debate heats up over a possible Brexit (Britain leaving the EU), it is interesting that Switzerland has given voting rights to prisoners for decades without any outcry from the public.

4 MAY

It is my daughter's birthday today. When I rang her she confirmed that she had received the two cards I sent – one made by me using cut-outs from discarded cards and stickers provided by the wonderful officer Mrs Beck. The card caused a lot of amusement as I am not at all artistic and the card turned out looking pretty weird, but she loved it, or so she said. Maybe it is true what they say, that it is the thought that counts, but I had been really pleased with myself. The other was a very nice, more conventional birthday card very sweetly brought back from the outside for me by one of my fellow residents during her day out. Anyone who has not been to prison can simply not imagine how important these types of communication were for us. We absolutely depended on letters getting there on time and birthdays are so important, we had to get it right. Using two stamps to send two cards as insurance, hoping that at least one would get there was, we all felt, worth it. They both in the event made it. Happy mummy, happy daughter, thank you Post Office.

Tricia, who also works for Working Chance during the week, asked me to endorse a proposal she was putting together to raise some £25,000 to fund a project for going into Holloway and teaching young offenders employability skills. I spent the weekend reading the terms of reference, loved it and wrote a note of support. I typed it in the IT room and printed it twice, and Tricia took it with her the following day. She had already made it to a shortlist of three after presenting to a group of possible investors who are part of what is known as the 'Funding Network'. They had to then put a few more things together and go and present again to see if they would get the final funding. After my release I found out from Jocelyn Hillman, the head of Working Chance, that they did. Jocelyn had taken two of ESP's young residents, May and Sam, to the final presentation. Both of them had received an indeterminate public protection sentence when they were just sixteen and they did a splendid job presenting the case. Real heroes. I hope they do well now that they have been released. When I had left, Sam was finishing an Access course for which she was getting external study leave, and was trying to decide where she should do her degree in psychology; like any other sixth-former she was finishing her exams and waiting anxiously for her results and final confirmation of offers.

5 MAY

In the afternoon I was visited by my great friends Philip and Stephanie Maltman, and my daughter and grandson. Philip, a painter, has been painting me a new card every week and I now have a marvellous collection which I intend to frame in a big tableau, naming it 'The Prison Cards'. I noticed that his colours were becoming richer and more rousing as the date of my release neared – although I may have just imagined it. Philip also manages the Dulwich independent bookshop, which seems to be getting all sorts of prizes, and I have benefited greatly from his choice of books, which have been coming to ESP on a very regular basis. Today, however, it's my turn to give him books: I have packed most of my papers and books to send home early and ease the pressure on my last day. The officers who look after the visitors helped me pack them and have them neatly labelled and put aside for my friends to collect at the end of the visit. It looked really funny seeing them cart five black prison rubbish bags through the visitors' car park home with them. (These bags still surround me in my study, mostly unopened. They have acquired sentimental value.)

As it is Greek Easter I had service with the chaplain after my visitors had left and then after dinner I settled down to watch the football. We beat Man United 1–0. Man U had many chances but Chelsea played better and should have been given a penalty, too. It was good to see Lampard playing throughout. Now, of course, Mourinho is sure to come back.

6 MAY

I rather got on with Leyla, a blonde, fair girl of Turkish-Cypriot origin. She had become an expert hairdresser and had offered a number of times to cut and colour my hair but we could never find the right time.

When I walked into Butler's this afternoon carrying food trays, she asked me a favour and I quickly obliged. She wanted her boyfriend to come and see her but was worried about how she would persuade him. It turned out he was Greek. She wanted to tell him straight, come to see me, but in perfect Greek. So I took her through the words 'come to see me' in Greek. I didn't think it was that hard. In fact, it is really easy: 'ella na me this'. And yet it took an hour and a half of practising, me saying the four words again and again, with everyone joining in to get it right. In the end it worked and he did come the following weekend.

7 MAY

I met with the HDC board today including the same lady I had met at my risk-assessment when I had first arrived. This was a less officious affair with Dee, my probation officer, Mo, from education, senior officer Mr Brown and my personal officer, Miss Callaghan, in attendance. Everything seemed to be going well though we are still awaiting the checks on the property from the local authority. They don't envisage any problems, however, and we're all set for a Monday release date after the governor has signed the application and the arrangements for my curfew have been agreed. The usual times are 7 p.m. to 7 a.m. but they can be changed if there is a good reason, such as work hours that can't be accommodated within that timeframe. The shortest a curfew can be is nine hours.

Conditions for the curfew vary depending on the service provider, the instructions of probation and the governor who signs the HDC licence. The security company providers come to fix the tag on day one of the HDC date (any time between 3 p.m. and midnight). Some people get use of the garden, others are just allowed from the front door to the back door, even if they smoke – one of the residents was apparently told that despite the fact they had children in the house they should just open the back door, stand just on the inside smoking and blow out. One of my friends, who was leaving after me, heard that this is what she was also going to get, which for her was tough as she had to run a farm with her husband. She described to me how she would have to stand with one foot in and the rest of her body leaning out for hours at a time trying to scare preying birds and foxes away from their chickens until her husband came home. She asked if she could complain about this just before she was due to leave ESP and was told that yes, she could, but that she would have to stay in prison beyond her HDC date while the complaint was being investigated. Not surprisingly she chose to let it go.

I said I was very pleased with the help I had received and that my stay in ESP had taught me a lot. They all wished me luck for the future.

8 MAY

I collected my licence today and discussed the final curfew restrictions, which seem reasonable. I agreed that I would ring if I encountered any problems. As it happens I never did; everything worked well and efficiently though I have heard from other ex-offenders that they were contacted by the security firm on a number of occasions as their monitor was showing them not to be there. In the case of one woman I know, her monitor continued to play up and after a few such mishaps she complained and they came and changed it. The bad news was they turned up just before midnight to replace it, waking everyone up. On another occasion I was told by a politician who had gone to prison for a few months that while on tag the security company accused them of having run away when they were in fact at that time with their proba-tion officer. I am sure there are lots of examples when things go wrong and ESP was sensible to warn us in advance and offer help if it were needed.

9 MAY

Spoke today to a lovely new girl in the Butler's Room, twenty-five years old, quiet, intelligent-looking, who had been working in the kitchens since arriving from a closed prison a few weeks earlier. She told me how she had gone to a club and had been searched. She had a few grams of cocaine on her – she says she had no intention of selling them but said to the police that she intended it for her use and that of her friends. And that did it for her.

She was on bail for a whole year and when it came to put in a plea she was again advised to plead guilty on the grounds that she would get a suspended sentence – well, she didn't and the judge said she had to go to prison because drugs are such a bad thing. She is convinced that if her case had been heard in a court other than the one in the sleepy town where the court hearing and sentencing took place she would have been let off. And for an evening's outing that went wrong her career has been ruined. Clearly she shouldn't have been carrying any drugs. But she felt she had learned nothing in prison; she was already well educated and when she got out she would have to start all over again.

Another girl with her, also twenty-five, was in for

a similar reason but for slightly longer. In her case, although it was a similar story, she had a few more grams of cocaine on her but pleaded not guilty as the charge was for possession and supplying. The second part of the charge was not true, she claimed, so she pleaded not guilty but in her view it was difficult for the jury to say anything other than guilty as she certainly was of the first part of the charge. She felt true anger at the system as she insists she had no intention of sharing or selling. In both cases they had made a silly mistake but you wonder how many other girls do a similar thing every night and just don't get caught.

10 MAY

My last healthcare check and my third and last hepatitis B injection. I had a nice chat with the nurse. My weight has stayed down, amazingly; I will leave prison 4 pounds lighter than when I entered. It must be the lack of alcohol; since I am getting the taste for puddings there may be something to be said for selling a diet book that is very simple and easy to follow. I might call it the prison diet: keep off booze and eat as much as you can get your hands on, three meals a day, nothing in between (throw those biscuits away) and as much pudding as you can stomach. Crucially you must remain active through the day and avoid slumping in front of the TV watching mindless soaps. That should guarantee staying skinny forever.

11 MAY

With a break in the weather, I had one last lovely long walk round the lake and the estate before an intense chat with Liz and Craig, the gym instructor, about

life and the future. Then half an hour of rowing, a
frantic rush to have a shower without burning myself
before brunch and then extra helpings of scrambled
eggs (put on my plate while the chef wasn't watching
or pretended not to), before I tackled my belongings.

Nigel, the officer at the reception desk, and I spent
about an hour putting most of what I was taking
home in a huge rucksack my son had brought in and
sorting out the bags I would be sending home via
my visitors (more books) that afternoon. Then I had
the pleasure of my last visit in prison, this time from
David and Lisa Buchan and Baroness Stedman-Scott
of the charity Tomorrow's People, for whom, while
senior managing director at FTI Consulting, I had
provided one of the first free economic evaluations
under the auspices of Pro Bono Economics, a charity of which I am a patron, of Tomorrow's People's
programme to get difficult 16–18-year-olds jobs. At
the end of my very last visit, David and Lisa kindly
took five of my bags away and dropped them at my
house; my daughter put them in the study where they
mostly still remain, alongside the previous lot.

We celebrated my final evening of bingo and then
enjoyed a cheese feast in my room, with presents given
out to everyone. It was stuff I had bought from the
canteen – cheese for Sarah, tobacco for Amy, Cadbury
sticks for Judy, coffee for Sue, more Kit Kats for Liz,
cereal for Charlotte. I also gave out food I had hoarded
from our 'grab bags' which I didn't like, mainly biscuits
and health cereal bars, and, of course, stamps; I included
lots of stamps in little thank you cards I had somehow
managed to obtain or had made myself. There were lots
of kisses to people I would not see in the morning and
also little thank you notes left for the staff.

The process felt quite businesslike at times, especially as I sorted out my accounts. Whatever was left in my balance, plus the £46 that everyone gets on release, would be transferred to my external bank account. I kept some money for last-minute phone calls but in the end, despite ringing everyone I could think of, I was still left with £14 of unspent phone money, which you cannot get back or transfer to anyone else who may need it.

Was I emotional? Maybe, but I didn't let it show. I was desperate to get back to my children and friends, so they could see that I was OK and stop worrying about me as they had done since I'd first entered prison. But I also knew that I would miss my fellow residents and maybe, strangely, also the simple routine of prison, knowing full well that life on the outside would not be easy. I knew I had to face photographers and the media, both of whom would follow my every move and document every success or failure. There would be many challenges as I tried to return to some form of 'normality'. My experience, however, was eye-opening and I knew it would stay with me forever; it would shape how I thought of the world and how I behaved in it. And I would never forget it – or my fellow residents.

12 MAY

My last full day. Aanjay and Alison lovingly squeezed me some orange juice and I had three pieces of toast and jam before completing my dining room duties.

At my last church session I discovered I wasn't the only one leaving: the chaplain, Tony, announced to a stunned congregation that he was leaving for Ford open prison at the end of the month. We agreed to stay in touch and I have since heard that Sally, a lady with whom I spent a lot of time, has taken over the post temporarily, which is so well deserved and I am sure she will look after the girls really well.

CHAPTER 6

BACK HOME

13 MAY

D-day. I should have been released on HDC on the twelfth but the way the system works, you cannot leave on a weekend or a bank holiday but have to wait until the first working day after it. So, I was allowed to leave on Monday 13 May. I can still to this day not understand why this is so. It used to be that if the date fell on a weekend you could be released on the Friday but that had been stopped relatively recently – again I don't understand why, unless it was the result of yet another law and order campaign.

Still, as the big day approached the girls had been constantly asking how much longer I had and how I felt. Of course, I was thrilled but I had to keep calm. Come each departure, however, the excitement among the girls is palpable. Why? First of all, you leave via the front door, the only time you are allowed to do that during the entire stay there, and not from the back, which is how you arrived. I hardly cared but for the other residents that seemed to matter a lot. The superstition was that once they left, they were not to look back as that would mean they would be returning at some stage.

More importantly, the departure was finally proof that you could really leave the place for good. For the residents each departure brought their own closer so although there were many tears as friends parted there was also hope. In my case I had very few of their problems – I had a home of my own, loving children, I had not benefited from my crime so there was nothing to pay back financially, I did not owe anything except my court case costs, whatever they ended up being, and I had had huge support from people on the outside. Obviously I had to rebuild my career but I felt that my experience could also be put to good use for my fellow residents and others in the system.

I was able to focus on the real immediate issue causing a lot of excitement among residents and staff: the photographers had gathered outside once more. Amazingly, some of them had been there since the previous weekend thinking I was being released then and were 'casing the joint' to find the best position from which to take their pictures.

But we had a cunning plan. I had already taken advantage of the previous two visits from relatives and friends in the preceding weekends to give back ten big prison rubbish bags of books and papers, writing pads and diaries, and some clothes so I would be left with the bare minimum on the day. That was helpful since I had accumulated a lot of stuff. Aside from the very many books – generous friends clearly thought I would be bored stiff without anything to read – what took up a lot of space were letters. After the huge postbag I had been given following my sentencing, I had been receiving an average of fifteen letters, e-mails or postcards a day during my entire stay at ESP. Many

I had replied to but so many others I intended to reply to on my return home.

Receiving so many letters had its pitfalls. Many of my women friends wrote to me daily, sometimes twice daily, scribbling on cards while on the bus, on the tube, on airplanes to visit their ailing mother in Cork, from London and then from Italy and back from London, with the result that I became utterly confused about the sequence of events in their lives, with letters arriving at different times depending on where they were posted from.

My great friend Boni would send me little summery cards with flowers on while other people kept me informed of life on the outside. Michael Littlechild, godfather to one of my sons, came to visit me early on but then went off on his travels. As chief executive of GoodOperation, a company that I helped set up and that advises others around the globe on corporate social responsibility, Michael is almost never at home and postcards started arriving from exotic locations, which fascinated my fellow residents. I had his name on my list of allowed numbers and at the various times I tried to get hold of him he was picking up his mobile while having dinner in Poland, Kazakhstan, Cambodia, Uganda, you name it. The postcards from him were incredibly colourful and very funny. My friends seemed to have rediscovered writing, which they had forgotten to do in the era of e-mails, and were relishing it. In fact a number have continued to write since. But what fascinated me is the fact that writing a proper letter brought forward the need for people to open up; despite having warned them that staff read everything that comes in, a couple of male friends started using me as an agony aunt and over five pages of tightly knit handwriting would divulge all their problems. I would respond with an equally long letter – although I knew full well that staff wouldn't be able to read my difficult handwriting, I was optimistic that my friends would have more time and inclination to decipher it. Hopefully they did and my advice was heeded – but maybe not. It seems that months of using a pen had actually reduced my ability to write legibly and in desperation my friends Jane and Mike Cooke teamed up with everyone and, on behalf of my friends, sent me a book called *Improve Your Handwriting*. Not very subtle! It had no effect and I left it to the library when I exited ESP.

My handwriting did cause extra problems for the staff, who were supposed to read some 5 per cent of what goes in and out, but in fact seemed to me to be reading everything. I once entered the centre office with a letter I wanted to make sure caught the 9 p.m. post deadline. I had made it, they said, but they had just been talking about my very difficult handwriting. Indeed, I could see one of the officers leaning over the desk reading one of the letters I was sending out who turned and laughed and said: 'Actually, the only words I can read in this letter are Ann Widdecombe!' I had mentioned her to a friend as she had just written a positive little piece in her column in the *Daily Express* defending me against some attack and I was really grateful. It was only then I realised how difficult their job of reading my mail must be. Even more troublesome must have been the letters I was sending out in Greek and French which I can only assume they just classified as even worse handwriting rather than something in a foreign language, given that no one questioned me about them.

Not that I was the only one with bad handwriting – many an hour was taken up deciphering people's addresses. Street names were particularly bad so we resigned ourselves by common agreement on a number of occasions in my room that I had no choice but to ring my office and ask Ava, my long-suffering ex-secretary, to see what street was associated with the postcode, which was just about discernible. Often we turned it into a game, passing the letter around and guessing and outguessing each other. You have to keep going in whatever small way.

Back to our cunning plan. It was very simple: get up early, straight after the 5.30 room check by the officers, have breakfast if there was time, bring my remaining stuff down to ensure a final check against my inventory of clothing and books (each day something arrived it had to be recorded by hand and itemised in an ever-expanding form and then counter-signed by me – and then the same process was carried out the other way so they could cross out each item one by one as I was leaving) and then we'd make a quick dash into the car of my solicitor, who had been warned to come early and park at the back.

While managing a quick breakfast (my friend Aanjay had the wonderful squeezed orange juice ready for me) the TV in the dining room was already showing the photographers outside. Well, we missed them all. My solicitor arrived just before 7 a.m. and the wonderful officers who had made the plan guided us through the back and down an alleyway that eventually led to a main road at the back of ESP, which we took, and we left the grounds almost immediately.

In the rush I forgot various things, in particular a threadbare green towel that I had taken with me from home when I packed for Holloway, which both my sons used at different times while they were boarders for a while in prep school (I was a great one for recycling everything, which you have to do when you have five children). I wanted it with me for sentimental and nostalgic value as there were labels on it with both their names. With every wash in ESP more of the towel would come off by the day but it was just still usable by the time I was leaving – and unfortunately it was left still hanging drying on the radiator below the window next to my bed. It was found later in the laundry room by one of the girls who was due to leave shortly after me. She very kindly returned it all washed and cleaned and neatly folded. What a relief to be reunited with it. I will never be able to throw that towel away.

We left unnoticed except for one lone photographer who seemed to have stationed himself by the crossroads at the back – the only one to have thought of it. Leaving before the usual hour of 9 a.m. we came as quite a surprise to him; he got up from his sitting position (maybe he had in fact been lying down as he probably slept the night there) and tried to focus on us and took a couple of pictures through the car windows. I suspect they were of bad quality and he was not able to sell them. But he must have warned the others and soon after, as we were driving through the beautiful Kent country roads, calls started coming through to my solicitor asking gently for confirmation of whether I was still in the building or had left – of course we had – and they all legged it to Clapham to join the growing throng of photographers already stationed outside my door.

But the thought that went through my head, as we were driving home and getting stuck in the usual early morning rush hour traffic on the A20, was that despite the constant attention and the difficulties that would still completely prevent me returning to normality, I still in reality had it easy by comparison to so many I had met. It is so obvious to me that for women, much more than for men, prison is only a small part of what they have to suffer. The punishment is not over when their sentence ends; consider the children taken away, the loss of home, loss of prospects, the shame and family breakdowns, all of which make any sentence they have to serve disproportionate to the offence itself. Women on the whole, again much more than men, are as much victims as perpetrators of crimes. Most of their crimes are non-violent and women offenders usually pose no threat to society.[113] I determined to write about what I'd learned and become involved in the exposing of the illogicality of keeping women in prison and the immense direct and indirect costs of separating women from society when alternative ways of dealing with them, such as through community service orders, seem to be used very sparingly.

I arrived home to be greeted by a large number of photographers and journalists. My solicitor read out my statement saying how glad I was to be home, that I wanted to thank my family and friends but also the prison staff and my fellow residents who I got to know well in East Sutton Park and that I now intended to resume my career as an economist.

Into my home at last and there were lots of hugs with the kids and close friends. Two Serco employees turned up at 4.30 p.m. and the tag was fitted easily. That evening the whole family came for supper and it was glorious – I had been asked what I fancied and they all prepared food for me that was just amazing. As I looked around the table at all my children, their partners and my grandchildren, I considered my future. Even with reasonable skills and a good track record, convictions and popular perceptions do matter. In the weeks that followed I would have knocks, privileges and other distinctions taken away as people followed rules, and my confidence and image would be greatly affected. I knew, however, that I would receive so much more in terms of support and extra chances. Possibilities would open up that would go some way towards restoring my faith in human nature. I hope my fellow residents get similar support when they come out.

14 MAY

My daughter's theatre company had been using my house for the past two weeks, rehearsing for a production of *A Midsummer Night's Dream*. They were all so brilliant but there were lots of young people around and the noise they were making was incredible. When they were going through the sword-fighting scene in the living room upstairs I feared the ceiling would fall on my head as I was sitting in the kitchen right underneath it. In many ways it was perfect to have them around as it really helped me readjust to life outside. They were incredibly sweet. No one asked anything – not that I would have minded.

That night, more food was prepared for me in what would become a pattern for the following two months while my tag was in operation. People would visit practically every night for eight weeks laden with food, puddings, drinks, flowers and the like – the house was continuously full of flowers after I returned home. Even the postman said it was good to have me back when he delivered the morning's mail.

15 MAY

It was the Europa League final. In any other year Chelsea fans would have sneered at that competition but we actually took it seriously as it ended up being the only trophy we were likely to get, having exited the FA Cup in the semi-final when we lost to Man City. We joked in ESP that since the game would be a few days after I got out I might just be able to make it to Amsterdam and back before the curfew. I knew it couldn't happen but my fellow residents took it seriously and made anxious questions to their relatives on their daily phone calls to see what time the game was scheduled for and therefore whether it was at all feasible for me to get to the match. Well, kick-off was not until 7.45 p.m. so they realised that even with the best will in the world and if planes were on time, I wouldn't be able to make it. There were lots of jokes made about how I would be ringing Serco from the air blaming it all on air traffic control. They knew by then how keen I was on Chelsea and we made a pact that if I watched *The Voice* from home they would in return watch the final, so at least we would be close in spirit. I hope they kept their side of the bargain. I kept mine.

16 MAY

A full dress rehearsal for *A Midsummer Night's Dream* was held in the private crescent at the front of the house. All the neighbours came, bringing their own chairs and umbrellas as it rained a bit at times, but it was brilliant. I could hear my daughter's voice loud and clear while sitting by the front steps of my house which was as far as I was allowed on my curfew days after 7 p.m. The neighbours loved it and the company took the play and *As You Like It* round the country. I caught it in a matinee at Russell Square Gardens two weeks later with lots of other friends, getting back home just in time for curfew that night.

18 MAY

A difficult decision to make: would I have enough time to get to Oxford and back to watch my son, who is studying there, act in the Jez Butterworth play *The Winterling*? Given I had to consider the tag, the only chance to see it was on the Saturday matinee on the last day of the show. I agonised about the logistics: should I leave at the interval? After Act 3? How hard would it be to escape unnoticed without interrupting the play? We discussed it all week long and my son was petrified that I might get stuck in traffic on the M40 and miss my curfew time. In the end I chickened out on the grounds that the last thing I wanted to do was have a son possibly worrying more about me than his performance. To make up for my absence, I sent lots of family members instead, including my brother who had come especially from Greece.

19 MAY

This afternoon my son and I went to watch Chelsea in their last game of the season. The game started at 4 p.m.; we beat Everton and finished safely in third place, so Champions League again next season. There were lots of handshakes from the other fans, the odd kiss and I got a warm welcome back – and we forgot all about timing. We got stuck in a terrible traffic jam trying to cross Albert Bridge and got home with one-and-a-half minutes to spare before curfew.

29 MAY

Back to business and my first public speaking engagement was arranged to take place at the Official Monetary and Financial Institutions Forum (OMFIF), a financial sector think tank, at the Armourers' Hall in the City of London. I was to be the respondent to the Croatian central bank governor, who was to explain his country's thinking in advance of them joining the EU on 1 July, the first new country to join since Bulgaria and Romania in 2007. There was much frantic brushing up on recent developments, based on little idea of what the governor was likely to say. The talk was so very important for my reputation and I was keen to go back to what I was doing before prison as quickly as possible. I survived it (just) and without incident; it was great to work on familiar ground again and everyone was so very kind and supportive.

13 JUNE

Kristiina Reed, who was helping me with my research, and I met with Gill Arupke, the CEO of Penrose, a charity which runs a number of projects which rehabilitate and reintegrate ex-offenders, drug users and people with mental health issues back into the community and help them to stop reoffending. I was keen to discover what charities in general were doing to help offenders and more specifically to see whether there were any lessons to be learned from Penrose's experience in Lewisham, where the charity is paid by results for keeping offenders (many of whom are also arrested and charged by the police for illegal drug offences) out of prison for more than twelve months. In particular, I wondered how evaluation actually worked in this field.

It turns out that the first problem the charity faced was that the full number of offenders with a drug-related problem was not known; unless they were already in treatment there was no data shared by the various agencies involved in helping offenders. The police are also reluctant to share the information they have with partner agencies as they see it as strictly confidential. This, Penrose argues, makes it very difficult for any agency to map out the required staff structure needed to meet whatever demand there may be for the service.

Penrose runs a number of residential units varying from the pretty open to the quite restrictive depending on the court orders the residents have received. In their first evaluation Penrose found that the reoffending rate of those helped by the charity was some 5 per cent – and this was without the charity doing what I feared, which is creaming off the easiest cases and ignoring the rest. So this is encouraging.

Whether you would achieve similar success rates if rehabilitating services for offenders were contracted out to private companies or charities (operating within a pay-by-results scheme), as proposed by Chris Grayling in his Transforming Rehabilitation agenda,[114] depends on a number of things which may just not be available.

First, you need baseline data so you can actually measure the improvement you are effecting, which in itself faces the aforementioned problems. Second, you need to be able to calculate proper attribution; in other words you need to have an agreed concept of 'additionality', an economic term that calculates the actual extra impact of the intervention that has achieved the result. Yet if the economy improves at country or local level and offenders are now able to get jobs, which wasn't the case before, the chances of reoffending tend to reduce and the problem becomes one of identifying the extra impact of the intervention in improving reoffending rates outside the effect of the general improvement in economic prosperity. Third and most important, there is the issue of who can in fact provide the service. Payment by results requires charities to have a large cash flow so, as they can't borrow much from the banks, except on mortgage, they need to have large reserves if they are to play a significant role in looking after offenders on behalf of the government if probation services are cut.

The fear is that it will only be the large private firms that can raise cash easily while the smaller specialist firms, often with the most innovative ideas and greatest effectiveness, may not be able to compete to take on this job. The trick would be to negotiate, if possible, with the government, an upfront payment to cover costs of providing the service while the payment by results based on reduced reoffending rates becomes a 'bonus', or alternatively to try to imitate the experience of St Giles Trust, a similar outfit to Penrose, through the issuing of a social impact bond. This is a social fund for which returns are based on results, in the case of St Giles, for example, by reducing reoffending in Peterborough.

There is a lot of excitement about the potential

availability of finance for this purpose and on 26 June, nearly a fortnight after my meeting with Penrose, I chaired a big conference on social finance organised by employment charity Tomorrow's People. The discussion at the conference, however, reinforced my view that charities, especially small ones, will struggle to raise enough funds to compete with the bigger private firms in looking after large numbers of offenders and ex-offenders. And they will also need to improve their own competences if they are to manage large projects of the sort envisaged by the government, something organisations have been trying to help with. City livery companies like the Worshipful Company of Management Consultants and others who work closely with the Centre for Charitable Effectiveness at the Cass Business School provide pro-bono assistance to charities in various areas of their operations. Pro Bono Economics, a charity of which I am a patron, was set up to provide expert economic evaluation support to other charities and provides them with free economic input by drawing resources both from private organisations and from the Government Economic Service.

One Whitehall charity that has been reaching out to help the prison community is the Whitehall & Industry Group (WIG), run by my ex-colleague Mark Gibson from the BIS. WIG offers a range of opportunities to bring business, government and the not-for-profit sector closer together. The idea is to share expertise, broaden networks and develop talent. WIG tells me that it has recently placed civil service fast-streamers with charities such as RAPt, Revolving Doors, Catch22 and the Irene Taylor Trust, all of whom provide rehabilitation support to offenders and ex-offenders. These are all very interesting charities. The Irene Taylor Trust, for example, has been delivering its music-in-prisons programme since 1995 whereby music is used to inspire change in individuals. In the past eighteen months it has extended its work to include 'through-the-gate' support to ex-prisoners and delivers projects with young people at risk of offending in the community. Interestingly WIG has recently been working with the trust to appoint a business development manager to look at the income stream from its music-in-prisons programme.

What most charities working in this sphere need help in is how to measure the returns they are getting – and the measurements are inevitably 'soft', in other words qualitative rather than 'hard' quantitative ones, but soft outcomes also matter and are important. Dan Corry of New Philanthropy Capital, a consultancy providing services to the charity sector, told me that in his view it is a myth that you can calculate a social cost by comparing £1 spent on, say, mental care with £1 spent on preventing drug abuse. Indeed there are surprisingly few such evaluations around. This is not a view shared by all. An impact evaluation carried out for the charity Penrose shows that 'for every £1 invested in support-focused alternatives to prison, £14 of social value is generated to women and their children, victims and society generally, over a ten-year period'.[115]

But other evaluations are much softer though no less important for that. A 2008 report on music in prisons for the Irene Taylor Trust, for example, based on a series of interviews concluded: 'The findings thus far show that the music in prisons project has beneficial effects on well-being, relationships, learning

capacity and motivation.'[116] The authors argue
that further work does need to be done, and the
project extended but the impact on prisoners is real.
Significantly they draw a link from their work on
the impact of music courses on other aspects of a
prisoner's behaviour which is particularly important
in terms of setting prisoners on the path of improvement and ultimate rehabilitation and reduced reoffending. The report draws on earlier research which
points to 'a relationship between an individual's
sense of self-efficacy and confidence to participate
in educational activities'. They therefore concluded
that the 'project clearly does impact on individuals'
feelings of self-efficacy, as well as engaging those
individuals with limited or undeveloped educational
skills who may not have succeeded in a traditional
education setting. This leads us to surmise that the
music project creates a pathway for some inmates to
engage in the skills training that they so obviously
need.' The conclusions are useful in that regard but
even here the authors are suggesting that there needs
to be a lot more work and that of course generalising
is difficult as clearly not all prisoners are right for
this kind of approach.

So what will happen next? So far the Ministry of
Justice proposals to outsource most of the prison
probation system have been greeted with guarded
optimism by charities. I have no idea how it will all
pan out in the end but the charities I spoke to hoped
that it would work better than the Work Programme,
which contracted out Jobcentres to private firms and
paid them by results. This concluded with scandals
of providers fiddling the results and creaming off
the easier-to-place jobseekers, ignoring the rest in

the process. But it looks like opinion in the charity
sector remains highly divided. Clive Martin, director of Clinks, the umbrella body for criminal justice
charities (and not to be confused with the Clink
restaurant charity) discusses in the influential *Third
Sector* magazine the possibility of some voluntary
sector organisations becoming the prime provider of
those services rather than being sub-contractors to
large private companies as has been mostly the case
with the Work Programme. However, Andrew Neilson,
director of campaigns for the Howard League for
Prison Reform, says: 'The MoJ wants to drive down
costs, improve quality, and introduce a new system,
all on a tight timetable ... It has bitten off more than it
can chew.'[117]

The justice select committee has moved into that
debate, too, arguing in its 13 July report that the
problems of payment by results may lead to perverse
incentives, particularly in the provision of appropriate gender-specific services as women 'are often
classified for probation purposes as presenting
a lower risk of reoffending or harm, but have a
higher level of need requiring more intensive and
costly intervention'. The committee is in favour of
'commissioning services for women offenders separately, and for applying other incentive mechanisms
to encourage not just a reduction in reoffending, but
also diversion from crime'.[118]

My hope is that both the third sector and the
government have learned important lessons from
the Work Programme and that they can put these
lessons to good use to help women. It is crucial that
the Ministry of Justice initiative succeeds for charities, prisoners and the public purse. If charities can

form consortia to bid for contracts, the expertise they are able to bring to their work will only bring better outcomes for the criminal justice system.

16 JUNE

Today's *Observer* featured an article by Yvonne Roberts, a journalist but also a trustee for Women in Prison who had spent time after my release filling me in on the work of the various charities operating in this field. The article discussed the death of a mother who hanged herself after going to prison for a second time rather than sell her home and dislocate her children in order to pay back some £17,000 she had embezzled from her employers to help her repay loans. Roberts was making very strongly the case that vulnerable women should not be sent to jail but that a community service with a later opportunity of being able to work again and pay money back slowly may well have been hugely preferable for all concerned in that instance. And it probably would have been a much better answer for her daughters, who are just two of the tens of thousands of children a year affected by mothers going to jail.

When I bought the newspaper that morning, in the queue was a young black man who asked me outright whether I was Mrs Pryce, then introduced himself and shook my hand. He asked in front of everyone whether I had indeed gone to jail and how it had been for me and then asked whether the women in prison had tried anything on me. He then proceeded to say that surely I would have hit them back if they had attacked me as I looked like a fighter! He finished by saying how nice it was to have met me. I kept my cool – I didn't worry about him asking all these questions in a loud voice in front of everyone. I had been impressed by Erwin James, the ex-offender and well-known commentator and journalist, telling me when I met him that I should keep my head up high. In any case no one had quite followed our conversation as the place seemed to be packed with eastern Europeans buying phone cards and travel cards who didn't much care what was being said and the young Pakistani chap behind the counter wasn't paying any attention either. No, what struck me was the perception that women are violent and that women's prisons are dangerous places, both things which for the most part are not true.

The public is uninformed. A recent survey suggested that people thought that women in prison were there mostly for violent crimes, just like men, but the numbers of women imprisoned for such crimes is only a small percentage of the overall total. And women die in prison not because of fights but because of depression. Data suggests that up to 80 per cent of women in prison suffer from a variety of health disorders, which are brought about by abuse in childhood, homelessness, domestic violence and drug-related issues. And they are jailed for non-violent crimes in the main, such as handling stolen goods and shoplifting, serving generally short sentences for petty offences. As they are generally left without support they often reoffend – some 49 per cent of women with sentences under twelve months reoffend within a year and have a high reconviction rate of 58 per cent. All campaigning bodies would want to see the perceptions of that young man who talked to me in the corner shop about women in prison changed. This is not to say that there aren't any violent incidents but there are a lot less than imagined and the numbers committed by women in prison have been going down.

But it is a common perception. I probably thought exactly the same two years ago, even a few months ago, and if I had watched the recent programme on BBC called *Prisoners* which covered life in Holloway, among other prisons, I would have got a very frightening view of what goes on in female prisons if I hadn't been in prison myself. According to an Ipsos MORI survey conducted in 2008, when those surveyed were asked whether they believed crime was rising (which figures suggest is not the case), 57 per cent said they believed it was because of what they see on television and 48 per cent said it was because of what they read in tabloid newspapers.[119] This suggests a serious degree of misrepresentation of the issue on behalf of the press and TV channels. Looking into the portrayals of women offenders in prime-time TV crime dramas, one piece of research found that in a single series of the popular American programme *CSI*, 36.4 per cent of characters committing offences were female and of these offences 70 per cent were for homicide.[120] Although this was higher than several other programmes, it nonetheless plays a role in public misconceptions. In a 2009 Ipsos-conducted survey, when members of the public were asked if they felt more threatened by men who commit crime, women who commit crime, or both, 58 per cent said that they felt threatened equally by both.[121]

The same 2009 Ipsos survey revealed that 34 per cent of respondents mentioned violent crime when asked which types of crime they felt threatened by, and that about half of the respondents felt there was no difference in the likelihood of committing crime between

men and women.[122] These answers would suggest
quite a large discrepancy between what the public
thinks about female offenders, that they are just as
likely as men to commit crimes and just as threatening, and the reality, that women are much less likely
to commit crime and much less likely to commit
violent crimes as the prison population figures
demonstrate. Indeed, another investigation revealed
that although crime has gone down significantly over
the last ten years, only 4 per cent of people believed
it had done so for the last twelve months in 2010.[123]
When it comes to how offenders should be sentenced,
65 per cent of the public believe prison would be effective in preventing crime and disorder. Yet, in addition
to this there is widespread support for better mental
healthcare (80 per cent in favour), making amends to
victims (79 per cent in favour), unpaid community
work (76 per cent in favour) and better treatment
to tackle drug addiction (74 per cent in favour).[124]
Furthermore, an ICM poll in 2010 showed that
80 per cent strongly agreed that centres addressing the
root causes of crimes committed by women, where
they can also work in the community, should be available.[125] Similarly, approximately two thirds of people
believe that for non-violent and non-serious offences,
alternatives to prison are more appropriate.[126] Finally,
regardless of offence a similar number thought
alternatives were more appropriate for offenders
with children.[127]

The trends suggest that although the public endorse
tough sentencing by the courts people do tend to react
to information rationally if they are given the correct
facts. A senior civil servant recalls a survey in the early
1990s which, almost as would be the case now, found

that most people when asked thought that if anything sentences in general were too lenient. When the question was put to them another way, with the crimes actually explained, the verdict was that the sentences were in fact too harsh.

25 JUNE

Baroness Whitaker, with whom I co-chaired a design commission enquiry into design education a year ago, wrote to me in prison and was the first to send me the famous Corston Report, which duly arrived in a brown envelope at East Sutton Park and was delivered to me without incident. She later arranged for me to meet Baroness Corston in person as soon as possible after my HDC release.

The three of us met at the peers' entrance of the Houses of Parliament but then walked all the way through the building to Portcullis House for lunch in the Adjournment restaurant. Three women lunching together attracted some attention and Jack Straw shouted out my name as we were going to our table and gave me the regards of his wife, Alice Perkins, who used to be a colleague at the civil service. My very good friend Stephen Glover was at the next table having lunch with David Davis. It was so nice to be back in town. And so good to hear Jean Corston so passionate and knowledgeable about the issues of women offenders.

4 JULY

Another visit to the House of Lords but this time to embark on a completely different mission. I was asked soon after I was released to give expert evidence to the House of Lords European Union economic and financial affairs select sub-committee on the eurozone. I duly arrived at 10.30, was greeted by the clerks of the committee at the Black Rod entrance and then brought up to committee room 3. I was joined by my old friend Ruth Lea, who I knew from her early days in what was then the Department of Trade and Industry but who was now at Arbuthnot Banking Group, and by Professor Stephen Haseler from the Global Policy Institute.

I only realised that this was not going to be an ordinary meeting when I was approached by a group of journalists who were lurking outside the entrance to the committee room. They introduced themselves as political sketch-writers from various newspapers, asked me how I was and then followed us in. I don't think the sub-committee, chaired by Lord Harrison, who I knew of old, and containing people like John Kerr, ex-permanent secretary in the Foreign Office, and Patrick Carter, who had written a lot about prison reform, has ever had so many people from the public attending any open hearing for a technical session that was also televised live on the parliamentary TV channel. The poor sketch-writers all had to listen patiently to the technical discussions as I and the other panel members answered the questions posed by the learned lords before we were finally, an hour and a half later, invited to join their lordships for coffee at the House of Lords bar – without the journalists. Some nice words were written about my contribution the next day but the fascination seemed to be mainly with trying to guess where my tag might be hiding around my body. I had by then, following my release from ESP, already given talks on Europe, participated in panels, chaired events, written the odd

piece for the papers and was generally getting back
to what I do best, namely commenting on economics. My prison sentence had not been mentioned by
anyone and no journalist had asked any questions
about it when I appeared on platforms. Given the
day's interest, however, I couldn't fail to wonder how
easy it would be for me and the other girls I met in
ESP who were due for release to get back to normality.

8 JULY

While waiting for James Timpson this morning at
the entrance of the Charing Cross Hotel to discuss
the policies towards training and employing offenders and ex-offenders in his company, a lovely porter,
a young half-Italian, half-Spanish guy, started to chat
to me. He was very happy with the world and told me
how much he had learned since he came to London. 'I
love my job,' he told me. 'I love London. I love talking
to people and helping them. Can I help you?'

'Of course,' I said, 'Where would you suggest I go
for coffee with my friend who is about to join me?'
'Don't worry at all,' he said, 'I will take you up to
the breakfast room with great views over Trafalgar
Square and will get you the best table.' As soon as
James arrived he did exactly that. Up he led us, into
the breakfast room, cleared a space for us on the best
table by the window, had a quick chat with the wait-
ers and he was gone.

The service was impeccable. I learned a lot from
James and he gave me plenty of help and sugges-
tions of who to talk to further. An hour and a half,
and quite a few cups of coffee and tea, later we tried
to pay the bill. No payment required, they all said.
However much we insisted they refused to let us leave

any money, not even a tip. 'This has never happened to me before,' said James. 'Ever.'

10 JULY

I had a mid-morning meeting with Roma Hooper of the charity Make Justice Work at some wonderfully understated club on Shaftesbury Avenue; the problem was, I couldn't find it, that is how understated it was. Finally I pushed the doorbell on an unmarked door and went up the flights of stairs into a large, airy and packed restaurant area half an hour late.

After chatting with Roma for a few hours, I was off again to a lunchtime event at the Centre for the Study for Financial Innovation (CSFI). I arrived only a minute before it was due to start and to my surprise was ushered to the platform by its director, Andrew Hilton, as apparently I was meant to be part of the panel. Panic!

On my return home on the almost empty upper deck of the number 88 bus the woman sitting in the front row recognised me and said she and the congregation in her church had been praying for me throughout the service. It is probably what got me through the previous terrifying hour and a half on a panel in front of lots of City experts, all keenly watching my performance knowing full well where I had been and why. Fortunately, it went well and I thanked the lady on the bus for her prayers.

11 JULY

My last day with the tag. Serco were meant to come between 10 p.m. and midnight according to the licence document I was given at ESP when I was leaving. I met my colleagues from my previous job for coffee in the Strand after a lunch and they advised me not to risk being late returning home. All thoughts of going briefly to Bastille Day celebrations at the French Embassy in Kensington Park Gardens were abandoned to ensure I didn't mess up on the last day; traffic on Chelsea Bridge on the way back could have made me late for my curfew.

Back at home I settled in for the evening and began cooking for the people who were coming for dinner to celebrate with me. This time it would be the ESP pork and sausages bought by my children nearly three months earlier during family day and kept in the freezer for me ever since, earmarked to be cooked on my unconditional release date... And then, to my delight, two ladies from Serco turned up at 7.30 p.m. Nice and early. They took my tag and monitor off super efficiently and there I was, free. I didn't quite know what to do with myself, so resumed cooking. In theory, I was still on curfew until midnight. Although no one could monitor me anymore, I decided to stay put.

My sentence finally at a close, a number of things have become clear to me and I end this part with a summary of my thoughts on the prison system. So at the end of four of the most charged months of my life how am I feeling and what do I think? The most important personal lesson I have learned is that love and support of family and friends are precious beyond belief. The second is that the women I met in prison were as much victims, often of men, as they were guilty of crimes which in countries not driven by atavistic media-generated retribution and revenge would not lead to costly and wasteful imprisonment. The third lesson is that despite the impressive

network of academics, reform organisations, think
tanks and support groups, the cause of reforming prisons is very far down the political agenda.
The main parliamentary spokespersons for reform I
encountered were all unelected peers well into retirement age. (No ageism is intended as some of the best
and most vigorous of our parliamentarians are peers
over sixty-five but great reform movements need
the energy of youth and belief that a cause will help
advance a political career.) Few MPs, or rising ministers or shadow ministers, seem to show much interest
in reducing the number of women sent to prison each
year either to serve a sentence or on remand. There
are MPs who do make the occasional speech or ministers who claim, no doubt sincerely, that they would
like to improve prisons but the massive increase in
the prison population and the extent to which prisons
release so many who only go on to reoffend suggests
that the good intentions mentioned by ministers do
not translate into policy or practice.

As an economist I was staggered at the obvious
reforms needed in such a tiny part of the government services. Clearly more work needs to be done to
evaluate different approaches and the extent to which
some of the issues relating to women also apply to
many of the men who receive custodial sentences,
but it is surely clear that the present system does not
work. A politician who is able to find a way to explain
why a different approach is needed and how it will
bring benefits for the taxpayer and the economy as a
whole, would be criticised by rent-a-quote colleagues
who clamour for ever harder sentences and write to
the police, ministers and CPS demanding action and
imprisonment for anyone they don't like. If such a

politician exists, he or she, like the great parliamentary reformers of the past, would have to take on all the conventional wisdoms about prison but in the end would render the country a significant service. He or she would have to point out that the cost–benefit analysis does not stack up – in its crudest form, despite an annual cost of £6bn for our judiciary system, the cost of reoffending alone is estimated, as shown by the various references throughout this book, to be anywhere between £9bn and £13bn. The other indirect costs of putting people away are enormous and in the imprisonment of mothers in particular we create more potential problems that increase the likelihood that their children will offend and become a cost to the economy themselves. Crime costs society dear. But the threat of a custodial sentence itself is not enough of a deterrent and there is evidence – as I have shown and as appears in more detail in the chapters that follow – that prison itself tends to lead to more rather than less offending overall.

So, finally, it comes down to leadership. Of course there are many pressing causes to tackle. As society grows more unequal and less generous, the welfare of a small percentage of people, such as women prisoners, may seem less of a priority. But it is obvious to me that in this strained financial environment we find ourselves in, prison reform that saves the taxpayer money in both the short and long term is a must – and surely only a win-win situation. And hopefully, armed with those facts, a real movement for change will emerge that challenges the clichés of those who dictate the public agenda. One day we will say with pride that our prisons are only for those who need to be locked away to prevent real harm. Home curfews, electronic

surveillance, education and training, support for jobseekers, and coordinated help for better parenting and
mental and health problems will be more important
to the police, CPS, judges and ministers than pressing
the conveyor belt button that sends so many women
(and men) to prison.

PART TWO

CHAPTER 7

THE ECONOMIC COST OF KEEPING PEOPLE IN PRISON

As an economist my professional life has been devoted to using economic analysis to suggest ways of achieving more and better output from poorly allocated resources. Often this has led to difficulties as the exposure of losses, bad management and poorly allocated capital reveals that a traditional time-honoured way of doing things is inefficient.

As the reader who has come this far will realise, I have been deeply impressed by the moral, social and – in a world where such qualities are undervalued and even scorned – the sheer do-gooding impulses of those who work on prison reform and those who help newly released individuals find work, a home or a meaning in life.

In the second part of this book, I want to explain why an economic evaluation of our prisons is not only long overdue but can contribute to a better system and so I ask the questions: are we receiving value for money and what does a cost–benefit analysis of the prison system reveal?

So, let us start with the costs. While tolerating the Whitehall-speak and abundance of acronyms, one must be aware that each report, each academic investigation, each think tank publication can produce slightly different figures. Yet some grasp of the bare facts is needed. We know that the 2010 spending review undertaken when the coalition came to power required the Ministry of Justice (MoJ) to reduce its Departmental Expenditure Limit (DEL) from £8.3bn in 2010/11 to £7bn in 2014/15. Some £460m of cuts have already taken place, mostly by cutting legal aid and staffing levels, and by closing a number of courts. In total, the National Offender Management Service (NOMS) alone was told to achieve total savings of £650m from its budget of £3.4bn by 2015. To put this into perspective, the total NOMS spending on women's prisons in 2011/12 was some £173.7m for a population of 4,154 women prisoners on average during the year.[128] Cuts to the prison budget led to the Prisoner Officers Association warning in 2011 that prisons were being put at serious risk of riots, jeopardising the safety of both prisoners and officers,[129] which echoed the opinions of a number of independent monitoring boards around the country. The Public Accounts Committee also raised concerns in March 2013 that the depth of the cuts may lead to greater reoffending.[130]

In addition the 2013 spending review announced in June demanded a further cut of between 8 per cent and 10 per cent in 2015/16 to the MoJ's DEL. Ministers anxious to please David Cameron had already volunteered these cuts before the review figures were announced in detail. A good way to reduce budget pressure would be to reduce the number of prisoners to average west European levels. If doing the right things for a minority of prisoners can actually achieve all these benefits and we then add to that the impact on mental health and the contribution to the economy made by the women themselves, the benefits can be much greater.

There are six areas of costs which need to be examined:

1. THE COST OF PRISON AGAINST OTHER ALTERNATIVES

There are different calculations for costs incurred by prisons depending on any additional spend that may be needed and there are differences in costs between short-term and longer-term sentences. In general, however, the alternatives to prison are much cheaper. A written answer published in Hansard suggested that the average cost of a prison place for a woman was £56,415 in 2009/10, not including expenses on healthcare or education.[131] The cost of a short-term prisoner is probably lower than this but it still compares poorly with the approximate cost of providing a community order such as curfews and tagging (without taking account of gender) of £2,800. The MoJ also estimates that the cost of providing holistic support through a women's community centre is in the region of £1,360 per year.[132]

If a year in custody for a woman costs the prison service £56,000, then the average short-term sentence of three months costs some £14,000. If we then compare that figure with the average cost of providing a community order or a community centre (say, £2,000), the difference compared to three months in prison is approximately £12,000. Moving 1,000 women from prison into community service would therefore instantly save nearly £12m per annum, which is close to 7 per cent of what is currently being spent on women's prisons per annum. Even on the more expensive calculation of £5,500 per annum for intensive twelve-month community service,[133] the difference in savings from the three-month custodial cost of £14,000 is £8,500 per prisoner per annum, so the saving for 1,000 women is £8.5m per annum. The savings one could make if one were diverting to community orders, say, 10,000 prisoners (men and women) could easily top one hundred million pounds. And this only considers the benefits of direct costs as a result of switching from custodial sentences to community orders, and nothing else, in other words any reduced reoffending, impact on children and wider societal benefits.

Business consultancy Matrix Knowledge Group calculates that if offenders with drug abuse issues are diverted from custody to community service with intensive supervision and drug treatment, society saves some £60,000 per offender in costs over the offender's lifetime. Of course, not all drug offenders are suitable for transfers to other services. But Matrix calculates that if the offender is diverted to residential drug treatment instead, that can produce an even larger lifetime cost saving to society, which they calculate at £200,000 per offender. Matrix concludes that if such a move had been done for those offenders given a custodial sentence of up to twelve months in 2007 a saving of £980m could have been made.[134]

2. COMMUNITY ORDERS ARE FOUND TO REDUCE REOFFENDING

The current system clearly is not working. The figures show that in 2010, 45 per cent of women leaving prison were reconvicted within one year.[135] This is particularly stark given that 26 per cent of women in prison have no previous convictions. So sending women to prison has the perverse effect of increasing the likelihood of offending.[136]

According to the MoJ's own statistics, when you compare similar offenders who have committed similar crimes, those who are given a short prison sentence (of fewer than twelve months) are 6.4 per cent more likely to reoffend than those given community orders, and 8.6 per cent more likely to reoffend than those given suspended sentences.[137] Again, take the MoJ figures as before that show that the average cost of a prison place for a woman was £56,415 in 2009/10, not including expense on healthcare or education.[138] The approximate cost of providing a community order (without taking account of gender) is £2,800, while the MoJ estimates that the cost of providing holistic support through a women's community centre is in the region of £1,360 per year.[139] If we assume for a moment that the length of a community sentence were to equal the length of a short prison sentence, that means that by using short prison sentences instead of community sentences, we are currently paying in the region of twenty to forty times more, to increase reoffending by 7 to 8 per cent. This may not apply to all people currently receiving custodial sentences but considering that the total cost of reoffending is estimated to be between £9.5bn and £13bn per year[140] and that custodial sentencing increases the reoffending rate by 8 per cent more than community orders, then by ignoring the alternatives on offer we could be costing society dear.

3. SEPARATING OFFENDERS FROM THEIR FAMILIES LEADS TO INCREASED LONGER-TERM COSTS TO SOCIETY

People who stay in touch with their families and

have proper relationships tend to reoffend far less than those that don't. For most mothers (and some fathers) not being separated from one's children also reduces the need for children to be taken into care, potentially saving hundreds of millions a year. The issue of care itself is not insignificant. A 2011 study into the unit costs of health and social care analysed four case studies of children in the care system with additional needs.[141] These case studies provided illustrative examples of the broad costs of children with additional needs ranging from low to high using standard examples of typical cases. What these case studies showed is that the economic costs to society of imprisoning women with children stretch far beyond the basic prison costs related to the female offender. The studies show that the costs of placing a child in state care can range from c.£40,000 (over a fourteen-month period) for a straightforward uncomplicated placement of a child with no additional needs to c.£525,000 (over a twenty-month period) for a child with highly complex care needs.

Between October 2011 and December 2012, 12,251 women were received into prison.[142] A conservative estimate by the Home Office suggests imprisonment results in approximately 17,240 separations of mothers from children per year.[143] If 12 per cent of separations result in local authority care, that would suggest 2,040 children per year enter the care system as a result of imprisoning mothers. If each of these generates a cost of £174,642, then this adds up to a total of £356m. If we take the minimum costs of £34,284 per child per year, then the total is still £70m. Although all these children may not stay in care for a whole year, many do because of the difficulties faced by mothers attempting to secure a care order to regain custody after imprisonment.

Furthermore, this is just for one year, and does not take into account the long-term possibility that the child will enter the criminal justice system – 24 per cent of prisoners were taken into care as a child. Neither does it take into account the biggest cost, which is that it vastly increases the child's likelihood of becoming a NEET (not in employment, education or training). Indeed a report by the New Economics Foundation calculated that imprisoning women who have committed non-violent offences incurs costs for the state of £17m over a ten-year period because of the children who become NEETs. Children in care also have a much higher propensity to become offenders themselves.

4. CHANGING SENTENCING GUIDELINES WOULD SUBSTANTIALLY REDUCE NUMBERS SENT TO PRISON AND THE SUBSEQUENT COSTS

The prison population for England and Wales reached an all-time high of 88,171 in December 2011. At the same time, Scotland's reached a record high of 8,420 (a higher proportion of their population). However, the figure for England and Wales has come down slightly in the most recent figures, for the week ending 30 August 2013 to 84,066, 3 per cent lower than the year before.[144] This is a good sign, though the numbers in prison are still large having risen steadily since the Second World War. A sharp increase in the prison population since the 1990s has led to the current bursting point – on average it has increased by 3.6 per cent each year since 1993.

And it really is at bursting point. At the end of May 2013, seventy-two prison establishments were deemed overcrowded – that's 57 per cent of the estate – with nine operating at over 150 per cent of their certified normal prison capacity. We send more people per 100,000 of the population to prison than any other country in western Europe. This makes no sense. There needs to be an urgent review to ensure that the substantial increase in prison numbers can be reversed and returned to the levels experienced some twenty years ago, where the numbers were half of what they are now, and perhaps continue then to decline. The increase in the amount of prisoners has made no sense at a time when crime rates are decreasing; the larger number of prisoners mostly reflects changes in custody rate and longer sentences imposed on offenders.[145]

5. INVESTMENT IN EDUCATION AND IN HELPING PEOPLE TO GET JOBS HAS ONE OF THE HIGHEST RETURNS IN TERMS OF REDUCING CRIME AND REOFFENDING

Not only is there a direct correlation between education and offending which demonstrates the large return on the £100m or so a year that is spent by the Department for Business, Innovation and Skills (BIS) but a link now seems also to exist between paid employment and offending. What is more, the impact of the reduction in benefits that people at work no longer need and the taxes they would pay, which will flow into the exchequer both through work and also through VAT as purchasing power increases, is rarely considered. And the economy will benefit from higher productivity; those that can work should not be wasted. The improvement in mental and physical health because of employment also has obvious benefits.

Indeed, if society was serious about reintegrating

offenders, it would be sensible to take the 'criminal' label off people who commit crimes who are not a threat to society. This would ensure they re-engage with their communities a lot more smoothly, incentivise them to educate or re-educate themselves and therefore become productive members of their community.

6. SELLING OFF THE ESTATE

In a study undertaken by Kevin Lockyer in 2013, Policy Exchange argued that much could be saved by closing old prisons and replacing them with fewer 'mega' prisons, each one housing many more prisoners than at present. A lot more could be saved by selling the real estate prisons occupy in a move akin to the army selling its barracks as it slims down. This could raise substantial sums for investment in local prisons while some of the 'horrid' ones, as Nick Hardwick describes Holloway, could be sold for their prime locations in the centre of towns. Other places, such as smaller local 'resettlement' prisons, could be acquired by private operators and charities or leased to provide community support for offenders, ex-offenders and other women in need of help and guidance and mentoring.

All of these areas will, of course, benefit from further research and analysis. The opportunity cost alone of wasted resources must be immense. The discrepancies in the data available are sometimes frustrating and contradictory but there are some clear messages. More needs to be done and soon to ensure that reforms to the justice system begin with looking at the evidence available and end with savings to society. The following chapters look at some of this evidence and suggest where some of the attention for reform should be focused.

CHAPTER 8

WHY PRISON IS NOT A DETERRENT FOR CRIME

The theory of deterrence is based upon the idea that offenders rationally calculate the potential benefits of committing a crime, and then weigh them against any possible punishment they might receive, to decide whether the risk is 'worth it'. In reality, this presumes that crime is the result of rational decision making. Actually, we need to consider the concept of 'deterrability', in effect, the offender's capacity (or willingness) to think through the process. Many crimes are carried out 'in the heat of the moment', without much time to think of the potential consequences. Some are a product of risk taking or thrill seeking. Many offenders lack the cognitive skills to think through the consequences. Indeed, 40 per cent of women prisoners are classed as learning disabled or bordering upon having a learning disability, which could affect their decision-making abilities in various ways.[146]

More than this, we need to consider the possibility, at first counter-intuitive to those of us who usually obey the law, that punishment actually leads to more crime. Findings are at best mixed as to whether legal sanctions reduce, increase or have no effect on crime levels. Indeed, research suggests that a variety of other factors come into play in determining whether punishment acts as a deterrent, including the individual's drug or alcohol use, their decision-making capacity, their natural level of impulsivity, and the extent to which they feel connected to society as a whole, not to mention an array of different situational factors and circumstances that make offending more or less likely. As one review concludes: 'After careful perusal of the literature, one cannot but be struck by the fact that the effect of sanctions or sanction threats is far from homogenous and depends on several other factors.'[147]

Academia has provided us with a number of possible explanations of why punishment may lead to increased offending for some people. Labelling theory, for example, suggests that the criminal justice system as a whole is deeply stigmatising and may lead to increased offending by excluding people from society, preventing people with a criminal conviction from getting work or suitable housing, or more profoundly by altering how they see themselves.[148] Regarding the latter point, it is argued that if you tell someone often enough that they are 'bad', sooner or later they start to see this as a fundamental part of their identity. Labelling somcone a 'criminal' or an 'offender' can become a self-fulfilling prophecy. Meanwhile, using punishment to make offenders feel 'ashamed' of their behaviour could unintentionally reinforce the deeply felt sense of shame experienced by many offenders resulting from the various forms of childhood abuse they may have suffered. This reinforcement could worsen all sorts of mental and emotional health problems, substance misuse and other self-destructive behaviours. In addition, various programmes acknowledge the central role of shame in reinforcing the cycle of addiction. Dr Brené Brown, Professor of Social Work at the University of Houston, perhaps expresses it most succinctly: 'Shame corrodes the very part of us that believes we are capable of change.'

Similarly, 'defiance theory' suggests that offenders who feel excluded from, or unjustly treated by, wider society may actually be *more* likely to reoffend as a result of any punishment they have been given. The punishment may in effect reinforce the effects of previous experiences where they have felt victimised, unjustly or unfairly treated or denied opportunities available to others. This may be especially so if they feel that in their cases the correct legal processes have been ignored or the punishments given were 'unfair' in some way.

On the other hand, a punishment is more likely to prevent further offending for individuals who share a close bond with society and who generally have an otherwise positive relationship with the criminal justice system.[149] In essence, it seems that punishment works to deter those who are most likely to follow the law anyway. For those from deprived, chaotic or abusive backgrounds, however, punishment could actually serve to reinforce the very problems that lead to offending in the first place. In such situations, it is clear that a more constructive solution is required, where the offender is given the resources and support to turn their own life around.

So it would seem the formulation of punishing people to prevent further offending is not as straightforward as we would wish. Having said that, we do know that in general some interventions are more likely to deter crime than others. Research has repeatedly shown that longer sentences have no effect as a deterrent. Rather, it is an increased likelihood of actually being caught and receiving a punishment (of whatever harshness) that leads to lower crime rates.[150] If we are interested in evidence-based policy, the argument is clear: don't waste money on harsher sentences. Instead redeploy resources towards ensuring that the likelihood of being caught visibly increases. It is also worth noting, however, that increasing police numbers indiscriminately is unlikely to have an effect either, whereas 'specific, targeted and visible police work' may.[151] The implication here is that, in order for punishment to act as a deterrent, resources must be used intelligently and in a focused manner.

That is the theory but what about the practice? Clearly prison has little impact on repeat offenders who go in for short sentences. One senior civil servant, who had worked in the Home Office and had looked after prisons and sentencing policy, confirmed that when he was working on policy in the 1970s, the analysis of various experiments carried out at the time found that the propensity of people to reoffend was much the same, whatever the sentence they received – prison, probation, fine. That pointed to the desirability of the cheapest and least damaging sentencing policy. He recalls that when he worked for the Advisory Council on the Penal System, weekend imprisonment was discussed to avoid disrupting employment, as is done in other European countries such as the Netherlands. But the prison service was not keen on the idea because of the administration costs of managing a Friday arrival and Sunday departure. In our 24-hour, seven-days-a-week world it seems odd that a measure that would reduce costs to the taxpayer cannot be implemented because it does not fit in with existing staff shift patterns.

Ministers never like the 'soft' advice they receive. Then

as now there was an insatiable media-driven appetite for 'prison works' and 'tough on crime' slogans from politicians. Willie Whitelaw's 'short, sharp shock' was a classic of the kind. The theory is that by putting young offenders in a tough regime for a short period they would not wish to return to it. This idea was imported from the US (as is so much of the UK's approach to penal policy) but it produced no better outcome than any other sentencing options.[152] But, as the ex-Home Office official told me, the civil servants knew that the act made ministers and the tabloid newspapers feel better.

As with much to do with prisoners and the criminal justice system, public perception plays a part in hindering reform. Prison education for example is often depicted as a reward for criminal behaviour, rather than a service with a wider social benefit. And yet it is clear from research that any help, such as education while in prison but also on the outside, leads to improved chances of employability, cuts reoffending, reduces longer-term costs to the overall system and allows people to contribute properly to society. In a speech at a conference in 2012, Chris Grayling said that one third of all offenders leaving prison need help to find housing and half of them need help to find jobs.[153] That is a huge number of people considering there are nearly 200,000 admissions through the gates every year – admittedly many prisoners go through more than once.

Ministers are reluctant to tackle this view, but Frances Crook of the Howard League explained to me that strong leadership from above is needed to change attitudes and drive through reform. And therein lies the whole crux of the matter. The politicians want to be tough on crime but being tough on crime has resulted in an increase in the number of acts which are now classified as an offence and in longer sentences, which has only led to a huge increase in the number of people in jail. The number of people in jail has practically doubled over the last twenty years though this has been slightly reversed in the past two years.[154] Prison is an expensive place to send people and if you add the costs of the police investigations and CPS and court costs, it becomes even higher – and this increases still further once you start adding the indirect costs of the impact on the individual and society as a whole. And of course crime itself costs society a great deal. If prison does not act as deterrent for crime and does not reduce reoffending – which it seems not to have an impact on, in fact quite the reverse – then something needs to change.

But the perception, often encouraged by politicians of both the right and the left, is still, overwhelmingly, that prison works. In fact, the argument is being made that crime has gone down precisely because we are putting more people behind bars.[155] Indeed it is true that as the prison population doubled, crimes halved over the same period. Law and order 'enthusiasts' therefore argue that this demonstrates beyond reasonable doubt that in fact prison acts as a deterrent – in other words that crime has fallen because we have put more people in prison. But that would be wrong. As I discuss, no study has shown a significant causative link between prison numbers and a fall in overall crime – of course there are specific areas where police activity if targeted can have a big impact. But in general, as Nick (now Lord) Stern told me, causality between crime and punishment is tenuous at best and the deterrent element of a sentence has very little influence on crime. What matters are other things.

One is the economic environment – the better the economy is doing and the more people are employed, the less incentive there is to commit a crime. And indeed, the drop in crime occurred during the past two decades in a period of fast growth. During the recession that followed in 2008, one would have expected crime to rise but unusually for a period of decline and then stagnation employment levels have remained higher than expected and this probably accounts for some of the reason why the rise in crime didn't happen.

A second reason, as Nick Ross explains in his book *Crime*, is technology. Investment in smarter tills has reduced levels of theft; car security and new designs, for example better car locks, trackers, no removable radios, have helped car crime figures drop. House burglaries are falling because insurance companies now insist on window locks before they insure a property.

Another factor is demographics. Most crimes are committed by those aged sixteen to twenty-four; the peak age for offending is in fact twenty-four. If that age group becomes smaller, or grows less rapidly, then this leads to a declining trend. Crime, unlike other vices, seems to decline with age.

The long prison sentences prescribed to offenders – in an effort to placate public opinion, which is in turn fuelled by the media – makes very little difference to those taking the decision to commit a crime. People ask themselves few questions before committing an offence, except one: will I be caught?

So if prison does not work, either as a deterrent for crime or as a means of reducing reoffending, then it cannot be fit for purpose. So what does work?

CHAPTER 9

WHY EDUCATION AND EMPLOYMENT MATTER

When looking at the costs of keeping people in prison I stressed that one way of reducing reoffending and hence further costs to society was through education and employment. I saw the desire of girls to educate themselves while in ESP, their frustration when they were not able to do the courses they wanted or had to repeat what they had done before because they had moved to a prison which was under a different education contractor. I witnessed their excitement at passing tests and the difference in mental attitude and ambition for the future that acquiring a job while in prison, whether as a volunteer or on a paid basis, made. Their whole attitude changed and their outlook on life was dramatically altered. One day they were fidgeting, worrying about what would happen to them next and the following day their eyes were shining at the pleasure of having succeeded in an interview and securing a job that might transform their lives. It didn't always work that way, and there were disappointments, but the opportunities given were certainly better than the alternative.

Indeed many of the inmates I met in Holloway and ESP needed basic numeracy and literacy skills and had clearly already been failed by the education system when on the outside. In my view they needed to be properly looked after while in prison to help them become more employable, prevent reoffending and therefore serve society more effectively. And given its importance, education should not be an 'earned' privilege but part of the rehabilitation package. And women should be, as at least they were in ESP, paid the same 'prison wage' for being in education as they would if they were working, therefore providing an incentive for the women to learn. Education really made a difference to the women at ESP. I saw nothing more moving than a forty-year-old lifer coming out of a classroom and shouting at the top of her voice for all to hear that she got fifty out of fifty in verbal reasoning. That really showed the role learning can play in building self-esteem.

Rod Clark, a former civil servant and now the head of the Prisoners Education Trust, whose purpose it is to support prisoners to rehabilitate through learning, is vociferous about the importance of education. In 2012, the trust received 3,180 applications from offenders for distant-learning courses and approved and hence enabled 1,889 of those applications to access funding to study 408 different subjects varying from the basic to the more advanced.[156] In Rod Clark's view, the evidence overwhelmingly demonstrates that education is a better route to reintegrate offenders into society because it drastically improves the chances of finding a job. In addition, as the Corston Report has emphasised, women in particular also urgently need help with certain life skills because of the higher prevalence of substance abuse, mental health problems and domestic responsibilities among them, as well as the effects of domestic violence.

Responsibility for the budget for prison education transferred to the Department for Education and Skills (DfES) in 2001. But this shuffling of responsibility from one building in Whitehall to another only added to confusion as there was no overall strategy because it wasn't clear who would be leading progress. The creation of the National Offenders Management Scheme (NOMS) in 2004, which was supposed to be responsible for offenders and their rehabilitation throughout their sentence, further exacerbated this confusion. Among Whitehall staff, NOMS was soon known as Nightmare on Marsham Street, which is where the Home Office is based. Education services are now commissioned through the Skills Funding Agency's Offender Learning and Skills Service (OLASS), which spends over £100m each year. The responsibility has now transferred to the Department for Business, Innovation and Skills (BIS), for which I worked until late 2010. Whatever its imperfections, a report on education and crime, which looked at the cost effectiveness of education, found educational interventions provided value for money and had a very positive impact upon offenders.[157] What this study did was look at a cohort of male offenders given custodial sentences in 2005 and the impact of educational and vocational courses on reoffending. The estimates of the benefits they came up with were substantial. Provision of education for that particular cohort was estimated to reduce the £2bn of total reoffending costs to society in the first year post release by 25 per cent. The studies they used suggest that prison education and vocational interventions can produce a net benefit to the public sector of between £2,000 and £28,000 per offender and the estimated net savings to society when victim costs are included are between £10,500 and £97,000 per offender.

The authors of the report point out the studies undertaken by the Matrix Knowledge Group, which formed the basis for this work, are by no means definitive but do nevertheless suggest that the return can be significant. Interestingly, the studies were all based in the US and there is an urgent need to assess whether the benefits are as high (or higher) in the UK. The methodology used was to construct an economic model built upon the review of the effectiveness of the educational and vocational interventions in prison in terms of the resultant short-term change in offending and then to extrapolate the change in reoffending over the lifetime of the offender and value the saving in terms of both public sector and victim costs. A spokesperson for the charity Prisoners Education Reform tells me that the procedures the MoJ have now developed to analyse levels of prisoners' subsequent reoffending via their own 'Justice Data Lab', which should provide a mechanism for testing the impact of statutorily funded prison education programmes in the UK; a very welcome move. Whichever way you calculate it the savings can be significant and the return on the £100m which BIS spends every year on prisoners' education can be enormous.

Education is also a crucial factor in preventing first-time offences. The 2005 report on prison education urges the government to 'focus on improving education provision for the almost 50 per cent of students who do not achieve 5 A–Cs at GCSE, and particularly the 5 per cent that leave school without any GCSEs'.[158] As this group has a much higher likelihood of entering the criminal justice system, interventions in early years are shown to have a bigger effect than interventions in teenage years once a student is already failing. MoJ statistics on newly sentenced prisoners suggest that more than half of male prisoners and two thirds of female prisoners have no qualifications at all, and a large percentage had been unemployed before they entered prison.[159] Perhaps some of the budget currently spent on prisons would be of more use if it were spent on educating young people, therefore reducing the chances of offending in the first place.

The most important purpose of funding education is to increase the chance of securing a job. The correlation between not having a job and committing a crime is very strong. The general economic argument on how education may affect crime is as follows: there are 'income effects', in other words as education increases the amount one can earn, a) it makes it less likely that one will go needy and therefore feel the need to commit a crime and b) crime tends to reduce its attractiveness as there is more to lose if one gets caught committing a crime – although one caveat of course is that the opportunity to commit white-collar crime increases. But in truth many petty crimes are committed by people in poverty or on low incomes. A second point is that young people do not tend to think about the long term and instead aim to satisfy their short-term needs. This is particularly the case for young people who leave education early; the earlier they enter a world based on employment the more likely they are to commit an offence. In economic jargon they have a

very high discount rate, in other words they discount
the future heavily and so are more likely to undertake
risky behaviour such as crime, because they can't or
won't think about the consequences.

Academic research also suggests that higher levels of
education tend to reduce crime and can not only yield
a significant benefit to society but can be a key policy
tool for achieving reductions in crime rates. The UCL
and LSE academic economist Steve Machin worked
with colleagues to link crime data from the Offenders
Index database to education data from the annual
Office for National Statistics General Household
Survey. Their conclusions are very interesting: for every
10 per cent increase in the average school leaving age
convictions drop by 2.1 per cent. Further still, every
1 per cent reduction in the proportion of people with
no qualifications would yield economic benefits of
between £23m and £30m a year after ten years.[160] It is
not hard to see that savings can be substantial and run
into the hundreds of millions of pounds if the target of
improving qualifications is set a bit higher.

But getting jobs so that the income earned starts
to make people less likely to want to tempt fate and
offend requires both knowledge and other employability skills. There is little opportunity to exercise
the key skills that employers value such as communication skills and a demonstrable work ethic and, as
offenders become institutionalised, their skills subside
still further and their chance of future employment
inevitably recedes.

Giving people the skills to be re-employed and
reduce reoffending is a no-brainer but the quality of
education can make a difference. Rightly, in my view,
over the last decade the emphasis has shifted from

simply providing 'basic skills' to those that help with 'employability', but some critics suggest this neglects broader holistic education objectives that contribute to a person's rehabilitation, contribution to society and desistance from crime.

Barriers to successful education programmes include overcrowding and constant transfers between prisons. I heard of many cases where a prisoner was not able to finish a course they were very keen on because they were suddenly transferred elsewhere where that course was no longer available or, even if it was, files did not transfer with them or there was a different contractor and they had to start again – sometimes many times over. This is particularly the case for women as there are few women's prisons around and a move may mean going to a completely different area many hundreds of miles from where they were before and under a new service provider. There is also the problem that when they leave prison without having completed a course there isn't always the possibility to get the funding to finish it on the outside. Portable distance learning tailored to individual requirements as part of a package of learning is an obvious part of the solution. The use of ICT for online courses is another. One development has been to pursue the 'virtual campus' as a web-based resource allowing prisoners to continue education programmes in different locations, and into probation. After its trial, it is now being rolled out throughout the prison service. However, there seems to be little exploration of how education may cater for prisoners on short-term sentences, who are also most likely to reoffend. Finding a way to support the education of these women after release must be a priority.

The Prisoners Education Trust noted a reduction early in 2013 in applications from prisoners for degree courses completed through the Open University; if numbers continue to lower this would be a worrying development. Prisoners like everyone else have to apply for funding, which of course can be refused. The current attitude seems to be that vocational and degree courses should only be allowed if the prisoner is in sight of coming out of prison so they have a direct impact on their employability – this in my view makes sense for vocational courses but not for those that longer-term prisoners can benefit from, as Erwin James did while serving twenty years for two murder charges. After successfully completing distance learning courses funded by the Prisoners Education Trust, he has emerged as a writer, journalist and commentator and began contributing articles from the inside to *The Guardian* long before he was released. Under the current arrangements he would not have been able to undertake this study until the final years of his sentence.

So this trend needs to be watched. It would also be a shame if, because of budget constraints, there was to be a cut in the number of people who act as a link between the student in prison and the distance learning provider such as the Open University. Without that help undertaking such a course from prison, given the problems already in the system, becomes that much more difficult. BIS reassured me that while OLASS do not deliver higher education, they are obliged through their contracts in cooperation with the jail to facilitate and support learners who wish to study with the Open University and other institutions that provide distance learning. So while tutorial input is provided directly by peripatetic Open University tutors, the OLASS contractors are still expected to provide general mentoring and guidance to those wishing to take part in a higher education distance-learning course.

Prisoners may be reluctant to take higher education courses because of the high tuition fees. Access courses for prisoners preparing for higher education studies receive full funding from the Prisoners Education Trust (using funds supplied through a grant from BIS), which fully funds the costs of the Open University module, but prisoners then apply for tuition fee loans for the actual course they want to do on the same basis as everybody else. That saddles them with a loan; the spokesperson for the Prisoners Education Trust tells me that prison staff are in fact often reluctant to help prisoners acquire substantial student loan debt. And in any case it is more difficult in practice for inmates to organise such loans than for someone from the outside, and requires the prison, in cooperation with the OLASS contractor, to provide adequate access to IT.

The IT issue is a recurring theme. While I was in ESP I was struck by the unavailability of the internet – all that we could use were intranet sites or secure learning platforms such as those provided by the Open University. The lack of internet use was a great inhibitor to first, learning and second, the ability afterwards to reintegrate into society, especially for those who had a long sentence. I find it odd that in this day and age there can't be applications available that while still providing security nevertheless allow a prisoner to have access to what is out there both for educational purposes but also to ensure that they are then able to reintegrate with the community much more easily on release. The absurdity of the situation is made even starker when you realise that most open prison residents can access the internet anyway when on external visits or at work and it seems odd to deprive them of it in the few hours they are in prison.

But what would clinch the issue of the importance of education would be a proper econometric analysis that would prove 'beyond reasonable doubt' that education works in reducing offending, reoffending and cost to society. There are still difficulties. Analysis would be reliant on reported crimes only. Another problem is that data on crime statistics and educational outcomes is not generally held together in one place and therefore is not easy to match together to allow one to estimate the causal relation. The Ministry of Justice Data Lab proposal does provide a potential solution to this by matching data from education providers with offending data from the police national computer. The Prisoners Education Trust is currently working with the MoJ to assess the impact on reoffending of its provision of distance-learning programmes to prisoners. This is welcome but more progress is needed.

We know that education and higher skills increase the chances of employment which in turn should reduce reoffending. It sounds correct in practice but there is still some way to go to ensure the correlation is proven. What is emerging, though, is a link between employment and a reduction in reoffending.

A Ministry of Justice report looked at the impact (if any) that employment (measured by having a PAYE employment spell notified by a P45) has on reducing reoffending.[161] It compared the proven one-year reoffending rates for offenders who received a P45 denoting employment in the year following their release from custody with a matched comparison group of offenders with no P45 employment. For robustness of the analysis it minimised the differences it could find on the databases on other characteristics that might have explained different reoffending rates, though the possibility still exists that other non-recorded characteristics rather than employment may explain part of the reoffending rate differences. The exciting thing about this study is the way it used linked data from the MoJ's data linking project, which brings together data on offenders from across the criminal justice system, with data that tracks the employment and benefit status of offenders, including that from the DWP and HMRC. That allowed all sorts of things to be taken into account such as drug and alcohol misuse though this restricted the sample to data coming from 'OASys', the assessment system used by prisons and probation services to measure the risks and needs of offenders under their supervision. This also meant that the study only considered serious offenders whose attitudinal data is held on the system; in addition, low-paid people below the tax threshold and the self-employed were not included in the data. Also, given that in the report's terminology reoffending is measured as 'any offence committed in the twelve months after release from custody which receives a court conviction, caution, reprimand or warning in the twelve-month period or within a further six-month waiting period', it could be argued that there are likely to be many undetected or unrecorded offences which are by definition not picked up in the analysis.

Nevertheless, despite all these caveats, the study points to a number of statistically significant results which I quote below:

- Offenders who got a P45 form, a piece of paper that officially welcomes them back into employment at some point in the year after being released from custody, were less likely to reoffend than similar offenders who did not get P45 employment.
- For custodial sentences of less than one year, the one year proven reoffending rate was 9.4 percentage points lower for those who found P45 employment after release than for the matched comparison group.
- For sentences lasting one year or more, the one year reoffending rate was 5.6 percentage points lower for those who found P45 employment than for the matched comparison group.
- The time from release until the first reoffence was longer for offenders who got P45 employment than for the matched comparison group, who did not get P45 employment.

The study concludes that 'there are limitations to this analysis which are highlighted in this report. However, the magnitude of the estimates of the reduction in reoffending and their statistical significance, alongside the results of the sensitivity analysis we have conducted, means we are confident that P45 employment has a positive impact on reducing reoffending.'

This is all very encouraging. There is undoubtedly more work that needs to be done in the UK by using matched data to take this further and extend it to a wider range of offenders. But it is becoming increasingly clear that education and employment are key in achieving a reduction in reoffending. And yet the amount of effort made in this area is almost nonexistent. The MoJ has a prison budget of some £2.6bn year but only just under £100m is being spent on education, and very little on careers and employment help. Even in ESP, despite its positive approach to education and employment, women faced difficulties accessing paid jobs; while I was there the lady who was supposed to arrange interviews for residents to get jobs after they left prison was almost never available – I am sure for purely legitimate reasons – and many appointments were cancelled. And some girls reported that the ESP advisory office in the 'out of bounds' cabin made signing on at the Jobcentre seem an arduous task. I know of a number of women who didn't bother to sign on because of the advice they were given. Given the win-win scenario from providing education and support for employment for offenders, it makes no sense to discourage people from trying to find a job. Quite the opposite.

CHAPTER 10

ALTERNATIVES TO PRISON FOR WOMEN

On 19 June 2013, I received texts and calls from friends informing me that there was going to be a BBC Radio 4 *Woman's Hour* special on women offenders in advance of the justice committee's publication of their review of women in prison. One of the issues that would be discussed was alternatives to prison. I wondered whether they were going to cover at all the situation in other countries and draw comparisons. The statistics for and attitudes towards women in prison seem to vary greatly from country to country. I had been intrigued by attitudes in places like Italy where apparently there are very few women in prison as the belief is that they should not be separated from their children and they are instead put under what they call 'house arrest'. This is clearly not restricted to women as ex-Prime Minister Silvio Berlusconi at one point faced house arrest as well, in this case ostensibly because of his age, according to news reports.

Worldwide there are approximately 625,000 women and girls held in detention, including those convicted and those on remand, out of a total of about 10.1m prisoners serving sentences or in custody.[162] Of

these women about one third are in the USA. Out of
the total prison population, the median percentage
of women in prison worldwide is about 4.45 per cent,
with Africa generally being just under and Asia being
a bit over. There has been an increase in the number of
women in prison worldwide of 16 per cent since 2006,
particularly driven by the USA where there has been an
increase of 23 per cent. Europe as a whole has actually
had the lowest increase – only 6 per cent.[163]

While the collateral effects upon children of imprisoned mothers are felt throughout the world, there
is difficulty in making direct comparisons between
countries since information on whether a detainee has
dependants is not consistently checked throughout the
world, and when it is the information is often not very
transparent or reliable. However, in the USA, approximately 54 per cent of the prison population are
parents to a child under eighteen years old,[164] resulting
in somewhere between two and three million children
with a parent in jail.[165] Of these there is a huge racial
difference with one in fifteen Afro-American children having at least one parent in prison, compared
to one in 111 for white children.[166] In New Zealand
47 per cent of female prisoners had dependent children and 35 per cent were sole carers.[167] And in the EU
800,000 children are separated from an incarcerated
parent on any given day of the year.[168] And the data
for the UK is amazingly depressing. The female prison
population has increased hugely, partly because of
harder sentences and also partly because women tend
to break court orders – often given for offences that
carry no custodial sentence in the first instance – and
are then sent to prison. In many instances, the reason
for breaking probation or curfew has tended to be

related to providing care for their children, causing them to miss their court or probation appointment. Of course, fathers also care for children but, as one ex-prison governor remarked, it was telling that it was overwhelmingly women who were taken to court for not paying the household's television licence or for rent arrears or for their children's truancy. And of the children affected by their mothers being in prison, only 9 per cent are in fact cared for by their fathers while their mother is away. At least one third of the women in prison with children are lone parents by comparison to only 9 per cent for the population as a whole. And the number of children affected is huge. Figures for 2009 suggest that during that year some 200,000 children in England and Wales had at least one parent in prison at some point during the year, and this compares with just 64,999 children in care in that year and 36,610 on the Child Protection register. In one year, more than 17,240 children are believed to have been separated from their mother due to the mother being sent to prison.[169]

But some countries are seeking alternatives and in the Netherlands the number of community service sentences more than doubled between 1997 and 2007, moving from 14,485 to 32,590. A 2010 study in the Netherlands investigated the rates of recidivism of those sentenced to community service compared with short-term imprisonment of up to six months and found that for different crimes, and over different lengths of time after the sentence had been completed, the rate of reoffending for those who served on community service was lower than those who had been imprisoned.[170] The evidence from the UK paints the same picture: community services on average have lower rates of recidivism and of course cost a lot less by comparison to keeping people in prison. Even if community orders produced similar reoffending rates to custodial sentences they would be worth it for the lower cost alone.

One solution to the problem of family separation proffered is to attach women's units to men's prisons. Campaigners I spoke to worry that the disadvantages of this drastically outweigh the advantages. There has traditionally been very little women-specific training for officers. In East Sutton Park we were sharing the officers with HMP Blantyre for men. It was obvious when new officers would come or relief officers would arrive to fill in when ESP was short staffed during holidays that they had no experience of women's open prisons or of women themselves. They had little idea of the rhythms and specific needs of a group of incarcerated women. The example of Durham prison was mentioned to me by both a previous governor of a women's prison and an ex-probation officer. A women's unit was attached to Durham prison but women ended up being ignored and treated like second-class citizens. If there were staff shortages or trouble in the men's units, activities for women were just stopped. The unit has since closed.

Women's Breakout, a representative body of forty-seven women-centred services across the country which offer community alternatives to custody specifically designed for women, argues that in order to prevent and reduce crime committed by women, what works best are gender-specific approaches, which understand women's specific needs and are delivered by women-only community-based organisations. To me that seems so sensible but the rhetoric from the government continues to be very much a male-centred one not specifically designed for women or other 'minorities' – and women are a minority because of their small number in prison.

But what to do with women remains a real issue. The United Nations Rules for the Treatment of Women Prisoners and Non-custodial Measures for Women Offenders (also known as the Bangkok Rules) and the Human Rights Act, which the Conservative Party have said they will abolish if they win the next election, both dictate that the courts should take dependent children into account when sentencing. The various pressure groups claim that this is rarely done and the evidence I collected while in ESP would seem to confirm that. Debbie Cowley, who runs Action for Prisoners' Families, told me, 'One of the really important things about families of offenders is that their needs for help are caused by the actions of the state that send the mother (or father) to jail.' She argues that families are the main source of support for prisoners and cutting those ties makes little sense. Naturally, not all families are perfect but acknowledging the existence of the family unit and using it cleverly is something that should be duly considered when sentencing women offenders.

In a powerful article in the *New York Times* in August 2013, Piper Kerman, who herself served eleven months for a drug-related offence in prison, argued that women convicted of such offences should not be sent to prison. The immediate spur for her article was the decision of the American Federal Bureau of Prisons to close a women's prison facility close to New York and send women prisoners a thousand miles south to Alabama. Ms Kerman talked of a new programme under development called JusticeHome, which was started by the Women's Prison Association in New York City. It is aimed at allowing women offenders to stay in their homes with their children while under close supervision and receiving help from case managers in relation to jobs, education and parenting. It is estimated that this costs about $15,000, hugely less than it would cost to put them in prison for a year. It not only assists women to rehabilitate but also keeps the family together.[171]

It is encouraging to read such sensible arguments in the *New York Times* even if the cynic in me says that the chances of changing US penal policy are not high. But there is a strong argument that most women should not be in prison at all. I was pleased to hear Sir Alan Beith MP, the chair of the justice select committee, acknowledging on that *Woman's Hour* programme on 19 June that community sentences requiring women to attend community centres were a good alternative for women, who in general receive very short prison sentences because their crimes are usually petty. How many MPs or voters know that 50 per cent of female offenders have committed a crime on behalf of a partner, which is not at all the characteristic of a male offender? What is more, as we have seen, the benefits to society of not separating mothers from their children are immeasurable. In addition there are serious issues about the mental health of the women who end up losing their children, which in itself becomes a cost to society and to the economy.

Children are rightly seen in a social context. All prime ministers pledge 'family friendly' policies and since most are parents of young children their inclination to care for the most vulnerable in society should be well intended. Of late, there have been court cases involving celebrities accused of paedophile incidents. There have also been well-publicised court cases about gangs of men grooming young girls for prostitution. And one fact emerges again and again: it is children in care who are most at risk. It would seem logical to do all in our power to reduce the number of children taken into care yet every time a judge sends a mother to prison the statistics show that the chances of the children left parentless being taken into care are high. The court system is not divorced from wider society. A modernised system would invite the police and judges to consider the costs – both financial and social – when giving women either custodial or non-custodial sentences, and the resulting impact upon the children of those sentenced.

Alan Beith accepted that most women serving short sentences received no benefit at all from going to prison. They were given no education, no drug rehabilitation; they went straight back to the community from which they came with no money, often homeless; and they were likely to reoffend. He added that very short prison sentences do not help women whereas if you work with them in the community that can have an impact.

There is therefore a real reason to look at women as victims as well as offenders. As I have shown before, although a significant percentage of men report having been physically and emotionally abused when they enter prison, the percentage of women is far higher. But women are a minority – there is a relatively small number of them in prison, and the fear is that there will be less emphasis given in the future on their specific needs as they matter less in direct cost terms than men. But that, of course, misses the point. The indirect costs of keeping women in prison are immense. Ignoring women's needs makes no sense. Not surprisingly campaigners point to the lack of a legal requirement currently in the Offender Rehabilitation Bill to take the interests of women fully into account and have concerns that if this is still the case when it finally becomes an act there will be no guarantees at all that women's special needs will be recognised and properly addressed.

The Prison Reform Trust argues that since only 3 per cent of women prisoners are assessed as being a serious risk to the public the rest shouldn't be behind bars as it serves no social purpose except to appease populist demands for retribution. Indeed, in a pamphlet published by Lord Ashcroft, the influential Conservative donor and peer, entitled 'Crime, Punishment and the People', one reads the depressing assertion that 'even short sentences, though offering too little time for proper rehabilitation, give the public respite from the prolific offenders who commit the most crime'. Giving the public what they want not what they need is the mark of populist politics. The pamphlet makes the point that 'community sentences, the alternative to prison, command woefully little public support'.

This is hardly surprising if tabloid populism rather than rational policy drives the agenda. The zeal for retribution misses the point that most women offenders are victims as well as offenders and they have often offended precisely because they are victims. Former governors who spent most of their careers in men's prisons and then went to run a female prison spoke to me of their astonishment at what they found. Women in prison were vulnerable, in need of support, rarely the instigators of the offences they were alleged to have carried out and imprisoned because of the men in their lives. And the system had let them down by failing to recognise this.

The Women Offender Substance Abuse Programme (WOSAP) in Canada adopted a gender-specific strategy to help women with substance addictions and a moderate-to-high need for intervention. It was adopted in 2003 and by 2008 was shown to lower the likelihood of returning to custody. It was felt that this was particularly strong because of its multi-targeted approach and continuity of programmes. Post-release support (Community Relapse Prevention and Support) had a particularly pronounced effect showing that for those who received it there was only a 5 per cent return to custody, compared to a 38 per cent for those with no contact with the post-release programme.[172]

But although the data is there and campaigners go blue in the face repeating the facts about the pointlessness of locking up so many women, politicians have to be seen to be tough on crime whatever the outcome. But as Britain comes to grips with excess public spending perhaps better policy to protect the taxpayer can fuse with a more humane and smart politics on keeping women in prison. Ministers, if they are honest, know the money isn't there anymore. The huge expansion we have seen in the prison population of both men and women is against international trends at a time when crime is falling – at least as it is calculated as such – and the money is no longer there to keep so many people in jail.

So, for the moment at least, and for those men and women who don't pose a threat, community services or other types of non-custodial sentences which still require the offender to fulfil all sorts of conditions would seem to make a huge amount of sense from every possible angle – costs, links with family and community, work, all reduce reoffending in many cases. But selling it to the public is the hardest part of it. In order to appease this quest for retribution the politicians feel the need to demonstrate that punishment is very much part of the sentence. And that may be the undoing of any good efforts to improve the system and allow more women to stay out of prison.

Helen Grant, the justice minister at the time of writing with a responsibility for women's issues, talked in that same *Woman's Hour* interview of the need for community orders in addition to unpaid work and supervision. In fact, tagging is already given instead of a prison sentence in some cases and the courts have the power to impose all sorts of restrictions on the movement of offenders and place prohibitions on what they can do. Magistrates' courts tend to give community sentences and crown courts mostly custodial ones and there is a whole industry of organisations working on court diversion, i.e. keeping women in particular away from crown court and custodial sentences, which must be a good thing if it works. But I have been told of a number of instances where offenders (men and women) make it clear that they consider the community orders that might be imposed on them to be too onerous and they prefer to go to prison – whereupon the magistrates, if they think that the community orders are likely to be ignored, have no alternative but to send them to prison.

As Pat Carlen argues, because there are relatively small numbers of women in the criminal and penal systems, there is a narrower range of non-custodial facilities for women.[173] And whatever is imposed needs to be specific to individual cases. Curfews and tagging, particularly for vulnerable women, may mean that they cannot escape easily a violent or abusive man at night, adding to the chances of these women being recalled for breaching their community orders (only to escape their problems at home) and given a custodial sentence as a result for a crime that had not been considered appropriate for one in the first place. So the alternatives and guidelines given to courts will have to be thought out with care. It is very typical of policy makers to react instinctively to popular pressure without thinking of and assessing the unintended consequences of that policy.

Much will need to be improved to get to a better place in this area. As the *Woman's Hour* programme pointed out, at least when the judge imposes a custodial sentence he or she knows that there will be a van there waiting to take the offender to prison and the judge is safe in the knowledge that a place will be found nearby. In handing out a community sentence there is no guarantee that a community centre will exist and, if it does, what it is able to do. Magistrates also say that if they had a clear alternative that they believed in they would use it instead of a custodial sentence.

Yet the message that community orders are an easy option is perversely encouraged by ministers in their speeches. Speaking in the autumn of 2012, the prison minister Jeremy Wright attacked community orders; as he put it, 'one third of the orders have no punitive element included in them'. He announced a significant change in the guidelines to ensure that this was addressed. Maybe that is needed to change perceptions but it is difficult to change that view among the public if the minister himself suggests that community service is a soft option. And as most organisations that deal with these issues tell me, women doing community service are already hugely challenged: they also have to cope with their families, social services, housing issues, often drug rehabilitation as well as the educational challenges put on them by a community centre in the form of numeracy and literacy classes, parenting skills courses, assertiveness training, employability skills and the like. The result therefore is likely to be a perverse one as the more conditions are set the more likely the chance of them breaching some of the orders they are given increase considerably. If you add to this the extra pressures from cuts in legal aid budget and in the probation service and the reduction in flexibility of the system in terms of reporting and reacting to breaches of any orders, women are immediately put at greater risk of being sent to prison. A former probation officer told me that women usually breach conditions of bail or probation or miss a court appearance because of their children taking greater priority as they are often sole carers. But this could still be the best compromise one could reach at least to improve the women's lot and reduce the cost to society that normally wants retribution at any cost. Sadly we may not even get that far.

The public perception can be changed if the facts and the evidence are presented to them in an unbiased and reasoned way. A report produced in September 2011 on behalf of the charity Making Justice Work found that properly targeted community service orders made a huge difference. If they appropriately address the causes of offending they can effectively replace custody for those offenders and achieve a huge cost reduction for the community. But more importantly in the introduction to the report Peter Oborne, a political journalist and commentator not generally known for his left-wing views, states that 'I have always been uneasily aware that political correspondents such as myself report law and order issues in a false and often misleading way'. He acknowledges that one has 'to be a brave politician to take a liberal view on crime and punishment' but believes that there must be a deeper understanding of the truth about these issues, which are at present framed simply in terms of being 'tough' versus being 'soft' or 'weak' on crime. And one of the things that struck him first is that alternative options to prison, as they stood then, even before the planned changes announced by the current government, 'are not a soft option as so often portrayed'. He describes how a number of the offenders who were involved in this inquiry said to the team that it would have been much easier to have gone to prison for three months. He argued that while it is true that prisoners cannot commit crimes while they are in jail (at least not in the community; they can commit plenty in prison) prison does little to stop them reoffending (as said elsewhere, it may in fact encourage even more reoffending as it becomes an acceptable part of life) but that based on what he had seen 'they are far more likely to reoffend when they have served their term than those who have been given an alternative punishment'. He uses the example of a women's project in Bradford where the reoffending rate is down to between 5 and 10 per cent and the cost of helping one woman over twelve months, despite the extra services and support and intensive care given, is half what it would have cost to send her to prison for just three months.

Another report for the same charity, conducted by Matrix Evidence, part of the consultants Matrix Knowledge Group, touched on the cost-benefit of community service as against custody. It calculated the probability of young offender reoffending during what is known as Intensive Alternative to Custody orders (IACs), which combine community work and educational achievements with intensive probation supervision, to be 21.4 per cent. This compares with MoJ data that suggests that the probability of a young adult reoffending the year after they are released from custody is 58 per cent.[174]

As usual there are all sorts of issues with the data and the comparisons are not easy to make as there are differences in the data collection and the exact periods over which the reoffending is measured. One of the complications, as far as I can see, centres on the fact that community service data is collected on a case study basis and follows the offenders during the period that they are under their order whereas MoJ data looks at the probability of reoffending the year after release. Adjusting the calculations to be more in line with MoJ calculations of probabilities of offending in the year after release, using the MoJ compendium of reoffending statistics and looking at various different ways to adjust the data to be as consistent as possible with official statistics, Matrix came to the conclusion that community supervision orders probably reduce the reoffending rate by some 13 per cent and have used this to calculate the benefit.

Matrix calculates that providing intensive community orders for all eligible young adult offenders instead of custodial services would save some £500m over five years, which is huge. (Compare this with the proposal to cut winter fuel benefits for 115,000 British pensioners living in the Costa del Sol and other warm parts of Europe announced with great fanfare by George Osborne to save at most £30m per year.) These savings would reflect both the lower running costs and also the benefits to society from less reoffending. Matrix calculates that of the total savings £177m would be in what they term reduced costs of interventions; some £69m in reduced costs to the criminal justice system that will have to deal with fewer crimes; £29m of reduced costs to the NHS, which has to deal with all the mental health and other health issues connected to crime; and some £225m of reduced costs to the victims of crime. These costs are what Matrix calls 'real economic costs' that are completely avoidable. But there are other costs, too, like a policeman's time for example, which are called 'opportunity costs', in other words costs that will be no longer be required to be spent on issues connected with crime but can be spent more usefully elsewhere. Matrix estimates that the reduction in opportunity costs would save another £46m on top of the £500m.

We are of course talking here of a relatively small number of young offenders in prison, some 1,800. And yet the savings appear to be significant. If the majority of men and women on short sentences served non-custodial sentences, the savings could be enormous. And the indirect benefits in terms of all the other savings on crime and reoffending and families and employability would potentially be even greater.

In no way would I want to advocate that many men do not face similar issues to women. A number of them currently in prison are no threat to society, need help and should not be in jail. And a certain number are also prime carers; even if not many, they still very much want to keep in touch with their children. And the children benefit if they do. But the chances of becoming antisocial and resorting to crime seem to be higher for those children separated from their mothers.

The literature on women's vulnerability and the prevalence of victims among women offenders has been well documented in many reports, most notably in the Corston Report of 2007, which resulted in the funding of the first centre for women offenders and, in many cases, potential offenders. Women's Breakout, a representative body of forty-seven women-centred services across the country, which offer specific community alternatives to custody specifically designed for women, argues that in order to prevent and reduce crime committed by women what works best is gender-specific approaches, which understand women's specific needs and are delivered by women-only community-based organisations. Despite progress, funding for these centres in the future remains uncertain.

Indeed campaigners fear that the government's proposals to transform rehabilitation services – dubbed 'the Rehabilitation Revolution' – may mean that the centres could come under threat as changes to probation and rehabilitation services are made. This is a very urgent concern, since the centres are in a stage of relative infancy in demonstrating their effectiveness, and could in fact be rolled out further in future if they survive. One problem in evidencing their importance is that each is locally specific in its impact, and indeed many areas have no women's centre at all.

As such, the problem is not so much with sentencing law, but with the lack of alternative facilities and communication to those who pass the sentences about the benefits of gender-specific alternatives.

The recent report by the justice select committee on what has been done since the Corston Report argued that 'whilst reducing reoffending is one important goal, upstream diversion from offending and reduced frequency and seriousness of reoffending are also socially desirable outcomes which need to be valued by the criminal justice system'.[175] But they also argued that getting proper evidence of the impact of the centres is difficult because they are still so new. In addition to this, the committee concluded that 'the Ministry of Justice has failed systematically to collect information required to determine effectiveness. Data from individual projects indicates a strong impact, but because they are not comparable results there is no ability to determine and disseminate best practice.'[176]

But the evidence, such as it is, is nevertheless encouraging. As Roma Hooper of Make Justice Work stressed in her submission to the justice select committee's inquiry on women in the justice system: 'There should be a greater use of robust and demanding community sentences as an alternative to short-term prison sentences for lower level offences committed by women offenders.' In her view the government urgently needed to produce a strategy with the aim of reducing the number of women in custody, to ensure proper coordination across all government departments – not just the Ministry of Justice – with clear ministerial responsibility, accountability and a timetable for action.

So, coordination is an issue. No one any longer

seems to care about the overall impact of policy outside their tight departmental budgets. However difficult they were, I long for the return of a system of cross-departmental policy targets that force departments to work together – and for the targets to be better enforced than before so they aren't ignored. During the last parliament under Labour the government introduced a series of thirty public service agreements (PSAs) in their manifesto, which were meant to define the overall targets of the government during a single parliament, though some were meant to be achieved over the longer term – such as child poverty and energy – but with intermediate targets set along the way. When it came to power, however, the coalition government did away with this process.

In my view the removal of these PSAs accounts for some of the lack of coordination between departments, which has an effect upon the policies geared towards offenders. PSAs required close cooperation across departments, each one having to deliver part of the PSA target so that it could be achieved. It brought in some collective responsibility, in theory at least and in many cases also in practice. And the cooperation and achievements were in fact monitored by a division within the Treasury run by an ex-private sector senior official.

Each PSA was given to a director general who had to put together a board with similarly highly graded DGs from other contributory departments which had a stake in that target. This has now been lost and one of the problems when making the overall case for prison reform more generally and for women in particular, which is indisputable in terms of the wider benefits it might bring, is that there is no longer any real incentive for, say, the Department of Health to think about the impact of their actions on crime rates as this does not form part of their direct responsibility.

PSA 24 was to 'deliver a more effective, transparent and responsive criminal justice system for victims and the public'.[177] I wonder how many people knew this and what difference it actually made in the end. But whatever the PSA framework achieved, it must be better than no coordination at all, which is the impression one gets at times now. And it shows. The July 2013 justice select committee report on the progress on women issues since the Corston Report confirmed the need for coordination when it said:

> We were particularly struck by Baroness Corston's evidence that under the previous government it was not until a group of women ministers worked together to take issues forward that significant progress was made in this area. We welcome the fact that, after we announced our inquiry, the Secretary of State for Justice assigned particular ministerial responsibility for women offenders. Clear leadership and a high level of support from other Ministers will be essential in restoring lost momentum.[178]

I am completely in agreement with this. Everything I have seen and heard tells me that women are regarded as a minority that has to be dealt with but that the decision makers have little understanding of how to address the issues that affect women to ensure less cost to society in the wider sense. It isn't just a question of empathy or moral prerogative – although these things matter. What we need is a thorough look at the facts and, as it emerges, ensure that wherever possible any good practice also applies to men too where the gains might be even greater in terms of over-all numbers. But unless there is a drive from the top the current structure of responsibilities for our prison system will fail to address women's needs properly. Lord Ramsbotham spoke to me of the need to create a Women's Justice Board along the lines of what he perceives as a very effective Youth Justice Board for young offenders to drive change. In his view, 'much misery for women would have been avoided' if such a board had been set up. He is encouraged, however, by the fact that after twelve to fourteen wasted years, during which little progress has been made, Sadiq Khan, the shadow justice minister, has finally called for such a board to be set up. I must admit I was never a great believer that just getting the right structure to deal with an issue is the answer as often bodies are formed to placate campaigners. They tend to create bureaucracy but no real intelligent action. But better to have tried and failed than not tried at all. And the issue is too big and the cost to society too large for things to be left as they are.

My journey into the world of women in prison was never intended. But what happened happened. I have learned far more about how the state apparatus works than I knew from my time in government. Sadly the higher up the hierarchy you go the more uncaring powerful people can be. I found those at the bottom, the prisoners, the prison staff, the marvellous people who campaign for reform and help with reintegration, to have warmth, humanity and sheer British decency that reminds me why I love my adopted country. This book is a modest contribution to a bigger debate. If it helps persuade one person in power to understand why sending so many women to prison is a counter-productive waste it will have served its purpose. If the book encourages one employer to hire a woman who has left prison, I will be delighted. The book places on record my admiration for those who work in the world of prison reform and who help women enjoy fulfilled lives after prison. The criminal justice and prison system is devised by men, run by men and does a great disservice to British women. One day the other half of the population will have prosecutors, judges and a sentencing and prison regime that moves beyond retribution and contributes to rather than subtracts from society.

THANKS AND ACKNOWLEDGEMENTS

In the process of writing this I have been particularly lucky to have spoken to Jenny Earle at the Prison Reform Trust; Deborah Coles from Inquest; Rachel Halford from Women in Prison; Yvonne Roberts, trustee of Women in Prison; Roma Hooper at Make Justice Work; Jackie Russell at Women's Breakout; Debbie Cowley and Clare Dean at Action for Prisoners' Families; Rod Clark and Nina Champion at the Prison Education Trust; Frances Crook at the Howard League for Penal Reform; Sir Gerry Acher, previously with the KPMG Foundation; Matthew Taylor and Rachel O'Brien at the RSA; Liz Padmore of the Hampshire Hospital NHS Trust; David Elliott and Gill Arupke at Penrose; ex-Holloway probation officer Liz Hogarth; ex-Chief Inspector of Prisons Lord Ramsbotham; the current Chief Inspector of Prisons, Nick Hardwick; Baroness Corston, who produced the seminal Corston Report on Women in the Judicial System; Baroness Whitaker of the Design Commission, who introduced us and sent me the Corston Report to whet my appetite for all this while I was in prison; Tony Hassall, ex-governor of Holloway; Clive Chatterton, ex-governor of Styal prison; ex-offenders Mark Leech and Erwin James, both now celebrated writers and commentators who were extremely kind to me and encouraging on release.

From the academic side, Nicola Padfield at Fitzwilliam College, Cambridge; Professor Loraine Gelsthorpe at the Institute of Criminology in Cambridge; and Lord Stern at the London School of Economics, in many ways an inspiration to me, who helped me in my search for arguments against prison as a deterrent. I am grateful to Sir Brian Bender, Mark Gibson, Ian Jones, Claire Durkin, Richard Price, Carole Willis, Mark Conaty, Jonathan Portes, Andy Ross, Bill Jeffrey and Joan McNaughton, all ex-civil servants who gave me some wonderful insights and also great support. Also, Tory Rothschild at Give a Book; Edwina Grosvenor at Clink; and Antony Oering, now chaplain at Ford Open. And then, of course, James Timpson, who enthused me with his very generous and positive attitude towards employing ex-offenders and who furnished me with a huge number of contacts; and Jocelyn Hillman, Ondine Upton and the entire team at Working Chance, the charity that specialises in finding quality employment for women offenders and ex-offenders, who have not only helped me with the research but also invited me, while I was still in prison, to become their patron – which of course I have accepted.

I am also grateful to the prison staff and the chaplains, in both Holloway and ESP, who made 'an unbearable situation almost bearable'; my fellow residents for their kindness and friendship; and those friends on the outside who have since helped me return to some sort of 'normality' while giving me their unconditional support. George and Ann Courmouzis, and Lydia and Takis Argyropoulos have been a great source of strength for me, as have Stephanie and Philip Maltman; David and Lisa Buchan; Boni Sones; Christos Pitelis; Jenny and Arthur Beesley; Chris Pryce and Janet Payne; Jane and Mike Cooke; David and Jessica Fletcher; Sarah Webb; Ed Beesley; Rob Toogood; Joyce Acher; Kate Barker; Luisa Affuso; Mike Bottomley; Alexandra Shulman; Jane Atkinson; Michael Littlechild; Geik Chew; Martin Deutz; Guy Warrington; Alexis Konstas; Monica Clancy; Elisabeth Kelly; Rupert Dove-Meadows; Merelina Dipack-White; Gil Duff; Catherine Roche; Nick Butler and Rosaleen Hughes; John Gieve; Mike Jeans; Jamie Stevenson; Roger and Belinda Hood; Kitty Ussher; Geoff and Melanie Llewellyn; Peter Bottomley; Gill King; Leslie Johnson; Alan Johnson; Tony Halmos; Alex Kedros; Alex Jan; Nikos Sideris; Kate Winn; Mandy Hutley; Gordon Stoker; Sue Owen; Andrew Hilton; David Marsh; Bronwen Maddox; Patricia Hewitt; Serena Simmons; Yasmin Alibhai-Brown; Satjit Singh; Ian Bonny; Noorzaman Rashid; Alan Broomhead; Patrick Chapman; Liz Walker; David Peregrine-Jones; Barbara Linder; Betty and Chris Sanders; Neil Williamson; Brian Parry; Gordon Dickerson; Phil and Gill Sutcliffe; Nick Talbot; Julia King; Leo Martin; Tay Cheng-Jim; Karen Dunnell; Suzie Funell; Sarah Green; Anthony Elliott; Janet Paraskeva; Jon Duke-Evans; Dan Corry; Rebecca Harding; Stefan Stern; Kathy Newman; Becky Milligan; Neil Sherlock; Romilly Weeks; Tim Leunig; Robert Chote; Richard Portes; Abhinay Muthoo; Flavia Lambert; Natalie Pham; Eleni Meleagrou; Don

Stillman; Paul Lejot; Catherine Donelly; Rosamund Urwin; Guy de Jonquieres; Diane Fortescue; Hamish McRae; Richard Davies; David Campbell; Neil Lerner; Colin MacCabe; Kate Aan de Weil; Martin Donnelly; Alan Budd; Joanna Donaldson; Heather Stewart; Lucy Thomas; Graham Haache; Andy Haldane; David Penfold; Marjan and Robert Johnson; Andrew Smith; Marcus Miller; Costas Meghir; Katerina, Louis, Peter, Melina and Elisabeth Georgantas; Rachel Cable; Pippa Oakeshott; Patty Hemingway; George Houpis; Lina Talka; Simon Walker; Mary Strang; Phil Stephens; Fiona Woolf; Polly Toynbee; Stephen and Celia Glover; David Walker; Steve Jones and Norma Percy; Denise Kingsmill; Dave Ramsden; Debbie Stedman-Scott; Louka Katseli; Tony Burke; Neil Acheson; Marian Bell; Isabel Hilton; Geoff Reid; Ed Mayo; Bridget Rosewell; Daisy Fletcher; Mark Boleat; Alison Sprague; Mike and Jill Toogood; Ava Alleyne; Kristiina Reed and Ed Sankey; and the Biteback team, among many others.

Most importantly my children and their own families, whose love and support were the only thing that kept me (semi) sane throughout. I can only hope that this book gives something back by contributing positively to the debate and helping to ease the condition of so many women – and many men – who should at this moment not be in jail but either at home with their families or being properly looked after by social and health services in their communities.

Last and certainly not least, a big thank-you to Chris Osborne, who trusted me throughout this process, and to Robert Brown, my solicitor.

NOTES

1   Berman, G., Prison Population Statistics SN/SG/4334, 28 June 2013.
2   Social Exclusion Unit report, 'Reducing Reoffending by Ex-prisoners', July 2002.
3   Prison Reform Trust, 'Justice for Women: the Need for Reform', 2000.
4   HM Inspectorate of Prisons, 'Women in Prison', Home Office, Research Study 208, 2005.
5   Corston, J., 'The Corston Report', Home Office, 2007.
6   Ibid.
7   O'Brien, M. et al., 'Psychiatric Morbidity among Women Prisoners', Office for National Statistics, 1997.
8   Ibid.
9   Corston, J., 'The Corston Report', Home Office, 2007.
10   Hughes, M., 'Quarter of UK population will be on new police database', *Telegraph* online, 17 June 2011.
11   'Clegg "not proud" of conviction', BBC News online, 19 September 2007.
12   Ministry of Justice, 'Criminal Justice Statistics Quarterly Update to December 2012', 30 May 2013.
13   Farrington, D. P. et al., 'Criminal Careers and Life Success: New Findings from the Cambridge Study in Delinquent Development', Findings 281, Home Office, 2006.
14   Wallerstein, J. S. and Wyle, C. J., 'Our Law-abiding Law-breakers', *Probation*, 1947, 25: 107–112.
15   Short, J. F. and Nye, F. I., 'Extent of Unrecorded Juvenile

Delinquency: Tentative Conclusions', *Journal of Criminal Law, Criminology and Police Science*, 1958, 49: 296–302.

16   Office for National Statistics, 'Crime in England and Wales, Year Ending December 2012', 18 July 2013.

17   Ministry of Justice, 'Criminal Justice Statistics Quarterly Update to December 2012', 30 May 2013.

18   Ministry of Justice, 'Offender Management Caseload Statistics 2009', 22 July 2010.

19   Howard League for Penal Reform, 'Revealed: the magistrates' courts most likely to send women to prison', press statement, 9 July 2013.

20   Jewkes, Y., *Media and Crime*, London: Sage, 2004, p. 109.

21   Liebling, A., assisted by Arnold, H., *Prisons and their Moral Performance: A Study of Values, Quality and Prison Life*, Oxford: Oxford University Press, 2004.

22   Ministry of Justice, 'Safety in Custody Statistics 2008–09', 11 February 2010.

23   Ministry of Justice, 'Safety in Custody Statistics: Update to December 2012', 25 April 2013.

24   Ramsbotham, D., *Prisongate: The Shocking State of Britain's Prisons and the Need for Visionary Change*, London: Free Press, 2003.

25   Gesch, C. B. et al., 'Influence of Supplementary Vitamins, Minerals and Essential Fatty Acids on the Anti-social Behaviour of Young Adult Prisoners', *British Journal of Psychiatry*, 2002, 181: 22–28.

26   Crisci, A., 'The Prison Restaurant: More than just bread, water and porridge', BBC Food Blog, 25 April 2011.

27   Ministry of Justice, 'Costs per place and costs per prisoner by individual prison', NOMS Annual Report and Accounts 2011–2012, Management Information Addendum, 25 October 2012.

28   Hales, L. and Gelsthorpe. L., *The Criminalisation of Migrant Women*, Cambridge: Institute of Criminology, University of Cambridge, 2012.

29   Ministry of Justice, 'Prison Population Tables Q1 – January to March 2013', 2013.

30   O'Brien, M. et al., 'Psychiatric Morbidity among Women Prisoners', Office for National Statistics, 1997.

31   Edgar, K. et al., *Out for Good: Taking Responsibility for Resettlement*, Prison Reform Trust, 2012. See also Crewe, B., 'Prisoner Society in the Era of Hard Drugs', *Punishment and Society*, 2005, 7(4): 457–481.

32   O'Brien, M. et al., 'Psychiatric Morbidity among Women Prisoners', Office for National Statistics, 1997.

33   Ministry of Justice, 'Reoffending of adults: results from the 2008 cohort', 18 March 2010.

34   Ministry of Justice, 'Offender Management Caseload Statistics 2011', cited in Bromley Briefings, Prison Reform Trust, November 2012.

35   Williams, K. et al., 'Prisoners' Childhood and Family Backgrounds', Ministry of Justice, March 2012.

36   Soroptimist International, 'Reducing Women's Imprisonment', Prison Reform Trust, 25 April 2013.

37   Devlin, A., *Invisible Women: What's Wrong with Women's Prisons?*, Winchester: Waterside Press, 1998.

38   Ministry of Justice NOMS, Equalities Annual Report 2011/12, 25 October 2012.

39   La Plante, L., 'Vicky Pryce in prison: "If she keeps her head down, she'll be fine"', *Telegraph* online, 16 March 2013.

40   HM Inspectorate of Prisons, 'Women in Prison', Home Office, Research Study 208, 2005.

41   Home Office, 'Imprisoned Women and Mothers', Home Office, Research Study 162, 1997.

42   Taylor, R., 'Women in Prison and Children of Imprisoned Mothers: Preliminary Research Paper', Quaker United Nations Office, July 2004, p. 34.

43   Prison Reform Trust, 'Reforming Women's Justice – Final Report of the Women's Justice Taskforce', 2011, p. 11.

44   HM Inspectorate of Prisons, 'Women in Prison', Home Office, Research Study 208, 2005.

45   Department for Education, 'Children Looked After by Local Authorities in England Year Ending 31 March 2011', 28 September 2011.

46   Social Exclusion Unit report, 'Reducing Reoffending by Ex-prisoners', July 2002.

47   See: Howard League for Penal Reform, 'Voice of a Child', 30 September 2011.

48   New Economic Foundation, 'Unlocking Value: How We All Benefit from Investing in Alternatives to Prison for Women Offenders', 2008.

49   Murray, J. and Farrington, D. P., 'Parental Imprisonment: Effects on Boys' Antisocial Behaviour and Delinquency through the Life Course', *Journal of Child Psychology and Child Psychiatry*, 2005, 46(12): 1269–78.

50   Corston, J., 'The Corston Report', Home Office, 2007.

51   Morris, A. et al., *Managing the Needs of Female Prisoners*, cited in Devlin, A., *Invisible Women*, p. 19.

52   HM Chief Inspector of Prisons for England and Wales, Annual Report 2011–12, HM Inspectorate of Prisons, 17 October 2012.

53   HM Chief Inspector of Prisons for England and Wales, Annual Report 2011–12, HM Inspectorate of Prisons, 17 October 2012.

54   Written evidence submitted to the Select Committee on Home Affairs, 'Measuring the Quality of Prison Life', fifth supplementary memorandum by HM Prison Service, Home Office, June 2004.

55   Crewe, B. et al., 'Staff Culture, Use of Authority and Prisoner Quality of Life in Public and Private Sector Prisons', *Australian and New Zealand Journal of Criminology*, 2011, 44(1): 94–115.

56   HM Inspectorate of Prisons, 'Report on an announced inspection of HMP East Sutton Park 21–25 November 2011', Ministry of Justice, 2012.

57   Ministry of Justice report cited in Fradd, A. et al., *Managing Together: Improving Prisoners' Family Ties*, London: New Philanthropy Capital, 2011.

58   Celinska, K. and Sung, H., 'Gender Differences in the Determinants of Prison Rule Violations', *The Prison Journal*, Issue 207, 2013.

59   National Offender Management Service, 'Reducing Re-offending, National Action Plan', Home Office, 2006.

60   Robertson, O., 'The Impact of Parental Imprisonment on Children', Quaker United Nations Office, April 2007, p. 44.

61   Report quoted in: May, C. et al., 'Factors Linked to Reoffending: A One-year Follow-up of Prisoners who Took

Part in the Resettlement Surveys 2001, 2003 and 2004, Ministry of Justice Research Summary 5, 2008.

62 Estep, B. and Nicholles, N., 'Economic Study of Integrated Family Support Programme (IFS)', nef consulting, 2012, p. 14.

63 Wedderburn, D., 'Justice for Women: The Need for Reform – The Report of the Committee on Women's Imprisonment', Prison Reform Trust, 2000, p. 9.

64 Social Exclusion Unit report, 'Reducing Reoffending by Ex-prisoners', July 2002.

65 HM Inspectorate of Prisons, 'Women in Prison: A Short Thematic Review', July 2010, p. 63.

66 Hansard HC, 7 January 2010, c. 548w and 25 November 2009, c. 238w.

67 Social Exclusion Unit report, 'Reducing Reoffending by Ex-prisoners', July 2002.

68 Anderson, S., 'Summing Up: Revolving Doors Agency's Key Learning 2000–2009', Revolving Doors Agency, August 2010.

69 HM Inspectorate of Prisons, 'Women in Prison: A Short Thematic Review', July 2010, pp. 14, 65.

70 The Howard League for Penal Reform, 'Voice of a Child', 2011, p. 13.

71 Ibid.

72 HM Inspectorate of Prisons, 'Women in Prison', Home Office, Research Study 208, 2005.

73 Ministry of Justice, 'Offender Management Statistics Quarterly Bulletin, April to June 2010', 28 October 2010.

74 Ministry of Justice, 'Prison Population Tables Q2 – April to June 2013', 2013.

75 Citizens Advice Bureau, 'Locked Out: CAB Evidence on Prisoners and Ex-offenders', March 2007.

76 Devlin, A., *Invisible Women: What's Wrong with Women's Prisons?*, Winchester: Waterside Press, 1998.

77 Ministry of Justice, 'Offender Management Statistics Quarterly Bulletin, April to June 2012', cited in Bromley Briefings, Prison Reform Trust, November 2012, p. 22.

78 Ruthven, D. and Seward, E., *Restricted Access: Legal Information for Remand Prisoners*, London: Prison Reform Trust, 2002.

79   Nacro, *The Forgotten Majority*, London: National Association for the Care and Resettlement of Offenders, 2000.

80   Buckaloo, B. J. et al., 'Exercise and the Low-security Inmate: Changes in Depression, Stress, and Anxiety', *The Prison Journal*, vol. 89 (3), 2009.

81   House of Commons Justice Committee, 'Women Offenders: After the Corston Report'; Second Report of Session 2013–14, vol. 1, p. 70.

82   Ibid., p. 64.

83   Ibid.

84   Ministry of Justice, 'Green Paper Evidence Report, Breaking the Cycle: Effective Punishment, Rehabilitation and Sentencing of Offenders', December 2010.

85   Irwin, J. and Owen, B., 'Harm and the Contemporary Prison', in A. Liebling and S. Maruna (eds), *The Effects of Imprisonment*, Cullompton: Willan, 2005.

86   Mottram, P. and Lancaster, R., 'HMPs Liverpool, Styal and Hindley YOI: Preliminary Results', Cumbria and Lancashire: NHS Specialised Services Commissioning Team, 2005.

87   Mottram, P. and Lancaster, R., 'HMP Liverpool, Styal and Hindley Study Report', Liverpool: University of Liverpool, 2007.

88   Hansard HC, 9 January 2007, c. 548w.

89   Clay, N., 'An Exploratory Study into how Christian Faith Affects Experiences of Prison Life', Cambridge: Institute of Criminology, 2011.

90   Ministry of Justice, FOI, 72680, May 2011.

91   'Provisional estimate of benefit claims by recently released prisoners', Ministry of Justice/Department for Work and Pensions, May 2011.

92   Working Links, 'Prejudged: Tagged for Life', 2010.

93   'Making Prisons Work: Skills for Rehabilitation: Review of Offender Learning', Ministry of Justice/Department for Business, Innovation and Skills, May 2011.

94   Stewart, D., 'The Problems and Needs of Newly Sentenced Prisoners: Results from a National Survey', Ministry of Justice Research Series 16/08, October 2008.

95   OECD, 'Employment Rate for Women', OECD iLibrary, 16 July 2013.

96   Private interview with Working Chance.

97   Working Chance, 'How to Employ an Ex-Offender Guide', unpublished draft, July 2013.

98   Matrix Knowledge Group, 'Lifelong Learning and Crime: An Analysis of the Cost Effectiveness of In Prison Educational and Vocational Interventions', IFLL Public Value Paper 2, National Institute of Adult Continuing Education, 2009.

99   Barret, D., 'G4S and Serco: Taxpayers overcharged by tens of millions over electronic tagging', *Telegraph* online, 11 July 2013.

100 Gibb, F., 'Cutting legal aid bill could trigger riots in prison, judges warn', *The Times*, 5 June 2013.

101 Allison, E., 'Legal aid for prisoners does not need to be cut – it already has been', *The Guardian*, 23 April 2013.

102 Sparrow, A., 'Margaret Thatcher's funeral cost taxpayers more than £3m', *The Guardian*, 29 July 2013.

103 'Half of inmates use legal aid to complain: prisoners spending £500,000 a week on issues including sentences and discipline', *Daily Mail* online, 7 July 2013.

104 Ibid.

105 Ibid.

106 McClenaghan, M. and Doward, J., 'Staff cuts at CPS lead to delays, errors and waste, say legal experts', *The Observer*, 28 July 2013.

107 Williams, K. et al., 'Prisoners' childhood and family backgrounds', Ministry of Justice, March 2012 and Bromley Briefings, Prison Reform Trust, November 2012, p. 26.

108 Report by the Comptroller and Auditor General, 'Managing Offenders on Custodial Sentences', Ministry of Justice, HC 431, Session 2009–2010, 10 March 2010.

109 The Clink Charity, Report of the Trustees for the year ended 31 December 2012.

110 'Prisoner voting: MPs seek compromise on ban', BBC News online, 19 June 2013.

111 Ibid.

112 Written evidence submitted by the Prison Reform Trust to the Commons Select Committee, 'Barred from Voting: The Right to Vote for Sentenced Prisoners', February 2011.

113 Sentencing Council, unpublished statistics from the Ministry of Justice Court Proceedings Database 2009, cited in Bromley Briefings, Prison Reform Trust, November 2012, p. 33.

114 Ministry of Justice, 'Transforming Rehabilitation: A Strategy for Reform', 2013.

115 Penrose, 'Impact Report 2011', 2011, p. 6.

116 Cox, A. and Gelsthorpe, L., 'Beats & Bars: Music in Prisons – An Evaluation', Cambridge: Institute of Criminology, October 2008.

117 Third Sector, 'Analysis: "A step in the right direction" on probation service contracts', Third Sector online, 25 June 2013.

118 House of Commons Justice Committee, 'Women Offenders: After the Corston Report'; Second Report of Session 2013– 14, vol. 1, pp. 51–3, 58.

119 Ipsos MORI, 'Closing Gaps, Crime and Public Perceptions', 14 January 2008, cited in Bromley Briefings, Prison Reform Trust, November 2012.

120 Cecil, D., 'Dramatic Portrayals of Violent Women: Female Offenders on Prime Time Crime Dramas', *Journal of Criminal Justice and Popular Culture*,14 (3), 2007, School of Criminal Justice, University at Albany.

121 Government Equalities Office, 'Perceptions of Offender's Gender and Alternatives to Prison', Ipsos MORI, October 2009.

122 Ibid.

123 Home Office, 'Crime in England and Wales 2009/10', cited in Bromley Briefings, Prison Reform Trust, November 2012.

124 Prison Reform Trust, 'Public want offenders to make amends', briefing paper, 2011, London, cited in Bromley Briefings, Prison Reform Trust, November 2012.

125 ICM opinion poll for the Corston Coalition, 26–28 November 2010, cited in Bromley Briefings, Prison Reform Trust, November 2012.

126 Government Equalities Office, 'Perceptions of Offender's Gender and Alternatives to Prison', Ipsos MORI, October 2009.

127 Ibid.

128 Berman, G., 'Prison Population Statistics', SN/SG/4334, House of Commons Library, 23 February 2012.

129 Wright, O. and Morris, N., 'Cuts put prisons at serious risk of riots, say officers', *The Independent*, 28 December 2011.

130 'Prison cuts may see reoffending rise, say MPs', BBC News online, 5 March 2013.

131 Hansard HC, 4 April 2011, c. 642w.

132 NOMS Women and Equalities Group, 'A Distinct Approach: A Guide to Working with Women Offenders', Ministry of Justice, March 2012.

133 Make Justice Work, 'Community or Custody? A National Enquiry', 12 September 2011.

134 Matrix Evidence, 'Are Short Term Prison Sentences an Efficient and Effective Use of Public Resources?', Make Justice Work, 29 June 2009.

135 Ministry of Justice, 'Adult Re-convictions: Results from the 2009 Cohort', March 2011.

136 Ministry of Justice, 'Crime Justice Statistics: Quarterly Update to March 2012', 13 September 2012.

137 Ministry of Justice, '2013 Compendium of Re-offending Statistics and Analysis', 11 July 2013.

138 Hansard HC, 4 April 2011, c. 642w.

139 NOMS Women and Equalities Group, 'A Distinct Approach: A Guide to Working with Women Offenders', Ministry of Justice, March 2012.

140 Report by the Comptroller and Auditor General, 'Managing Offenders on Custodial Sentences', Ministry of Justice, HC 431, Session 2009–2010, 10 March 2010.

141 Curtis, L., 'Unit Costs of Health and Social Care 2011', Personal Social Services Research Unit, University of Kent, 2011.

142 Ministry of Justice, 'Prison Reception Tables', Offender Management Statistics Quarterly, 8 May 2013.

143 HM Inspectorate of Prisons, 'Women in Prison', Home Office, Research Study 208, 2005.

144 Ministry of Justice, Prison Population Statistics, weekly population updates.

145 Carter, P., 'Lord Carter's Review of Prisons: Securing the Future', Ministry of Justice, December 2007 and cited in Bromley Briefings, Prison Reform Trust, November 2012, p. 16.

146 Mottram, P. and Lancaster, R., 'HMPs Liverpool, Styal and Hindley YOI: Preliminary Results', Cumbria and Lancashire: NHS Specialised Services Commissioning Team, 2005.

147 Piquero, A. R. et al., 'Elaborating the Individual Difference Component in Deterrence Theory', *Annual Review of Law and Social Science*, vol. 7, 335–360, December 2011.

148 See: Becker, H., *Outsiders: Studies in the Sociology of Defiance*, London: Collier-Macmillan, 1966.

149 Sherman, L., 'Defiance, Deterrence, and Irrelevance: A Theory of the Criminal Sanction', *Journal of Research in Crime and Delinquency*, vol. 30, no. 4, 445–473, November 1993.

150 Piquero, A. and Paternoster, R., 'An Application of Stafford and Warr's Reconceptualization of Deterrence to Drinking and Driving', *Journal of Research in Crime and Delinquency*, vol. 35, no. 1, 3–39, February 1998.

151 Shepherd, J. P., 'Criminal deterrence as a public health strategy,' *The Lancet*, 17 November 2001.

152 Ungar, M., 'Nurturing Resilience', *Psychology Today*, 13 November 2009.

153 Centre for Social Justice, conference proceedings, November 2012.

154 Ministry of Justice, 'Population and Capacity Briefing', 2 November 2012 and HM Prison Sentence, Prison Service Annual Report 1992–1993, 1993.

155 Johnson, P., 'Violent crime is down. The prison population has doubled. Might there be a link?', *Daily Telegraph*, 24 April 2013.

156 Prisoners Education Trust, Annual Review 2012, 2012.

157 Matrix Knowledge Group, 'Lifelong Learning and Crime: An Analysis of the Cost Effectiveness of In Prison Educational and Vocational Interventions', IFLL Public Value Paper 2, National Institute of Adult Continuing Education, 2009.

158 Government Response to the House of Commons Education and Skills Committee Report – Prison Education, June 2005, p. 6.

159 Ministry of Justice, 'Compendium of Reoffending Statistics and Analysis 2010', 4 November 2010.

160 Machin, S. et al., 'The Crime Reducing Effect of Education', *Economic Journal*, vol. 121, issue 552, 463–484, May 2011.

161 A report – Ministry of Justice, 'Analysis of the Impact of Employment on Reoffending Following Release from

Custody, Using Propensity Score Matching', March 2013 – has come up with serious positive findings in this regard.

162 Walmsley, R., 'Prison Population List', 9th edn., International Centre for Prison Studies, University of Essex; Walmsley, R., 'World Female Imprisonment List', 2nd edn, International Centre for Prison Studies, University of Essex.

163 Ibid.

164 Written submission by The Osborne Association's New York Initiative for Children of Incarcerated Parents and The Committee for Hispanic Children and Families, Inc., cited in Robertson, O., 'Collateral Convicts: Children of Incarcerated Parents', Quaker United Nations Office, Human Rights and Refugees Publications, p. 11.

165 Newell, D. A., 'Risk and Protective Factors for Secondary Girls of Incarcerated Parents', *Family Court Review*, vol. 50, issue 1, p. 107, January 2012, cited in Robertson, O., 'Collateral Convicts: Children of Incarcerated Parents'.

166 Written submission by National Resource Center on Children and Families of the Incarcerated, cited in Robertson, O., 'Collateral Convicts: Children of Incarcerated Parents'.

167 Written submission by Action for Children and Youth Aotearoa, cited in Robertson, O., 'Collateral Convicts: Children of Incarcerated Parents'.

168 Eurochips website, cited in Robertson, O., 'Collateral Convicts: Children of Incarcerated Parents'.

169 Bromley Briefings, Prison Reform Trust, November 2012.

170 Wermink, H. et al., 'Comparing the Effects of Community Service and Short-term Imprisonment on Recidivism: A Matched Samples Approach', *Journal of Experimental Criminology*, 19 June 2010.

171 Kerman, P., 'For women, a second sentence', *New York Times* online, 13 August 2013.

172 Matheson, F. et al., 'Women Offender Substance Abuse Programming and Community Reintegration', Corrections Service Canada, March 2008.

173 Carlen, P., 'Women's Imprisonment: An Introduction to the Bangkok Rules', *Revista Critica Penal y Poder,* University of Barcelona, no. 3, 2012.

174 Hansard HC, 17 January 2011, c. 653w.
175 House of Commons Justice Committee, 'Women Offenders: After the Corston Report'; Second Report of Session 2013–14, vol. 1, p. 51.
176 Ibid., p. 55.
177 HM Government, PSA Delivery Agreement 24, October 2007.
178 House of Commons Justice Committee, 'Women Offenders: After the Corston Report'; Second Report of Session 2013–14, vol. 1.

INDEX

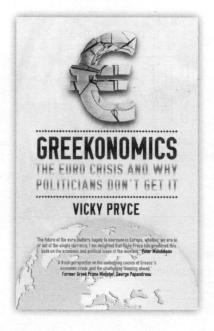

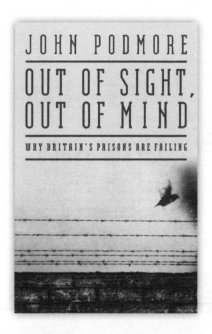

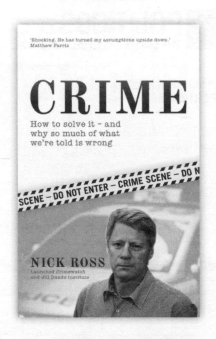